# Gender and Media Representation

# DIVERSE PERSPECTIVES ON CREATING A FAIRER SOCIETY

A fair society is one that is just, inclusive and embracing of all without any barriers to participation based on sex, sexual orientation, religion or belief, ethnicity, age, class, ability or any other social difference. One where there is access to healthcare and education, technology, justice, strong institutions, peace and security, social protection, decent work and housing. But how can research truly contribute to creating global equity and diversity without showcasing diverse voices that are underrepresented in academia or paying specific attention to the Global South?

Including books addressing key challenges and issues within the social sciences which are essential to creating a fairer society for all with specific reference to the Global South, *Diverse Perspectives on Creating a Fairer Society* amplifies underrepresented voices showcasing Black, Asian and minority ethnic voices, authorship from the Global South and academics who work to amplify diverse voices.

With the primary aim of showcasing authorship and voices from beyond the Global North, the series welcomes submissions from established and junior authors on cutting-edge and high-level research on key topics that feature in global news and public debate, specifically from and about the Global South in national and international contexts. Harnessing research across a range of diversities of people and place to generate previously unheard insights, the series offers a truly global perspective on the current societal debates of the 21st century bringing contemporary debate in the social sciences from diverse voices to light.

**Previous Titles**

- *Disaster, Displacement and Resilient Livelihoods: Perspectives from South Asia* edited by M. Rezaul Islam
- *Pandemic, Politics, and a Fairer Society in Southeast Asia: A Malaysian Perspective* edited by Syaza Shukri
- *Empowering Female Climate Change Activists in the Global South: The Path Toward Environmental Social Justice* by Peggy Ann Spitzer
- *Gendered Perspectives of Restorative Justice, Violence and Resilience: An International Framework* edited by Bev Orton
- *Social Sector Development and Inclusive Growth in India* by Ishu Chadda
- *The Socially Constructed and Reproduced Youth Delinquency in Southeast Asia: Advancing Positive Youth Involvement in Sustainable Futures* by Jason Hung
- *Youth Development in South Africa: Harnessing the Demographic Dividend* edited by Botshabelo Maja and Busani Ngcaweni
- *Debt Crisis and Popular Social Protest in Sri Lanka: Citizenship, Development and Democracy Within Global North–South Dynamics* by S. Janaka Biyanwila
- *Building Strong Communities: Ethical Approaches to Inclusive Development* by Ifzal Ahmad and M. Rezaul Islam

- *Family Planning and Sustainable Development in Bangladesh: Empowering Marginalized Communities in Asian Contexts* by M. Rezaul Islam
- *Critical Reflections on the Internationalisation of Higher Education in the Global South* edited by Emnet Tadesse Woldegiorgis and Cheryl Qiumei Yu
- *Exploring Hope: Case Studies of Innovation, Change and Development in the Global South* edited by Marcelo Sili, Andrés Kozel, Samira Mizbar, Aviram Sharma, and Ana Casado
- *Social Constructions of Migration in Nigeria and Zimbabwe: Discourse, Rhetoric, and Identity* by Kunle Musbaudeen Oparinde and Rodwell Makombe
- *'Natural' Disasters and Everyday Lives: Floods, Climate Justice and Marginalisation in India* by Suddhabrata Deb Roy
- *Rural Social Infrastructure Development in India: An Inclusive Approach* by M. Mahadeva
- *Globalization and the Transitional Cultures: An Eastern Perspective* by Debanjana Nag
- Neoliberal Subjectivities at Work: Conduct, Commitments, Contradictions and Contestations by Muneeb Ul Lateef Banday

**Forthcoming Titles**

- *From Mainstream to Digital: African Perspectives on Participatory Media Cultures* edited by Natalie Le Clue, Catherine Duncan, and Janelle Vermaak-Griessel
- *The Emerald Handbook of Family and Social Change in the Global South: A Gendered Perspective* edited by Aylin Akpınar and Nawal H. Ammar
- *An Introduction to Platform Economy in India: Exploring Relationality and Embeddedness* by Shriram Venkatraman, Jillet Sarah Sam, and Rajorshi Ra
- *Unveiling Identities: Navigating the Spectrum of LGBT+ Experiences in Southern Africa* edited by Tinovimba Pamela Patsika, Kammila Naidoo, and Paddington Mutekwe
- *Intersecting Inequalities in Jamaica and Beyond: Policy Solutions for the Global South* edited by Kevin Williams, Dacia L. Leslie, and Warren Benfield
- *Unearthing the Institutionalised Social Exclusion of Black Youth in Contemporary South Africa: The Burden of Being Born Free* by Khosi Kubeka

# Gender and Media Representation: Perspectives from Sub-Saharan Africa

EDITED BY

## MARGARET JJUUKO
*University of Rwanda, Rwanda*

## SOLVEIG OMLAND
*NLA University College, Norway*

and

## CAROL AZUNGI DRALEGA
*NLA University College, Norway*

emerald
**PUBLISHING**

United Kingdom – North America – Japan – India – Malaysia – China

Emerald Publishing Limited
Emerald Publishing, Floor 5, Northspring, 21-23 Wellington Street, Leeds LS1 4DL.

First edition 2025

**Reprints and permissions service**
Contact: www.copyright.com

**British Library Cataloguing in Publication Data**
A catalogue record for this book is available from the British Library

ISBN: 978-1-83608-409-9 (Print)
ISBN: 978-1-83608-406-8 (Online)
ISBN: 978-1-83608-408-2 (Epub)

INVESTOR IN PEOPLE

# Contents

# About the Editors

**Margaret Jjuuko** is a Professor of Journalism, Media and Communication Studies at the University of Rwanda's School of Journalism and Communication, where she coordinates the MA programme in Journalism, Media and Communication Studies. She is the current President of the East African Communication Association and a board member of the African Journalism Educators' Network among other professional affiliations. She is also the Principal Investigator for 'Preparing Media Practitioners for a Resilient Media in Eastern Africa' project (Rwanda chapter), which is funded under NORHED II. As an International Media and Communication Consultant, she has been instrumental in the development of the media in Rwanda, and the setting up of the Media Development Institute in South Sudan (2013–2015). Her research interests are in cultural studies in relation to media textual production and reception analyses in the areas of environment and climate change communication, political communication, gender and social justice, and information and communication technologies.

**Solveig Omland** is an Associate Professor at NLA University College in Kristiansand, Norway, where she teaches BA and MA-level courses in intercultural studies on intercultural communication, diversity, pluricultural Norway, methodology, representation, media, and culture and has led a study-abroad trip to East Africa. She has been Head of the Department of Intercultural Studies since 2016. Her research focuses on integration and inclusion, media and representation, intercultural competence, and religion among others.

**Carol Azungi** Dralega is a Professor, Department of Journalism, Media and Communication, NLA University College, Norway. She has recently co-edited and edited three books: Dralega, C. A., & Napakol, A. (2022). *Health Crises and Media Discourses in Sub-Saharan Africa*, Springer Nature; Dralega, C. A., & Napakol, A. (Eds.), (2022). *COVID-19 and the Media in Sub-Saharan Africa: Media Viability, Framing and Health Communication,* Emerald Group Publishing, and Dralega, A. C. (2024) *Digitization, AI, and Algorithms in African Journalism and Media Contexts*, Emerald Publishing. Her research interests revolve around information and communication technologies/media, marginalisation, and social change. She is involved in several research projects including Preventing violence-inducing behaviour in social cyber spaces (2022–2026); Preparing practitioners for a resilient media in Eastern Africa (2021–2026); and Capacity building for a resilient media in Eastern Africa (2021–2027).

# About the Contributors

**Theodora Dame Adjin-Tettey** is a Senior Lecturer at the Department of Media, Language and Communication at the Durban University of Technology and a Research Associate at the School of Journalism and Media Studies at Rhodes University, South Africa. The research projects she has been part of include the State of the Ghanaian Media report, a sustainable journalism in sub-Saharan Africa study and policy brief, the South African country report on government communications during the pandemic, a Konrad-Adenauer-Stiftung Foundation-funded study on global strategies to save journalism, and an Open Society Foundations-commissioned report on news consumption habits among non-elite audiences in the Global South.

**Manfred Kofi Antwi Asuman** is an Assistant Professor of Sociology and a Postdoctoral Researcher at the University of Western Ontario, Canada. He earned his PhD in Media Studies from Nelson Mandela University in South Africa. His research studies the lives of underprivileged people and media, how they use media, and how they make media to achieve communal development goals. He is a Former Visiting Research Scholar at the School of Journalism and Mass Communications at the University of Iowa and continues to serve as a member of its Global Media Studies Working Group.

**Mary Selikem Ayim-Segbefia** is a Lecturer in Broadcast Journalism at the Institute of Film and Television Campus of the University of Media, Arts and Communication in Accra, Ghana. Her research interests include women's autobiographical tradition, newsroom operations and processes, the nexus between women in media and gender, the safety of journalists, and fact-checking and verification.

**Aurelia Ayisi** is a Lecturer and Researcher in the Department of Communication Studies at the University of Ghana. Her current research specialisation is in digital communication, media, and information literacy with a focus on the intersection of these areas and issues of access, competencies, and the global disparities and trends that shape them. She holds an MA in Media and Cultural Studies from Loughborough University and a PhD in Cultural Studies from Bath Spa University, both in the UK.

**Emma Durden** is a Health and Development Communications Consultant and an Honorary Research Fellow at the Centre for Communication and Media in Society at the University of KwaZulu-Natal in South Africa. Her research focus areas include health communications, sexual and reproductive health, and theatre for development.

**Anne Anjao Eboi** is a lecturer in Media and Communication at Daystar University where she is currently heading the Department of Media and Film Studies. Anne earned her doctoral degree from Universiti Utara Malaysia. She recently featured as a panelist at the Pan-Atlantic University's Symposium titled, "Symposium on Media and Women Empowerment in Africa." Anne has authored several articles in refereed journals, book chapters, a book, newspaper articles, and short stories. Her research interests are in new/social media, gender and social justice, women and film, health communication, leadership, Artificial Intelligence, and general education topics. She also belongs to several professional bodies.

**Bimbo Lolade Fafowora** is a Postdoctoral Research Fellow at the School of Journalism and Media Studies, Rhodes University, South Africa, and a Research Fellow at Stellenbosch University, South Africa, where she earned a PhD in Journalism with a doctoral dissertation focussed on the construction and representation of women's political leaders in Nigerian newspapers. She is an alumna of the University of Ibadan. She is co-editing a special journal issue on digital media literacy in Africa with her host, Dr Priscilla Boshoff. Her research interests are media construction/representation, gender, politics, fake news and mis/disinformation, media literacy, disability, and digital inclusion.

**Sarah Gibson** is an Associate Professor in the Centre for Communication and Media in Society at the University of KwaZulu-Natal (UKZN), South Africa. She was previously appointed as Academic Leader of Teaching and Learning in the School of Applied Human Sciences and then as (Interim) Director of Teaching and Learning in the College of Humanities at UKZN. She is also the Assistant Editor of *Transfers: Interdisciplinary Journal of Mobility Studies*. Her research interests include cultural studies, the new mobilities paradigm, and critical theory. She is currently the Convenor of the Media, Culture and Society Working Group for the South African Sociological Association and is on the *South African Review of Sociology* editorial board.

**Denis Ikachoi** is a lecturer in communication, media and public relations and the chair of the Department of Media, Film and Communication at Maasai Mara University in Kenya. He holds a PhD in Mass Communication from Jomo Kenyatta University of Agriculture and Technology in Kenya and has presented papers at local and international conferences and published book chapters and articles in a variety of peer-reviewed journals. His research interests span media and society, media and gender, media audience studies, and digital media.

**Dianus Josephat Ishengoma** is an accomplished journalist and communication professional who serves as Academic Staff at the School of Journalism and Mass Communication, University of Dar es Salaam. He is currently pursuing a PhD in Media Studies at Nelson Mandela University's School of Language, Media, and Communication in South Africa. His expertise spans gender analysis, strategic communication, media production, health communication, and science journalism.

**Fred Kakooza** is a Senior Lecturer in the Department of Journalism and Communication at Makerere University. He specialises in media and communication research, broadcast journalism, multimedia journalism, and social media and lectures to both graduate and undergraduate students as well as supervising research and professional projects. He completed his PhD in Cultural and Media Studies at the University of KwaZulu-Natal and holds an MA in Journalism and Communication and a Bachelor of Mass Communication both from Makerere University.

**Samuel Kazibwe** is an award-winning Ugandan journalist, academic, and researcher. He completed BA in Mass Communication at Uganda Christian University, MA in Human Rights at Makerere University, and PhD in Cultural and Media Studies at the University of KwaZulu-Natal, South Africa. He is a Senior Lecturer at the School of Journalism, Media, and Communication at Uganda Christian University whose research interests span mass communication theory, media law, development communication, governance, and human rights. Kazibwe has also worked as a reporter, news anchor, talk-show producer/host, and news editor for several local Ugandan radio stations.

**Emilly Comfort Maractho** is an Associate Professor in the School of Journalism, Media, and Communication at Uganda Christian University (UCU), and her research focuses on media governance and media for development. She is interested in the broad intersection between media, democracy, and development, and, more specifically, media, gender, and social justice. She has taught at UCU since 2008 and at Makerere University for 14 years. She works extensively on capacity building (training), communication strategies, and policy analysis (legal and regulatory frameworks). She previously headed the Department of Journalism and Media Studies and was Director of the Africa Policy Centre at UCU. She serves as Chair for the Board of Directors of the African Centre for Media Excellence, the Editorial Board Committee of the Monitor Publications Limited – Nation Media Group Uganda, Media, Democracy, and Development Research Group at UCU, and the Uganda Media Women's Association.

**Jeanne d'Arc Mukamana** is a Lecturer in the School of Journalism and Communication at the University of Rwanda and a PhD candidate at the Centre for Communication and Media in Society at the University of KwaZulu-Natal, South Africa.

**Theodorah S. Munisi** is a former Tanzanian journalist and currently Lecturer at the School of Journalism and Communication at the University of Dar es Salaam. She has contributed to various local media research projects, including the Yearbook on Media Quality in Tanzania.

**Joseph Njuguna** is a Lecturer at the University of Rwanda's School of Journalism and Communication. He holds a PhD in Mass Communication from Jomo Kenyatta University of Agriculture and Technology in Kenya and has researched and published journal articles and book chapters on media and gender, journalism education, media and regional integration, artificial intelligence, and ICT4D.

**Terje Skjerdal** is a Professor of Journalism at NLA University College, Norway. He has researched African journalism since the early 2000s and has taught at various universities in East Africa and the Horn of Africa. He is Coordinator of the NORHED project 'Preparing Practitioners for a Resilient Media in East Africa' in partnership with Uganda Christian University, University of Rwanda and University of KwaZulu-Natal.

**Eva Solomon** lectures at the School of Journalism and Mass Communication at the University of Dar es Salaam in Tanzania. Her research interests span gender and the media; social media; media, development, and social change; and intercultural communications. She has published with such renowned international publishers as Taylor & Francis, Springer Cham, and Emerald. She is an Editorial Board Member of the *Studies in Media and Communication*, a Scopus-indexed journal based in the USA. She holds a BA in Mass Communication from Makerere University in Uganda, an MA in Journalism and Mass Communication from Tampere University in Finland, and a PhD in Media and Communication Studies from Freie Universitat Berlin in Germany.

# Foreword

Media plays an undeniably crucial role in shaping societal perceptions of gender, particularly in Sub-Saharan Africa, where traditional gender roles and socio-cultural norms are deeply entrenched. *Gender and Media Representations: Perspectives from Sub-Saharan Africa* is an essential contribution to understanding how these dynamics manifest in media portrayals and their implications for gender equality. Conferences, webinars, and workshops held across the continents have highlighted the relevance of gender representation, which resonates with many people's daily lives, not only in Sub-Saharan Africa but also globally. Discussions and research on gender and media will continue, as these topics are central to our lives.

This volume brings together insights from distinguished scholars and researchers, each presenting unique perspectives grounded in empirical research, cultural analysis, and theoretical frameworks. From presidential representation to gender-based violence, from political participation to professional opportunities for women in journalism, this work comprehensively explores how the media frames gender in various contexts across the region. The representation of women in media is examined through multiple lenses, such as political power, reproductive rights, participation in public life, and professional standing in the media industry. Through diverse topics, the book underscores the ongoing struggles for fair gender representation, highlighting both progress and persistent challenges.

The editors have brought together critical discussions and research findings that conceptualise participation as representation, interaction, and engagement in both traditional and new media. Media's growing power is evident across Africa, particularly through the widespread use of radio, the most accessible and affordable medium, which has been harnessed for gender empowerment and therapy in countries like Ghana, Kenya, Tanzania, and Rwanda. Community radio stations, both privately owned and public, have become enablers of women's empowerment by raising awareness on health, climate, politics, and business issues. These stations have also helped build resilience against gender-based violence, promoting empowerment for both men and women, as seen in Tanzania. Topics in this book range from gender representation in journalism and communication to the challenges of misrepresentation in AI-generated content and digital space communication.

While many media channels, such as YouTube, offer educational and therapeutic benefits, challenges remain, including online gender bullying and intimidation, which disproportionately affect women. This book provides suggestions to mitigate the negatives associated with online communication about gender. It also highlights how power imbalances in workplaces, universities, and society perpetuate a culture of silence, allowing injustices such as victim-shaming and blaming to continue. The research findings presented here offer tools to enhance inclusiveness and improve communication in these areas.

This book opens the door to understanding media not just as a reflection of society but as an active force shaping public opinion, gender roles, and societal norms. With a focus on Sub-Saharan Africa, it brings visibility to a region often underrepresented in global gender discourse. For academics, media practitioners, policymakers, and students alike, this book provides invaluable insights into the ongoing struggles for gender inclusion, equality, justice, and representation through the media in one of the world's most diverse and complex regions.

The editors have compiled a resource and provided the latest research findings on media and gender representations from countries such as Kenya, Tanzania, Rwanda, Ghana, and Nigeria. These chapters deepen our understanding of the lived experiences of African men and women, particularly in relation to their portrayal in the media. This volume offers valuable suggestions and recommendations for mainstreaming gender, eliminating injustices, and using digital communication channels to benefit humanity. Let us read this book to enrich both our academic and personal lives.

Juliet Macharia (PhD)
Associate Professor
Karatina University, Nairobi, Kenya

# Book Preface

This book, *Gender and Media Representation: Perspectives from Sub-Saharan Africa,* has been inspired by the ongoing collaborative capacity building project, *'Preparing Practitioners for a Resilient Media in Eastern Africa'*, between Norway (NLA University College), Rwanda (University of Rwanda), Uganda (Uganda Christian University), and South Africa (KwaZulu-Natal University). The project is funded by the Norwegian Agency for Development Cooperation (NORAD) with the aim to support North–South–South university partnerships on capacity development in inclusive higher education and research under NORHED II 2021–2026 programme.

The 'enhancement of gender equality and inclusion' is one of the four programme ambitions, which is a cross-cutting subject in our project. This project has been a remarkable opportunity to explore the intersection of media, gender, and representation, particularly in the context of Sub-Saharan Africa, a region where the struggle for gender equality is both historical and contemporary.

Our focus on gender representation in media stems from the understanding that media is not merely a tool of communication but a powerful institution that constructs, deconstructs, and reconstructs social realities. Throughout this book, you will encounter a range of case studies, theoretical explorations, and empirical research highlighting the ways in which media influences gender perceptions, from political coverage and representation to everyday portrayals of women in newsrooms and public life. Digital and technological trends and concerns are also covered.

The contributors to this volume come from diverse academic and professional backgrounds across Sub-Saharan Africa and beyond, each bringing a wealth of expertise in journalism, communication, gender studies, media ethics as well as traditional and new media. Their work illustrates both the progress and the setbacks encountered in the fight for gender equality in the media spaces. This book project, with its regional focus, aims to equip media professionals and scholars with the knowledge, tools, and capacities necessary to foster a more balanced, gender-sensitive, resilience media landscape in Sub-Saharan Africa.

As editors, we would like to acknowledge the immense support provided by NORAD through the NORHED II project, which has enabled the production of this important resource, and also The East African Communication Association and the AfroMedia Network for academic support. We also extend our gratitude to all the researchers/contributors, institutions, media professionals, and reviewers who have contributed to this volume. Finally, many thanks to Emerald Publishers for bringing this volume to the world. It is our hope that this book will inspire further dialogue, research, and action towards achieving gender equality in media and beyond.

Margaret Jjuuko (PhD)
University of Rwanda

Solveig Omland (PhD)
NLA University College

Carol Azungi Dralega (PhD)
NLA University College
30th October 2024.

# Introduction: Contextualising Media's Representations of Gender Issues in Sub-Saharan Africa

*Margaret Jjuuko[a], Solveig Omland[b] and Carol Azungi Dralega[b]*

[a]*University of Rwanda, Rwanda*
[b]*NLA University College, Norway*

> Feminist discourse on African media remains largely traditional – frequently critiqued as misogynistic – and anchored in patriarchal hegemony. (Dralega, 2016, p. 247).

## Introduction

Despite advances in civil rights and legal protections, restrictive gender stereotypes persist in many contexts. Media are among the most pervasive and powerful forces shaping how men and women are perceived in society. They play a key role in producing and reinforcing sociocultural expectations and pressures. Media are deeply embedded in daily life, influencing politics and the broader structures of power in every environment. Media content, whether intentionally or not, often perpetuates unrealistic, stereotypical, and marginalising perceptions as it infiltrates audiences' consciousness. Koenig and Eagly (2014) defined gender stereotypes as a dangerous streamlined concept of attitudes and behaviours positioned as normal and appropriate for men and women in a specific cultural sphere. Wood (2009, p. 86) identifies three key themes in the media's portrayal of gender: underrepresentation, which presents men as the cultural norm while women are rendered invisible; stereotyping, which reinforces socially accepted gender roles; and depictions of relationships between men and women that often emphasise traditional roles and normalise violence against women and other marginalised groups. These portrayals reinforce socially constructed gender norms and contribute to the normalisation of sexual harassment, rape, and gender-based violence (GBV), which disproportionately affect women – even within media institutions themselves.

Gender and Media Representation: Perspectives from Sub-Saharan Africa, 1–8

Despite the increase in visibility and voices of women in media content in Sub-Saharan Africa in recent years, women are depicted as passive and disinterested in the issues at hand more often than not (Akinbobola 2020; Jjuuko & Njuguna, 2019a). In her 2016 article 'Media, capacity building and gender parity: why we shouldn't look away', Dralega points out how feminist discourse on media in Africa has largely been conservative and is often described as 'misogynistic' and deeply entrenched in patriarchal norms. She argues gender inequality persists, particularly in the underrepresentation and misrepresentation of gender issues and employment, although women's absence in leadership, management, and ownership in media also needs addressing (Dralega, 2016). Socially constructed roles, behaviours, and attributes assigned to men and women strongly influence news media production and the resulting discourses, which often further reinforce gender stereotypes (Santoniccolo et al., 2023). How gender issues are integrated into the news production and consumption cycle is, needless to say, among the critical tests of a professional media.

In general, the female folk are stereotypically associated with the home and characteristics such as supportiveness, compassion, expression, warmth, whereas the male folk are stereotypically associated with agency (e.g. action, competitiveness, ambition, and assertiveness) and competence (e.g. intelligence and skill). Should their actions be inconsistent with these stereotypical norms, both genders are likely to experience a backlash from the media and their audiences. In the political arena, for instance, common gender stereotypes relate to how women leaders or politicians are perceived and represented by the media and in communication discourses in ways that undermine their potential as capable leaders (Campus, 2013; Ross & Byerly, 2014). In addition to claims of biased coverage of women's issues, research also has uncovered other unequal gender tendencies and irregularities within the media industry, including salary discrepancies, inequitable allocation of journalistic roles between male and female journalists, male dominance in management positions, and a general misconstruction of the concept of gender equality and its implications in the media (Santoniccolo et al., 2023).

The implementation of policies that create gender-inclusive environments in both media education and journalism practice is a key concern in media development in Sub-Saharan Africa. These policies aim to ensure that journalism equitably represents the views and aspirations of all members of society and fulfils its role as a watchdog and voice for all (Santoniccolo et al., 2023). Although many media houses have established gender policies, uncertainties about their operationalisation or implementation proliferate and foster incongruous handling of sexual harassment and discrimination cases (Akinbobola & Charles-Hatt, 2021; Ryan & Karen, 2019; Ward & Grower, 2020).

Similar gender issues impact media education not only in relation to students' admission and enrolment into journalism or communication training institutions but also in relation to the curricula (Akinbobola, 2020). In their gender audit of journalism institutions in eastern Africa, Dralega et al. (2016) found that these departments harboured negative attitudes towards gender mainstreaming and had gender insensitive curricular and supported limited gender research. In addition to the limited presence of women in journalism programmes in some of Sub-Saharan

Africa, several studies have revealed that the few women who study journalism rarely end up employed in the media sector (Akinbobola, 2020; Akinbobola & Charles-Hatt, 2021; Ryan & Karen, 2019). This trend is attributed to either the lack of interest or opportunities and inadequate investment opportunities in the sector. The few women who are highly motivated to proceed into the field are frustrated by gender inequalities (Akinbobola, 2020). Nevertheless, the growing global awareness of gender issues, especially in the Global South, has increased women's recognition and led to the integration of a module or two on gender into academic programmes (Akinbobola & Charles-Hatt, 2021; Jjuuko & Njuguna, 2019b).

Given the vital role of media in society, these issues raise concerns for gender equality and equity, and particularly about how media discourse represents and constructs them. Hence, this edited volume also engages the functions (and challenges) of media and communication in the promotion of equal representation of women and, to some extent, minority groups in Sub-Saharan Africa and teases out the interdisciplinarities between these sectors. The central thesis of this book is that how the media talks about its practices and how it actually practises the representation of gender issues requires scrutiny. The contributors consider not only the factors that influence the representations and constructions of these issues but also how particular issues are included in the discourse and others are left out. *Gender and Media Representations: Perspectives from Sub-Saharan Africa*, therefore, positions media as central advocates for social justice, particularly in relation to gender and minority groups and emphasises how the connections between media, gender, and representation inform and complement each other. The essays highlight the importance of building resilience among media practitioners and equipping them to navigate challenges, promote equitable gender representation, and advocate for broader social change.

Our central argument is that while media in Sub-Saharan Africa and the global South are strategically positioned to address such developmental issues as gender equality and social justice, current shifts, and trends in media and communication – both positive or negative – undermine their potential to promote democracy and inclusive development. Political and economic pressures, as well as the transition to digital media, have transformed media operations and audiences in ways that do not favour diverse representation. This transformation limits minority groups' perspectives, experiences, and knowledge in media content, employment, and consumption. This ultimately also excludes them from policymaking, planning, and decision-making processes. While technology has facilitated faster, more accessible communication across wider sections of society, it has also disrupted the quality of information and exacerbated social, political, and economic inequalities. It is crucial that we critically examine the role of media in shaping gender, identity, and representation from an African perspective (Santoniccolo et al., 2023).

## Key Concepts in This Volume

Although the collection of essays in this book employs a rich and diverse range of concepts that resonate with its core concerns, some are common: media, representation, gender, gender equality, gender equity, gender mainstreaming, empowerment, and GBV. 'Media' is used as an umbrella term for all channels or means of general communication, news or information, or entertainment in society and includes broadcast (radio and television), newspapers, and such social media platforms as X, Facebook, and YouTube. Media are central in a democracy because they provide the information based on which individuals make their own decisions. The media monitor the health of a democracy by publishing reports, agendas, and threats, reporting political, social, and economic decisions, and shedding light on public opinion (Jjuuko, 2023). 'Representation' refers to how groups or identities of people, voices, events, stories, and issues are included or excluded and constructed in media reports (Jjuuko & Prinsloo, 2014). It draws attention to why some of these issues are recurrently represented – and exclusions – why others are constantly ignored and, thus, excluded (Jjuuko, 2023). The representations are recognised as selective and structured by the values and the discursive practices of media institutions.

Gender, gender equality, and equity have public concerns since United Nations (UN) General Assembly Resolution 31/136 established the UN Decade for Women (1975–1985) on 15 December 1975. The UN-sponsored initiatives, events, and programmes engaged issues affecting women on the global scale, including remuneration equity, gendered violence, land ownership, and human rights. Gender has been defined as the socially constructed characteristics of men, women, boys, and girls. They include, among others, the social, psychological, cultural, and behavioural traits of being a woman, man, or other gender identity, including sex-based social structures and gender expression. In this project, gender equality and equity are both understood in the context of social justice. Equality demands that all human beings, regardless of their gender, be free to develop their individual capacities and make choices without the restrictions set by stereotypes, unyielding gender roles, or prejudices. Equity describes impartiality of treatment for women and men, according to their respective needs, and the systems that support it (EIGE, 2017). 'Gender mainstreaming', a process of assessing the implications for women and men of any planned action, including legislation, policies, or programmes in any area and at all levels, has been an approach to foster gender equality and equity in several societies (ILO, 2022). Such efforts have led to women's empowerment (Jjuuko & Njuguna, 2019a). The practice of 'empowerment' has motivated minority and underprivileged groups, such as rural women, to take control of their lives by giving people knowledge, skills, authority, and opportunity and holding them responsible and accountable for outcomes of their actions (Jjuuko & Njuguna, 2019a). Socially ascribed gender differences result in wide range of harmful actions perpetrated against people's wills because of their gender, and this volume refers to all those actions as 'gender-based violence'.

## Aims and Rationale

This edited volume offers critical contributions to the study of media, gender equality and equity, and social justice in Sub-Saharan Africa. It conceptualises issues of gender representation, gender equality, and social inclusion within the framework of gender mainstreaming, as defined by the UN SDGs (Goal 8) as well as the United Nations Office on Drugs and Crime (UNODC, 2013), which advocates for the inclusion of all marginalised groups, not just women (p. 7). The book provides insights into gender norms, roles, and the inclusion of diverse perspectives – women, men, and minorities – in policymaking, planning, and decision-making processes. It problematises current gender imbalances in media institutions and the media's role in representing these issues through national and regional ontologies and epistemologies. The various chapters showcase the wide range of considerations for media practitioners while researching or reporting on issues around gender in developing democracies and make significant contributions to our understandings of current trends and shifts in media representation. It brings together empirical research from several African countries – Ghana, Kenya, Nigeria, Rwanda, South Africa, Tanzania, and Uganda – to add depth through regional diversity and cross-country analysis.

In short, this collection offers a comprehensive analysis of the common reference points for achieving gender inclusion in Sub-Saharan Africa and can be a vital resource for educators and scholars because it provides new knowledge on how gender issues like women's leadership, political participation, and gender policies in media workplaces are framed within media discourses. Its approach aligns with the works of scholars like Gadzekpo (2009), who called for more feminist media scholarship in Africa, and more recent studies that explore the impact of economic and political factors on feminist media institutions (Adjin-Tettey, 2020; Dralega et al., 2016, 2022). Many contributions highlight the media's potential role in fostering resilience among practitioners, particularly through its capacity to combat inequality and promote gender balance in society. By synthesising global perspectives with African realities, the volume offers both theoretical and practical vantage points on the intersection of media, gender, representation, and resilience.

## Structure of the Book

The book is divided into two parts. Section I focuses on *gender representation, construction, and portrayal* and consists of eight chapters. Section 2 focuses on *digital media spaces and gender empowerment* and consists of seven chapters.

Chapter 1, titled 'Conceptualising Participation as Representation, Interaction, and Engagement', conceptualises 'participation' as representation, interaction, and engagement (RIE). Emily Comfort Maractho and Solveig Omland trace the central concepts in the study of women's participation in public life through the lens of the media and present and advocate for the RIE model. In Chapter 2 entitled, 'How the Tanzanian Press Portrayed the Country's First Female President Samia Suluhu Hassan in a Non-stereotypical Manner', Theodorah S. Munisi and Terje Skjerdal disclose constructive journalism practices within the Tanzanian media landscape, highlighting a gender-sensitive portrayal of the country's first female president, thereby challenging common socio-norms and previous studies. Denis Ikachoi's and Joseph Njuguna's Chapter 3 provides a content analysis of 'Media Representations of Women Candidates in Kenya's 2022 General Elections'. Their findings indicate that the frequency of coverage of female candidates was erratic and included only 'popular' candidates regularly, whereas male candidates frequently featured and dominated the front pages and editorials. In Chapter 4, 'Critiquing Language and Discourse in "Rwanda 20 Years On: The Tragic Testimony of the Children of Rape" Newspaper Article', Margaret Jjuuko demonstrates how the mode in which media represent events and subjects in conflict situations is likely to shape negative or positive views about them and have ideological effects on the represented. She argues that greater responsibility and ethical procedures are needed when reporting on sensitive matters related to such vulnerable groups as women and children. In Chapter 5 titled, 'Unveiling Voices and Visibility: Women's Engagement and Representation in Three Morning Prime-time Radio Shows in Accra, Ghana', Theodora Dame Adjin-Tettey, Manfred Kofi Antwi Asuman, and Mary Selikem Ayim-Segbefia report on their insightful case study of three radio morning shows' gender representations and women's engagement in those prime morning radio shows. 'Exploring the Affordance of Equality and Equal Opportunities to Female Journalists in Rwanda's Media' is undertaken in Chapter 6 by Margaret Jjuuko and Solveig Omland. They argue that gender mainstreaming in the Rwandan media should foster gender equality by developing capacity, inclusiveness, and non-discriminatory work environments. In a comprehensive review of literature on how abortion is communicated in the mass media, executed in Chapter 7, titled 'Communicating Abortion in the Mass Media: A Literature Review of the Challenges and Possibilities', Jeanne d'Arc Mukamana, Emma Durden, and Sarah Gibson systematically identify the challenges and possibilities as they unfold in literature. Aurelia Ayisi's Chapter 8, 'Mainstreaming Gender in Postgraduate Journalism and Communication Programmes in Ghana', concludes Section I. She investigates whether and how gender issues are taught in journalism and communication post-graduate programmes in Ghana and advocates for a gendered responsive curriculum to address the missing links in balanced representation and improve the status of women in media.

Section II of the book focuses on the use and abuse of digital media platforms (including broadcast and social media) in addressing gender inclusion, equality, and GBV as well as examining ways of empowering young journalists. In Chapter 9, Eva Solomon's 'Digital Storytelling in Social Media: A Cultural Activity and a Media Style in Fighting Gender-based Violence in Tanzania', draws on narrative and feminist theories to explore two key questions: What GBV themes are conveyed through DST, and how does DST help delineate GBV? In Chapter 10, 'Gender Mainstreaming in AI-enhanced Journalism Practice, Education, and Research in African Contexts', Carol Azungi Dralega identifies key gender-related issues in AI-enhanced media environments and proposes specific toolkits for gender mainstreaming. 'Digital Safety: Perspectives from Women Journalists in Uganda' by Fred Kakooza and Samuel Kazibwe in Chapter 11 highlights how digital spaces both empower women journalists and expose them to threats, violations, and harassment. Anne Anjao Eboi's 'YouTube Videos as Agents of Social Inclusion and Therapy Among Gender-based Violence Survivors', analyses the portrayal of GBV in YouTube videos from a Kenyan perspective in Chapter 12. Chapter 13, titled 'Community Radio in Building Resilience Against Gender-Based Violence in Tanzania: A Case of Radio Sengerema', by Dianus Josephat Ishengoma, calls for more radio programmes on GBV, involving local leaders in broadcasts and educating the public on cultural barriers to women's participation in decision-making. Joseph Njuguna reviews 17 journal articles on the empowerment of Kenyan women over the past decade, focussing on women from slums and rural, semi-arid areas in Chapter 14, titled 'Community Radio as an Enabler of Women's Empowerment in Kenya: A Systematic Review of Scholarly Evidence'. These women, often illiterate, information-poor, and culturally marginalised, possess significant untapped potential. Finally, in Chapter 15, 'Gendered Power Relations and Culture of Silence: An Exploration of Female Interns' Sexual Harassment Experiences in Nigerian Newsrooms', Bimbo Lolade Fafowora investigates how female interns cope with sexual harassment and the policies available for victims to seek justice and empower future internees.

The authors are not only experts in media and gender studies but also advocates for social justice and human rights who bring personal and professional experiences of discrimination to their analyses. The collection contributes significantly to the scant literature on media's representations of gender and related issues in Sub-Saharan Africa (including media institutions/newsrooms, media content, media curricula, among others) and is a rich resource for academics, media practitioners, policymakers, gender activists, and students. In short, these chapters will be valuable to anyone interested in identifying methodologies, procedures, and principles to make decision-making more deliberative such that men, women, and other minority groups can better connect their individual views to public debate that is non-discriminatory, inclusive, gender-sensitive, and open to diverse views.

For most media organisations in Sub-Saharan Africa, balanced gender representation is still a work in progress. Our contributors agree that concerted efforts to adequately sensitise stakeholders and measures to monitor and guide adherence are still crucial.

## References

Adjin-Tettey, T. D. (2020, October 16). The media have muted the voices of women during COVID-19: Can the tide be turned? *The Conversation*. https://theconversation.com/the-media-have-muted-the-voices-of-women-during-covid-19-can-the-tide-be-turned-148010

Akinbobola, Y. (2020). *Barriers to women journalists in Sub-Saharan Africa*. Fojo Media Institute and Africa Women in Media. https://urn.kb.se/resolve?urn=urn:nbn:se:lnu:diva-101111

Akinbobola, O., & Charles-Hatt, R. A. (2021). *Barriers to women journalists in Rwanda*. Fojo Media Institute, Linnaeus University.

Campus, D. (2013). *Women political leaders and the media*. Palgrave Macmillan.

Dralega, C. A. (2016). Media, capacity building and gender parity: Why we shouldn't look away. *Journal of African Media Studies*, 8(3), 247–249. https://doi.org/10.1386/jams.8.3.247_2

Dralega, C, A., Jemaneh, A., Jjuuko, M., & Kantono, R. (2016). Gender mainstreaming in media and journalism education – An audit of media departments in Uganda, Rwanda and Ethiopia. *Journal of African Media Studies, 8*(3), 251–266.

Dralega, C. A., Jjuuko, M., & Solomon, E. (2022). Caught between a rock and a hard place: COVID-19 impact on feminist media in Uganda, Rwanda and Tanzania. In C. D. Azungi & A. Napakol (Eds.), *COVID-19 and the media in Sub-Saharan Africa: Media viability, framing and heath communication* (pp. 19–35). Emerald Publishing.

EIGE. (2017). *Economic benefits of gender equality in the European Union: Report on the empirical application of the model.* https://eige.europa.eu/publications-resources/publications/economic-benefits-gender-equality-european-union-report-empirical-application-model

Gadzekpo, A. (2009). Missing links: African media studies and feminist concerns. *Journal of African Media Studies, 1*(1), 69–80. https://doi.org/10.1386/jams.1.1.69_1

ILO. (2022). Definition of gender mainstreaming. *Gender Equality Tool.* International Labour Organisation. https://webapps.ilo.org/public/english/bureau/gender/newsite2002/about/defin.htm

Jjuuko, M. (2023). Cultural studies and construction of developmental discourses in indigenous African Media. In P. Mpofu, I. A. Fadipe, & T. Tshabangu (Eds.), *African language media* (pp. 23–35). Routledge, Taylor and Francis Group. https://doi.org/10.4324/9781003350194-4

Jjuuko, M., & Njuguna, J. (2019a). The discourses of digital inclusion of women in Rwanda's media. A thematic analysis of *Imvaho Nshya* and *The New Times* newspapers. In B. Mutsvairo & M. Ragnedda (Eds.), *Mapping the digital divide in Africa: A mediated analysis* (pp. 131–150). Amsterdam University Press. https://doi.org/10.5117/9789462986855

Jjuuko, M., & Njuguna, J. (2019b). Confronting the challenges of journalism education in Rwanda in the context of educational reforms. *Scholarship of Teaching and Learning in the South, 3*(2), 49–67. https://doi.org/10.36615/sotls.v3i2.92

Jjuuko, M., & Prinsloo, J. (2014). The representation of the environmental crises on Lake Victoria in Uganda's media: A critical Analysis of the *Victoria Voice* radio documentaries. *Journal of African Media Studies, 6*(2), 213–229. https://doi.org/10.1386/jams.6.2.213_1

Koenig, A. M., & Eagly, A. H. (2014). Evidence for the social role theory of stereotype content: Observations of groups' roles shape stereotypes. *Journal of Personality and Social Psychology, 107*(3), 371–392. https://psycnet.apa.org/doi/10.1037/a0037215

Ross, K., & Byerly, C. (2014). *Women and media: International perspectives.* Wiley-Blackwell.

Ryan, C., & Karen, J. (2019). *Beyond prime time activism: Communication activism and social change.* Routledge. https://doi.org/10.4324/9781315181219

Santoniccolo, F., Trombetta, T., Paradiso, M. N., & Rollè, L. (2023). Gender and media representations: A review of the literature on gender stereotypes, objectification and sexualization. *International Journal of Environmental Research and Public Health, 20*(10), 5770. https://doi.org/10.3390/ijerph20105770

United Nations Economic and Social Council (UNODC). (2013). https://www.unodc.org/documents/commissions/CCPCJ/Crime_Resolutions/2010-2019/2013/ECOSOC/Resolution_2013-36.pdf

Ward, L. M., & Grower, P. (2020). Media and the development of gender role stereotypes. *Annual Review of Developmental Psychology, 2*, 177–199. https://doi.org/10.1146/annurev-devpsych-051120-010630

Wood, J. T. (2009). *Gendered lives: Communication, gender, and culture* (8th ed.). Thompson/Wadsworth.

Section I

# Gender Representation, Construction, and Portrayal

# Chapter 1

# Conceptualising Participation as Representation, Interaction, and Engagement

*Emilly Comfort Maractho[a] and Solveig Omland[b]*

[a]Uganda Christian University, Uganda
[b]NLA University College, Norway

## Abstract

This chapter presents and nuances central concepts in the study of women's participation in public life through the lens of the media. It is the centrality of politics and power that has captured the attention of researchers using various frameworks in gender and media studies. Yet, a focus on the participation of women in public life, more generally, through the lens of media has been in short supply. People's public life is often reflected in the media. Consequently, much research has been done to investigate how women are represented in the media, from content analysis, examinations of when and how they are sources, and studies into why women leave the newsroom, to name only some of the many research foci. Especially in a sub-Saharan context, research shows underrepresentation and misrepresentation of women through mediated platforms (Tamale, 1999). This chapter starts by asking whether there are additional or complementary approaches to understanding and getting more accurate insight into how women participate in public life. We conceptualise participation as representation, interaction, and engagement and present an approach to understanding and researching women in public life and media. We argue that these perspectives

Gender and Media Representation: Perspectives from Sub-Saharan Africa, 11–24
doi:10.1108/978-1-83608-406-820251002

will give a more accurate understanding of women's participation in public life, beyond politics and power.

*Keywords*: Participation; representation; interaction; engagement; women; media; public life

## Introduction

This chapter presents central concepts in the study of women's participation in public life, a well-researched topic that includes studies focussed on the interconnection between women, politics, and power, (Hughes et al., 2017), women and power in postcolonial Africa, and African women in politics and policymaking (Goetz & Hassim, 2003). Much research has been done to investigate how women are represented in the media from content analysis of women's portrayal in media and gender responsiveness in media products (Litho et al., 2012) to when and how they are sources (UMWA, 2016) and why women leave the newsroom (Kaija, 2013), to name only some of the research foci. The centrality of politics and power has captured the attention of researchers using various frameworks, but the participation of women in public life, more generally, through the lens of media, has been in short supply. Research shows that there is underrepresentation and misrepresentation of women through mediated platforms, especially in a Sub-Saharan context (Tamale, 1999) where fewer women contribute to the 'hard stories' like politics, economics, and security in national news (UMWA, 2016) and much fewer women are engaged in public affairs talk shows (Maractho, 2019; Mwesige, 2009). This chapter begins by asking whether there are additional or complementary approaches to understanding and getting more accurate insight into how women are represented by and participate in media and public life. By combining a focus on representation, interaction, and engagement (RIE) and introducing the RIE model, we hope to offer a more comprehensive approach to understanding women's participation in public life. We presume that research on women's participation that does not sufficiently engage with the ideas of RIE collectively may result in an incomplete valuation. Each of these aspects is necessary but insufficient to fully understand the depth and extent of participation in any area of public life.

The model builds on doctoral work using grounded theory to investigate not only the frequency of women's participation in media and public life but also the substance of their participation in a Ugandan context (Maractho, 2017). The three-phase research project comprised interviews with producers and presenters of 10 broadcast news media organisations, observation and content analysis of programmes run by the 10 media houses, and unstructured interviews targeting the life history of 25 women in public life, analysed using a grounded theory approach. The collected data for the development of the model focussed on six areas of women in public life: women in politics, public administration, medicine and public health, education and sports, business and economics, and law and advocacy. This rich data set helped expand the concept of participation while redefining the indicators of RIE.

This chapter further sharpens the RIE model and adds to the conversation on what it means to participate in public life and how it is often reflected through the media. The RIE model may present a fresh look at women's participation in public life and give meaning to some of the valuable concepts and how they may be utilised for the study of gender and media and, broadly, for other areas of participation. It attempts to answer questions about who participates, how they participate, and why, where, and when they may participate. The chapter offers a redefinition of participation encompassing three other broad concepts – representation, interaction, and engagement – all as forms of participation to provide a more accurate understanding of and a more holistic framework for studying women's participation in media and public life. This supplements existing contributions and is not intended as a comprehensive approach. We will first define the concept of participation and then demonstrate the value of the three concepts of the three-legged stool approach. Although the model emerged from research in a Ugandan context, we argue for its transferability to other contexts and foci of research.

### *The Concept of Participation*

Participation is a politically ambivalent and definitionally vague buzzword that, despite being 'irrevocably contaminated' by its mainstreaming, has 'been critical for decades in animating struggles for equality, rights and social justice' (Cornwall & Brock, 2005, pp. 1056–1057). Participation means being able to speak 'in one's own voice, thereby simultaneously constructing and expressing one's cultural identity through idiom and style' (Fraser, 1990, p. 69). A perspective on participation from development studies we find helpful is the concept of 'invited' and 'claimed' spaces (Cornwall, 2002). Whereas invited space refers to a more formal event where development agents create events for stakeholders to contribute, claimed space involves the poor taking control of political processes without being invited in. For instance, women may mobilise votes to participate in politics (claimed space) or get appointed into public office (invited). These concepts help us understand women's participation not only in public affairs programmes and public life but also in media. This chapter argues that participation is more than a manifestation of women's voice and visibility in media (representation). It also includes women in public life through consultation and conversation on media (interaction) and their quest for equal rights and political agency through the involvement and influence of the state and society using the media (engagement).

Women's participation in media is a multifaceted phenomenon. Roughly speaking, one can talk about two main areas of participation in media related to the kind of role that a woman plays, whether working in the media or contributing to media content (Maractho, 2017). Women in the media are professionals who contribute to media production and presentation in various ways, such as journalists, editors, researchers, managers, owners, and technical personnel. Women on the media describe those who are not employed by the media but contribute to setting the agenda on media through their work in public life and engagement in public debates. Utilising these non-exhausting categorisations might contribute to understanding their RIE (Fig. 1.1).

Maractho (2017) presented three categories applicable to navigating the landscape of women in media: (a) journalists and artists (e.g. hosting guests, reporting, presenting, anchoring, and producing current and public affairs programmes); (b) media managers (e.g. editors and programme managers); and (c) media owners. Women on media are not employed by media and are not media professionals but may be analysts (commentators) consulted by the media to provide their expert views or opinions on matters of public affairs in areas where they may be involved, featured as subjects (or part of a story in which they have no voice), and sources (eyewitnesses and those in possession of information relevant for a story). They are women in public life. Both women in the media and on the media are important indicators of representation. This approach allows for representation beyond image or the portrayal of women, which has been given much research focus. Therefore, women's representation in the mass media comprises women's access to and presence in the mass media, as well as their contribution to the production and consumption of the mass media.

## Women's Participation in Public Life

Women's participation in public life is a broad term that refers to their engagement in politics and policymaking. Fraser (1990, p. 70) argues that 'the concept of a public presupposes a plurality of perspectives among those who participate within it, thereby allowing for internal differences and antagonisms, and likewise discouraging reified blocs'. However, Thompson (1995, p. 55) sees public life as founded on the recognition of mutual interests and networks of association and emphasises its hegemonic basis of public life. In categorising women in public life, the idea of interests and networks were crucial.

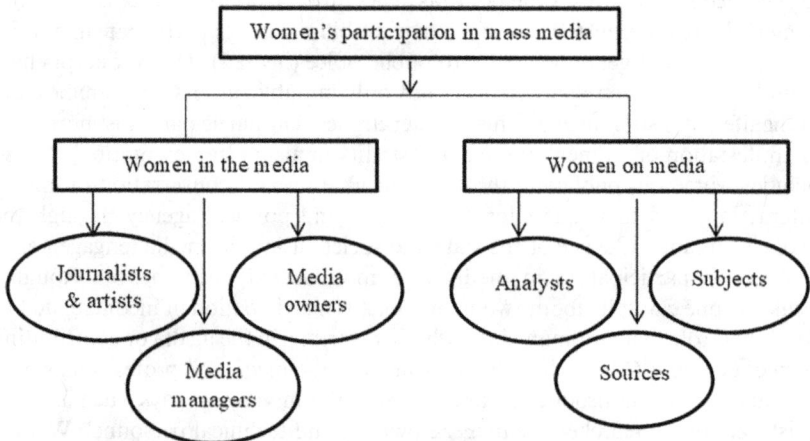

Fig. 1.1.   Women's Participation in the Mass Media.

From a Ugandan perspective, it is interesting to note that many strategies have been implemented in Uganda to increase women's participation in public life, for example, affirmative action and gender mainstreaming. Nevertheless, it remains unclear how this integration is reflected in the media. Maractho's (2017) analysis explored women's participation in public life through extensive interviews and a life history approach to inform the reconceptualisation of participation as RIE.

Although limited, media coverage can indicate women's participation in public life by highlighting their issues and roles as analysts and sources in public affairs. The absence of such representation suggests barriers for both women and the media despite the growing number of women in public life in Uganda. Six distinct areas were examined to assess women's participation in public life, namely women in politics (both national and local), civil service, education and sports, business and economics, medicine and public health, and law and advocacy. These are not the only areas of public life but are indicative of a broader realm beyond politics that has dominated research on African women in general and Ugandan women in particular. This categorical framework is an analytical tool that disaggregates the women on media and helps identify which women are in and on media.

The data suggest that women's participation in public life is better understood through the study of RIE, the three elements of the RIE model, each of which is a necessary but insufficient condition for an adequate analysis of participation in public life. We argue that this 'three-legged stool' anchored in the grounded theory work in a Ugandan context (Maractho, 2017) can contribute to further research and analysis of women's participation in public life. This builds from Houle's (2000) demonstration that 'participation in public debate which challenges the expectations of women's and men's roles in society therefore offers an alternative route by which women can participate in redefining their social status' (p. 149). As such, access to media that allows for participation becomes a gateway through which the media can play a meaningful role in changing the status of women. Participation is central for democratisation, development and public life. Because the modern media brings in a new kind of publicness beyond the traditional model (Thompson, 1995), it follows that our conception of participation should also change, to accommodate this new media.

The focus on negative portrayal of women politicians by female journalists (Tamale, 1999) relies on the assumption that women only weakly participate in media and public life, therefore victims of a male-dominated press, without recognising how much the mediated space has changed and affords better models of participation for women, beyond representation or stereotypical portrayal and symbolic annihilation, through interaction and engagement with the public now a common occurrence.

### Representation

In cultural studies, representation is interpreted as discourse, or in other words, the process by which meaning is produced and exchanged between members of a culture (Foucault, 1980). Hall is best known for his work on ideology and representation which shaped cultural and media studies. In the politics of signification

Hall (1980, p. 138) presents representation as a complex way in which the mass media present images and also engage in re-representing images with multiple meanings regarding race and ethnicity. Representation is further used to explain the gender gap in the media and why it matters by appreciating the differences in coverage of men and women. The concept and forms of political representation are greatly explored in the seminal work of political theorist Pitkin (1967), who describes it as the 'continuing tension between ideal and achievement' and argues that it behoves democracies to 'construct institutions and train individuals in such a way that they engage in the pursuit of the public interest, the genuine representation of the public; and at the same time, to remain critical of those institutions and that training' (p. 240). Pitkin proposes four distinct categories of representation: formalistic (authorisation and accountability), symbolic, descriptive, and substantive representation.

The marginalisation of women in media has long been debated and researched, and in an American context, the question of whether media coverage of women reinforces rather than challenges the dominant culture; their research showed that the representation contributed towards women's marginalisation in public life (Norris, 1997). Sreberny-Mohammadi and Ross (1996) note that there has been a significant lacuna in the analysis of how media presentations of politics are gendered and impact not only democracy at large but also the best strategies to increase women's political participation.

Some studies of women and media focus on the media's portrayal of women, especially women in politics (Tamale, 1999). This research examines women's representation in the media in terms of their visibility and voice. Instead of a singular focus on mass media, the study critically looks at women and how they negotiate for space 'in' and 'on' media. Studies from the Middle East provide rich examples of how women have used media to reconstruct feminism and gender issues and foster constitutional change (Sakr, 2004). In Uganda, women have relied more heavily on politics than media to advance their causes. This study assumes that such negotiations in public politics should be reflected in the media, yet women are underrepresented in media content in Uganda (Maractho, 2018). What emerged from Maractho's (2017) data reconceptualised and addressed women's participation from two angles: (a) access to and presence of women in broadcast media (visibility), and (b) the availability of women, gender, and women's issues on media (voice). The determinants of women's access to media, their presence, and which women are visible are crucial. For example, how many women are invited as guests and what range of public life do they represent? How many of the citizens who contribute to the talk shows are women and what areas of public life do they represent? What specific issues dominate the discussions related to women?

This chapter does not focus on any single form of representation but attempts to address the question of voice and visibility in analytical terms by integrating its different forms. Fig. 1.2 provides a conceptual measurement of representation using typological theory that can facilitate future research.

Pitkin (1967) asks interesting questions about representation: When should men feel represented? What counts as evidence that they are represented (p. 9)?

| | |
|---|---|
| C – Low voice, high visibility | D – High voice, high visibility |
| A – Low voice, low visibility | B – low visibility and high voice |

Visibility

Voice

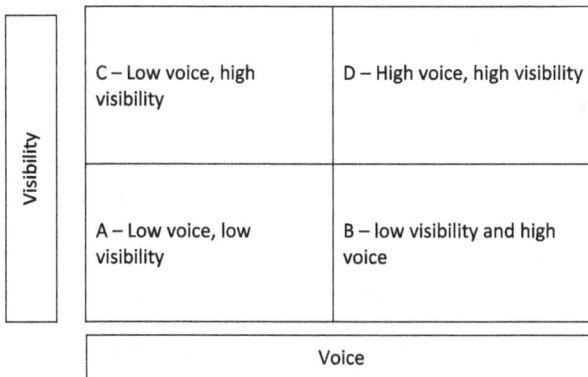

Fig. 1.2. Typology of Women's Representation on Media.

This section applies these questions to women. Women's representation on media refers to the proportion of women compared to men in and on media, particularly in current and public affairs programmes. This representation is assessed by their physical presence (visibility) or through their voice. Visibility reflects not only the extent to which women are physically present but also the range of issues covered in the media that are of specific interest to women in particular or related to gender, for example, women's rights and the marginalisation of women in society. Voice describes the range of women's perspective in and on the media, directly or indirectly, to hold decision-makers accountable or to amplify issues relevant to women's advancement.

Women's representation in the media can be categorised into four types that are determined by the relationship between visibility and voice: low visibility and voice (A), low visibility and high voice (B), high visibility and low voice (C), and high visibility and voice (D). Policy action should aim at moving women from categories A, B, and C to D using strategies that reflect each group's specific barriers to representation. Media serves as a lens to examine women's participation in public life and its influence on that participation.

If women in and on media use their presence to amplify and promote women's issues, then they have voice. What is more, the presence of a woman on a programme does not guarantee voice unless the topics discussed are about women, although their presence adds value by bringing in women's perspective. For instance, two women might be hosting a show on the civil service and not 'women's issues' or discussions about gender and women in particular. While women's issues are not clearly defined, the term refers to issues that affect or are important to women, what the media often calls 'soft' issues related to such social services as health and education as well as family and religion. While visibility portends presence, voice is agency.

Although the focus here is on women in the media and on media, women are not solely responsible for visibility. Stories about women covered by men also increase visibility. Men who 'speak for' women are giving voice to women, too. All issues are gendered, and training matters for women in the media

(Dralega et al., 2016). The question is whether participants on these programmes recognise and address gendered issues.

### Interaction

Thompson (1995) identifies three types of interaction between people and media: (a) face-to-face interaction, which occurs in-person; (b) mediated interaction, which uses such technical mediums as letters and telephone; and (c) mediated quasi-interaction, which is unique to mass communication. Craig (2004) explores how politicians and the news media interact and the nature of the power of the media to flag the media's value as a site for understanding participation in public life. This chapter presents interaction as adding value to representation through consultation and conversation and depicts who initiates contact. Interaction is crucial to capturing the 'political interactivity or mediated real-time feedback between political actors and citizens' that comprises both consultation and conversation. Indeed, as Davis and Owen (1998) argue:

> what distinguishes these communication forms from more traditional ones, such as newspapers and nightly television news, is the degree to which they offer political discussion opportunities that attract public officials, candidates, citizens, and even members of the mainstream press corps. (p. 7)

New media enhances the public's ability to become actors rather than merely spectators in media politics. This changes where we locate underrepresentation of women in the media because there are significant new opportunities available for women who had previously been excluded. Women can directly initiate and participate in media conversations through interactive affordances like text messages, call-in programmes, and social media chats that are embedded in programming. The RIE model emphasises 'the interaction between women and media to explore how dominant meanings about gender are created and how audiences interpret what they see and hear' (Sakr, 2004, p. 4). So which women are interacting with the mass media and in what ways (forms)?

Fig. 1.3 presents a typology of interaction that identifies four categories of how that women–media interaction plays out: low consultation and conversation (A); low consultation and high conversation (B); high consultation and low conversation (C); and high consultation and conversation (D). Communication is a form of interaction, and media interactivity is an increasingly salient feature of the media in question and other cultural trends as digital technology proliferates. This framework assumes that the programmes studied are interactive and use new media in a way that reflects media convergence. Fig. 1.4 illustrates the suggested typology of women–media interactions.

Women–media interaction is a function of both consultation (media-driven) and conversation (more often women-driven). In other words, interaction can redefine representation, enabling otherwise-excluded women to claim space in and on the media by joining the conversation in a variety of ways. This should

|  | C – Low conversation, high consultation | D – High consultation, conversation |
|---|---|---|
|  | A – Low conversation, consultation | B – low consultation, high conversation |

Consultation (left axis label) · Conversation (bottom axis label)

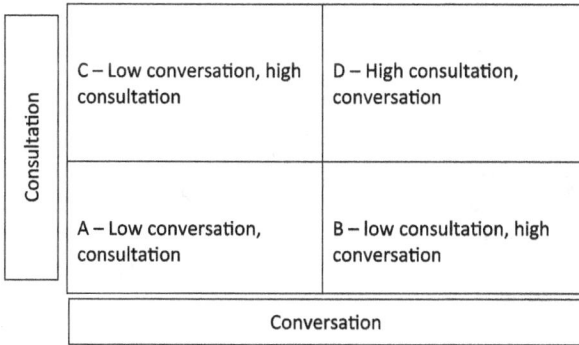

Fig. 1.3. Typology of Women–Media Interaction.

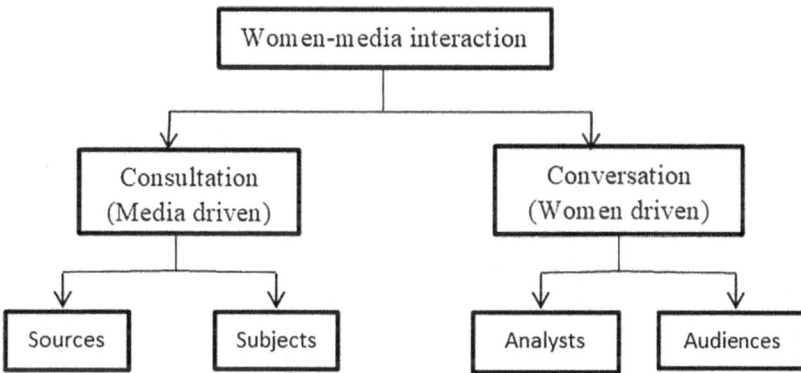

Women-media interaction
- Consultation (Media driven)
  - Sources
  - Subjects
- Conversation (Women driven)
  - Analysts
  - Audiences

Fig. 1.4. Women–Media Interaction.

demonstrate the pertinence to invited and claimed spaces (Cornwall, 2002) because women–media interaction addresses who initiates interaction. In consultation, the media include women by giving them a platform or covering women's issues. It measures how often women are consulted and the range of women's issues covered by the media, regardless of who is doing the actual reporting. Conversation refers to how and when women gain access to the media as citizens (analysts) and participants in public life (audiences) who use that access to increase their visibility and amplify their voices. Conversation is more dependent on women taking action (e.g. by either calling or engaging in newsworthy actions) that compel media to consult them.

Maractho (2017) showed that the women–media interaction most often involves women as sources, subjects, analysts, and audiences. Media-driven consultation of women depends on the media seeking women as sources and covering issues that make women the subjects of stories. Women who are not media workers may lack the opportunity to influence these choices. Conversation involves women participating in dialogue in or outside the media that shape their media presence. This can include active involvement in the discussion of politics, advocacy, and policy, so this approach allows for a deeper analysis than the assumptions in portrayal studies that only look at how women are re-represented in media text and images. As analysts, women often engage in activities outside the media that draw them into it. Women may buy airtime or produce advertisements to discuss issues. They can also get involved in the discussion through such other forms as calling into talk shows, using social media, and sending SMS text messages. The degree of media-driven versus women-driven interaction determines the extent and nature of interaction. Thus, conversation reflects women's ability to use the media to shape gender and women's issues and advocate for equal rights from both the state and society.

## Engagement

When women gain access to the media and are both represented and interacting, how they use this platform to benefit women is a matter of engagement. Engagement has 'rich potential for illuminating ways in which women are empowered or disempowered' (Sakr, 2004, p. 12). Women's engagement with the media is the ability of women to use the media through the current and public affairs programmes to influence policy and initiate state and societal responses to women's demands. For example, despite many challenges, Iranian women used the press to question gender constructions and gender relations and to call for a radical rethinking of law, policy, and the constitution, and similar trends of women's struggle for engagement with the press were seen throughout the Middle East (Khiabany & Sreberny, 2004, p. 15). Research on the Ugandan context indicates that after 1986, when the National Resistance Movement came to power, women's organisations began to engage with the media to address the negative portrayal of women and the underrepresentation of women's issues (Mukama, 2002, p. 148). This led to improved media representation of women and coverage of women's issues.

However, some questions remain unanswered in the literature. Based on the now-available data, we reconceptualise engagement as involvement and influence in shaping public debate and policy by critiquing state and societal structures that marginalise women through the media. This engagement promotes women's rights in the media and on media when they use it to question negative gender constructions and gender relations. There are four potential scenarios: low involvement and influence (A); low involvement and high influence (B); high involvement and low influence (C); and high involvement and influence (D). Figs. 1.5 and 1.6 illustrate this typology of engagement and women's engagement with the media in relation to the state, society and public life.

Involvement and influence are characterised by whether women's representation and interaction with media are media- or women-driven. Involvement can occur without creating direct change, whereas influence creates change. What is critical here is that engagement is a product of representation (visibility and voice) and interaction (consultation and conversation). There are not only two points of involvement, that is, in mass media and public life, but also two areas of influence, that is, of the society through its practices and of the state through policy.

| | | |
|---|---|---|
| | C – Low influence, high involvement | D – High influence, involvement |
| Involvement | A – Low involvement, influence | B – low involvement, high Influence |

| Influence |
|---|

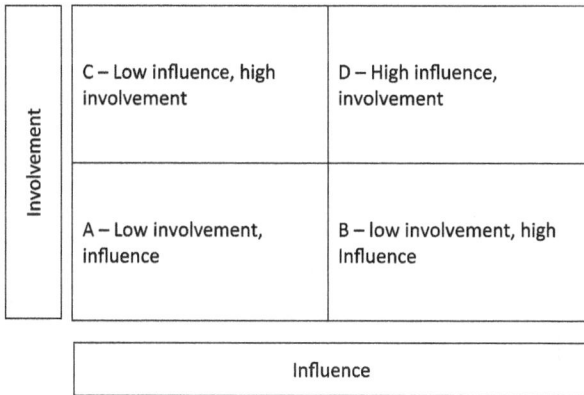

Fig. 1.5.   Typology of Women's Engagement with Media.

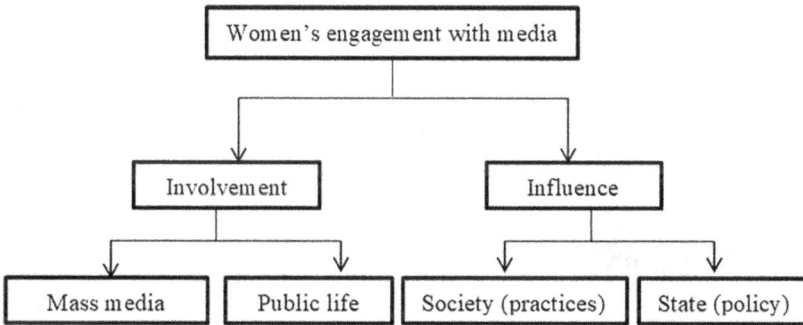

```
                  Women's engagement with media

          Involvement                       Influence

Mass media    Public life    Society (practices)    State (policy)
```

Fig. 1.6.   Women's Engagement with the Media.

An analysis of these two factors demonstrates the nature of women's engagement with the media and the extent of their success.

## The RIE Model for Research

Our aim for this chapter is to contribute perspectives and a model that illustrates the nature and extent of women's participation in mass media as an independent variable that, in turn, impacts women's participation in public life, the dependent variable. RIE are necessary but insufficient conditions for influencing women's participation in public life. Such external issues as policy, legal, institutional, and regulatory frameworks for both the media and public spheres also influence women's participation.

Study of representation without consideration of interactive media will overlook the new opportunities it affords women that, in turn, increase their representation on media. A study of interaction without consideration of who initiates a consultation or conversation may also miss crucial dynamics. And looking only at representation and interaction, we will likely overlook the variety of ways in

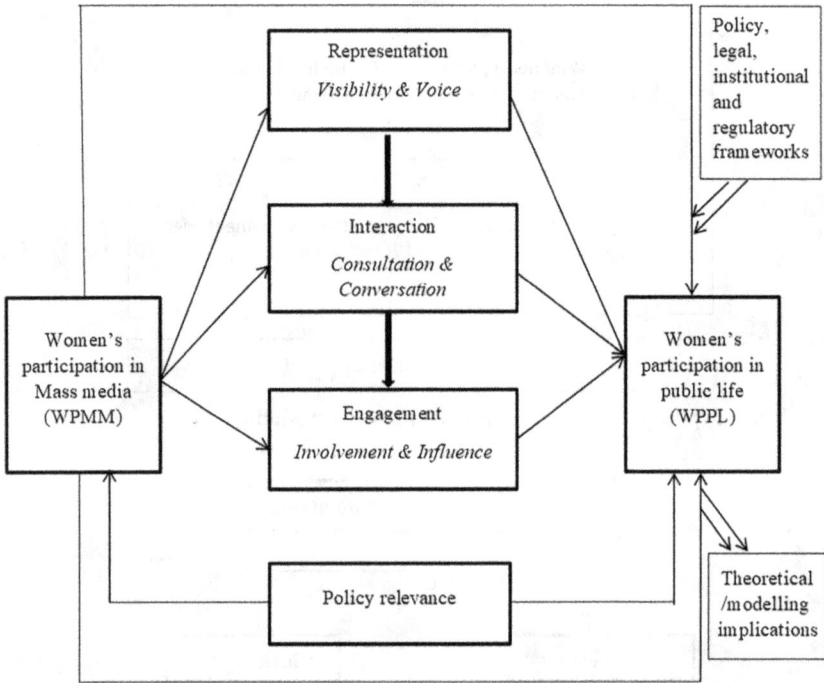

Fig. 1.7.   The RIE Model.

which women are involved in and influence the public space that, in turn, lead to their representation and interaction with media. Participation conceptualised as RIE provides a more holistic picture of women's participation.

We theorise that effective RIE in and on mass media facilitates women's participation in public life. These three dimensions of participation intersect to function and complement each other. What is more, they represent levels of participation, starting with representation, moving through interaction, and culminating in engagement, the final stage that influences policy and drives change for women. The degree of influence of participation in public life depends on the quality of each of these three factors. Ultimately, women's participation in the mass media increases women's participation in public life (Fig. 1.7).

## Conclusion

This conceptualisation of representation is a step towards creating an analytical tool for research on women's participation in media and public life. Giving meaning to the many concepts used in this research is of paramount importance. The chapter unpacks several concepts and discusses the dimensions and also the indicators of the concepts as derived from data and refined by literature.

A diagrammatical presentation of the conceptual framework that can be used for the analysis of participation as RIE is introduced. The relationships are clearly marked out with arrows. The key assumption, at this point, is that the mass media influences women's participation in public life and that depends on the nature and extent of participation conceptualised as representation, interaction, and engagement.

# References

Bucy, E. P., & Gregson, K. S. (2001). Media participation: A legitimizing mechanism of mass democracy. *New Media & Society*, *3*(3), 357–380.

Cornwall, A. (2002). *IDS Working papers 170: Making spaces, changing places: situating participation in development*. Institute of Development Studies. https://ids.ac.uk/pub-lications/making-spaces-changing-places-situating-participation-in-development/

Cornwall, A., & Brock, K. (2005). What do buzzwords do for development policy? A critical look at "participation," "empowerment" and "poverty reduction." *Third World Quarterly*, *26*(7), 1043–1060. https://doi.org/10.1080/01436590500235603

Craig, G. (2004). *The media, politics and public life*. Allen & Unwin.

Davis, R., & Owen, D. (1998). *New media and American politics*. Oxford University Press.

Dralega, C. A., Agaredech, J., Jjuko, M., & Katono, R. (2016). Gender mainstreaming in media and journalism education – An audit of media departments in Uganda, Rwanda and Ethiopia. *Journal of African Media Studies*, *8*(3), 251–266. https://doi.org/10.1386/jams.8.3.251_1

Foucault, M. (1980). *The history of sexuality* (R. Hurley, Trans.). Vintage books.

Fraser, N. (1990). Rethinking the public sphere: A contribution to the critique of actually existing democracy. *Social Text*, *25/26*, 56–80. https://doi.org/10.2307/466240

Goetz, A. M., & Hassim, S. (Eds.). (2003). *No shortcuts to power: African women in politics and policy making* (Vol. 3). Zed Books.

Hall, S. (1980). Encoding/decoding. In S. Hall, D. Hobson, A. Lowe, & P. Wills (Eds.), *Culture, media, language* (pp. 128–138). Hutchinson.

Houle, A. E. (2000). *Women and the public sphere: Exploring women's access to participation in a democratic society* [Ph.D. thesis, Queens University].

Hughes, M. M., Paxton, P., & Krook, M. L. (2017). Gender quotas for legislatures and corporate boards. *Annual Review of Sociology*, *43*(1), 331–352.

Kaija, B. (2013). Uganda: Women near parity but still leaving newsrooms. In C. M. Byerly, C. M. Byerly (Eds.), *The Palgrave international handbook of women and journalism* (pp. 315–329). Palgrave Macmillan UK.

Khiabany, G., & Sreberny, A. (2004). The women's press in contemporary Iran: Engendering the public sphere. In N. Sakr (Ed.), *Women and media in the Middle East. Power through self-expression* (pp. 15–38). IB Tauris.

Litho, P., Masagazi, M., Leko, P., Higenyi, J., Buyana, K., Nankya, J., & Lukanda, I. (2012). *An assessment of the Ugandan media's capacity to produce gender-responsive products: A focus on the New Vision Bukedde*. ILO.

Maractho, E. C. (2017). *Mass media, women and public life in Uganda: Interrogating representation, interaction and engagement* [Doctoral dissertation, University of KwaZulu-Natal].

Maractho, E. C. (2018). Determinants of participation in political communication in Uganda's broadcast media: Implications for women. In B. Mutsvairo & B. Karam (Eds.), *Perspectives on political communication in Africa* (pp. 79–94). Springer.

Maractho, E. C. (2019). (Re)producing cultural narratives on women in public affairs programmes in Uganda. *Journal of African Media Studies, 11*(3), 293–311.

Mukama, R. (2002). Women making a difference in the media. In A. M. Tripp & J. C. Kwesiga (Eds.), *The women's movement in Uganda: History, challenges and prospects* (pp. 146–163). Fountain Publishers.

Mwesige, P. G. (2009). The democratic functions and dysfunctions of political talk radio: The case of Uganda. *Journal of African Media Studies, 1*(2), 221–245.

Norris, P. (1997). Introduction: Women, media and politics. In *Women, media and politics*. Oxford University Press.

Pitkin, H. (1967). *The concept of representation*. University of California Press.

Sakr, N. (Ed.). (2004). *Women and media in the Middle East: Power through self-expression*. I.B. Taurus & Co. Ltd.

Sreberny-Mohammadi, A., & Ross, K. (1996). Women MPs and the media: Representing the body politic. *Parliamentary Affairs, 49*(1), 103–115. https://doi.org/10.1093/oxfordjournals.pa.a028661

Tamale, S. (1999). *When hens begin to crow: Gender and parliamentary politics in Uganda*. Westview Press.

Thompson, J. B. (1995). *The media and modernity: A social theory of the media*. Stanford University Press.

Tripp, A. M. (2015). *Women and power in post-conflict Africa*. Cambridge University Press.

Tuchman, G. (1979). Women's depiction by the mass media. *Signs: Journal of Women in Culture and Society, 4*(3), 528–542.

Uganda Media Women's Association (UMWA). 2016. Media and elections in Uganda. *A gender analysis of print coverage of the 2016 general elections in Uganda*. http://www.umwamamafm.co.ug/pdf

World Association of Christian Communication. (2015). 5th Global Media Monitoring Report. https://whomakesthenews.org/gmmp-2015-reports/

World Association of Christian Communication. (2020). 6th Global Media Monitoring Report. https://whomakesthenews.org/gmmp-2020-final-reports/

# Chapter 2

# How the Tanzanian Press Portrayed the Country's First Female President Samia Suluhu Hassan in a Non-stereotypical Manner

*Theodorah S. Munisi[a] and Terje Skjerdal[b]*

[a]*University of Dar es Salaam, Tanzania*
[b]*NLA University College, Norway*

## Abstract

Despite increased visibility, women politicians continue to confront gender stereotypes perpetuated by biases in media coverage and systemic barriers. This study investigates the gender representation of Tanzania's first female president, Samia Suluhu Hassan, in local newspaper coverage. The study asks two primary research questions: how prominent were the news articles about President Hassan and how was she portrayed in those articles? The quantitative content analysis of 414 news articles that appeared in the state-owned *HabariLeo* daily newspaper and the privately owned *Mwananchi* daily newspaper from March 2021 to March 2022 revealed slightly different approaches to President Hassan's visibility and portrayal. Whereas *HabariLeo* prioritised the president's visibility with front-page placement, *Mwananchi* offered more in-depth, below-the-fold analysis. The study establishes that ownership, editorial policy, and sociocultural constructs influence the newspapers' coverage. The study unveils not only positive gender representations of the president emphasising her authority and competence but also minor stereotypical representations in the coverage consistent with how President Hassan presented herself to the public using traditional gender roles. Overall, the study unearths favourable journalistic practices within the Tanzanian media landscape and a gender-sensitive portrayal of the country's first female president that challenges not only entrenched traditional socionorms but also previous research.

*Keywords*: Tanzania; President Samia Suluhu Hassan; media portrayal; gender stereotypes; *HabariLeo*; *Mwananchi*

## Introduction

The portrayal of women politicians in the media has become central to global discussions in our era of significant sociopolitical shifts and evolving perspectives on gender equality. Female politicians have undoubtedly gained visibility in the media coverage, yet their representation is still subject to biases in reporting and systematic barriers within the media industry and society writ large. Gendered imbalances are particularly evident in traditional societies where the media are accused of applying double standards to female and male politicians when they, for example, showcase the private lives and appearances of women politicians and induce emotional attachment. Unequal gender representation and biased coverage, however, are? evident also in international media portrayals of women in power, including heads of state, who have become subjects of biased media coverage (Zamfirache, 2010). Former German Chancellor Angela Merkel, former Prime Minister of New Zealand Jacinda Ardern, former Prime Minister of the United Kingdom Theresa May, former President of Liberia Ellen Johnson Sirleaf, and former Vice President of the United States Kamala Harris have all been stereotyped by local as well as global media. Women in leadership often face negative media portrayals that disproportionately emphasise personal attributes over other contributions to governance (Geertsema-Sligh, 2018; Raicheva-Stover & Ibroscheva, 2014; Van der Pas & Aaldering, 2020). The male politician is portrayed as a natural fit, whereas the female politician is portrayed as a contradiction or an oddity, as illustrated by such name-calling as 'Iron-lady' and 'Superwoman' (Aalberg & Strömbäck, 2010).

This chapter focuses on Tanzania to extend scholarship on media representations of female politicians with a non-Western point of view. Traditionally characterised by its patriarchal structures (Johannessen, 2006), Tanzanian politics experienced a significant transformation with the succession of its first female president in 2021. Samia Suluhu Hassan ascended from the position of vice president after the sudden death of her predecessor, President John Magufuli, during the Covid-19 pandemic in March 2021. The new president was soon celebrated for her government's proactive policies against the pandemic and a softer stance on civil society and the media, although restraints against the political opposition were sustained (Committee to Protect Journalists, 2024). Hassan is one of only a handful of women who have served as the head of an African state. At the time of writing (March 2025), Samia Suluhu Hassan is the only woman among 54 heads of state on the continent besides President Netumbo Nandi-Ndaitwah of Namibia.

The Tanzanian media landscape, shaped by historical, cultural, and societal norms, has traditionally operated within a patriarchal framework that mirrors male-dominated decision-making structures. In other words, Tanzanian media have often upheld gendered norms when covering female politicians (Johannessen, 2006). What is more, both public and privately owned media have faced challenges related to democracy, accountability, transparency, and independence, particularly during male presidencies. Prior to President Samia Suluhu Hassan's leadership, restrictive legislation like the Media Services Act (2016), along with media outlet closures, journalist intimidation, and online repression, hindered media freedoms (Holmén, 2023). This study examines President Hassan's representation in the state-owned *HabariLeo* and privately owned *Mwananchi* newspapers within her first year in office, from March 2021 to March 2022, using quantitative content analysis to explore her coverage's prominence and portrayal, including its portrayal of her leadership style, gender role, and personal life.

### *Female Voices in the Media*

Women's voices in the media are consistently underrepresented as sources, content producers, and commentators (Akpabio, 2017; Lukanda, 2021; Mitchelstein et al., 2020). In Tanzania, women constitute only 21% of quoted sources, aligning closely with the 22% average across Africa (Who Makes the News?, 2021). Globally, women represent about 25% of news sources. What is more, female voices are largely confined to softer topics, like gender equality and gender-based violence, whereas male voices dominate areas like politics, finance, and science. For example, women in Uganda are often marginalised in science coverage; although women author 23% of science stories, they feature as sources in just 5% (Lukanda, 2021). In Argentina, women are particularly underrepresented in popular beats like sports, politics, and crime reporting (Mitchelstein et al., 2020). Some Eastern European countries, however, show higher female representation (Josephi et al., 2019). For instance, Slovakia leads with 51% female authorship, followed by Czechia and Poland, though Hungary lags behind (Shevchuck et al., 2022). Research by the Global Media Monitoring Project, which has studied gender representation in multiple countries at five-year intervals since 1995, reveals that women are still often limited to sharing personal experiences, voicing popular opinions and offering witness accounts, rather than holding authoritative roles (Who Makes the News?, 2021). While there have been some advances in representation, ongoing challenges like objectification and stereotyping underscore the need for further progress towards gender equality in media portrayal.

Global research indicates that as societal attitudes and gender norms have evolved, progress has indeed been made towards more inclusive portrayals of women (Zamfirache, 2010), and initiatives like the United Nation's Sustainable Development Goal for gender equality have played important roles in challenging media stereotypes (Goswami et al., 2023). Stereotypes and reinforcement of traditional gender roles, however, remain prevalent, with women typically portrayed as caregivers, excessively emotional, or overly focused on appearance, while men are portrayed as dominant, strong, and independent (Santoniccolo et al., 2023).

In Tanzania, for instance, *Mwananchi* often depicts women as caregivers, victims, or sexual objects (Juppi et al., 2014). Similarly, in the Tanzanian tabloid *Ijumaa*, women are frequently portrayed as sexual objects (Elias, 2018). While sociocultural factors influence these portrayals, there is also potential to challenge these stereotypes when women are shown in positions of power, successful careers, and active citizenship (Juppi et al., 2014).

### Representation of Female Politicians

The portrayal of female politicians in news media often focuses disproportionately on their personal lives, appearance (both their physical features and such choices as hairstyle and dress), and family roles rather than their political achievements or policy positions. This tendency reinforces gender stereotypes, undermines credibility, and diminishes professional accomplishments (Sheeler & Anderson, 2013). In Bulgaria, for instance, female politicians are portrayed as women first and politicians second, and in Hong Kong, they are often depicted as idealised figures balancing leadership with traditional femininity (Raicheva-Stover & Ibroscheva, 2014). A study on media portrayals in Kenya highlights similar biases and the use of narratives that emphasise patriarchy, family roles, and controversy (Nduva, 2016). This focus on appearance denigrates their political competence and influences public perception.

Media narratives often depict female politicians as embodying maternal qualities, attributing traits like empathy, resilience, and communication skills to them (Garcia-Blanco & Wahl-Jørgensen, 2012). This is evident in coverage of leaders like former presidents Joyce Banda of Malawi and Ellen Johnson Sirleaf of Liberia, where themes of motherhood and leadership intertwine (Sihvonen, 2016). For instance, *Big Issue Magazine* in Malawi framed Banda as a nurturing figure, suggesting that her maternal instincts would safeguard the nation (Sihvonen, 2016). While motherhood may enhance public appeal and approachability, such portrayals also reinforce stereotypes that limit perceptions of female politicians. Studies indicate that women in top political roles face intensified scrutiny of their appearance and personal lives, with less emphasis on their political agendas (Aaldering & Van der Pas, 2020; Falk, 2010). Even in digital media, coverage of figures like President Hassan focuses on style and tone over leadership abilities, perpetuating biases that prioritise gender over competence (Solomon, 2023). This media framing of female leaders as 'female presidents' rather than simply 'presidents' contributes to societal norms that undervalue women's leadership by reinforcing gendered perceptions (Anderson et al., 2011).

## Women in Tanzanian Politics

Women's involvement in Tanzanian politics can be traced back to the struggle for independence from 1954 to 1961, when the Tanganyika African National Union (TANU) party was formed under the leadership of Julius Nyerere (Coulson, 2013). Thanks in large part to the work of activist, freedom fighter, and long-time supporter of Nyerere, Bibi Titi Mohamed, a separate women's section was formed within TANU to assist in the struggle for independence (Geiger, 1987), but no woman was appointed to the first Cabinet (Kairuki, 2018). In the 1980s, the Tanzanian government incorporated affirmative action to increase women's participation in the legislative assembly. In 1997, the constitution of Tanzania was amended to raise the proportion of female representation to 15% in Parliament and 25% in local councils (Meena et al., 2017). In 2020, the proportionate requirement was increased to 20% and 33%, respectively, and more women began to serve as ministers. In 2015, John Pombe Magufuli selected Samia Suluhu Hassan as his presidential running mate due, and the pair were re-elected in 2020. Despite the progress made in the political system in Tanzania, women politicians encounter persistent challenges emanating from entrenched sociocultural constructs and patriarchal systems (Makulilo, 2020). Hassan never ran for president. She was sworn in two days after President Magufuli's death on 17 March 2021. This marked a new era in the political system in Tanzania, and it also made history as the first country in East Africa with a female president.

Tanzania's media system has gone through four major phases: the German colonial phase (1885–1919), the British colonial phase (1919–1961), the postcolonial phase (or socialism phase, 1961–1992), and the democratisation phase (1992–present) (Sturmer & Rioba, 1998). After independence, the Tanzanian press was used to facilitate socialist *ujamaa* principles, whereas independent outlets were established with their own editorial policies during the democratisation phase. The establishment of the Tanzania Media Women's Association in 1987 aimed to increase women's participation at decision-making levels in the media. The formation of pressure groups like the Tanzania Gender Networking Programme in 1993 and the Media Council of Tanzania (MCT) in 1997 aimed to bring a new perspective to news coverage (Mushi, 2012). These initiatives have played a crucial role in promoting equal gender representation and encouraging women's involvement in the media. Yet the Tanzanian media still face significant challenges in the 21st century, some caused by poor quality journalism and some by infringements enforced by different presidents. News selection in Tanzania reflects assumptions about women's roles and status in society. A 2006 study found that when women appeared in the local media, 25% of the stories were about society (including politics), 36% about gender violence and harassment, 21% about relationships, and 18% about extraordinary women (Johannessen, 2006, p. 120). A 2013 study reported that male politicians featured more prominently in news articles and were quoted more than four times as often as their female counterparts (Juppi et al., 2014).

The violation of media freedom in Tanzania gained momentum during Magufuli's presidency (Cheeseman et al., 2021). Several laws were introduced that oppressed media freedom, including the Media Services Act of 2016. Newspaper licences were revoked for criticising the government, media outlets were suspended, and journalists were arrested and even abducted (Holmén, 2023). However, an Afrobarometer (2024) report lists Tanzania as a champion of media freedom in Africa from 2021 to 2023. This finding reflects how after President Hassan assumed office, her government amended policies in favour of media freedom. For example, four newspapers were reissued with publishing licences and the ban on specific online channels has been lifted (Holmén, 2023). Nevertheless, direct and indirect political interference remains well known, and the impact of the traditional cultural norms cannot be downplayed.

## Method

This study utilised quantitative content analysis to determine the prominence and portrayal of President Hassan in the local news. Replicability was guaranteed by employing standardised coding schemes and procedures. Two newspapers were purposively selected on the grounds that *Mwananchi* is a private newspaper and *HabariLeo* is a government-run newspaper. Both newspapers are published in Swahili, the official and most common native language in Tanzania. *Mwananchi* has a daily circulation of 32,000 newspapers, whereas *HabariLeo*, the government newspaper, distributes 6,500 copies daily (MCT, 2022). Both these newspapers are also relatively young. Although there was no private press before the adoption of multiparty democracy in Tanzania in 1992, by 2018, 175 newspapers were registered. Established in 1999, the private outlet *Mwananchi* has a slightly longer history than *HabariLeo*, founded in 2006. The most prominent independent publisher today is Mwananchi Communication Limited, a subsidiary of the Kenya-based Nation Media Group, and *Mwananchi* applies the same editorial policy as the group's publications in Kenya: to inform, educate and entertain its consumers (Primary data). Tanzanian Standard Newspapers, a state-owned organisation, publish *HabariLeo*. Both newspapers are headquartered in Dar es Salaam but have nation-wide circulation.

Systematic sampling identified 414 news articles from the two dailies (267 articles from *HabariLeo* and 147 from *Mwananchi*). All articles were published in the first year of President Hassan's term, from 19 March 2021 to 31 March 2022 and explicitly referred to the president in the headline. Only one news article was selected from each newspaper per day to avoid a sample too large for analysis. A systematic approach to article selection was followed: The article was ideally a front-page, leading news story about President Hassan. If there was no leading story about the president, then a secondary front-page story was used. When there was no story about the president on the front page, we shifted to the subsequent pages of the newspaper. When there was no news story about President Hassan in an issue, two stories were selected from one of the two following days. The search for a replacement article ended on the third day. This technique gathered 414 news articles for analysis over the 377 days.

Each story was coded using a predetermined codebook comprising variables in eight groups:

(1) Formal aspects and context data (e.g. date, title of article, and name and gender of author).
(2) News article salience as measured by size, photo, and the placement of article.
(3) Sources.
(4) Portrayal of gender roles.
(5) Description of appearance and personal life.

(6) Photos and image characteristics.
(7) Description of leadership qualities.
(8) Journalists' gender and its significance.

The second and third variables address research question one (prominence), and the fourth to eighth variables address research question two (portrayal of the president).

Two coders used SPSS to assign codes. About 10% of the 414 articles were pre-tested, and another 10% were coded for an intercoder reliability test that revealed confusion about the meaning of variables and which were mutually exclusive. After the coding variables were improved, a second intercoder reliability test resulted in kappa scores for front page (0.873), size of news articles (1.000), photo (1.000), topic (0.798), main source (0.884), main source gender (0.947), photo situation (0.937), and photo shots (0.934). Other variables were not tested because the kappa score is sensitive to skewed variables, that is, variables rarely present in the sample.

## President Hassan's Prominence

Our findings indicate a considerable difference in the prominence that each outlet gave to articles about President Hassan. Almost 70% of the stories concerning the president appeared as the main story on the front page of state-owned *HabariLeo* as compared to only 25% for *Mwananchi*. What is more, only 18% of *HabariLeo* issues had no front-page story about the president as compared to 54% for Nation Media's *Mwananchi*. Thus, although the president is highly visible in both news-papers, the government-affiliated outlet prioritises stories about her and her government. Placing President Hassan on the front page of the state-owned news-paper not only increases the head of state's visibility but also normalises women with executive power. The lower visibility of President Hassan in *Mwananchi* is arguably consistent with the Nation Media Group's editorial policy that its out-lets should 'not be driven by personal agendas nor practice excessive and con-tinuous personality-based journalism, but instead, they will practice issue-based journalism' (Nation Media Group, 2018). Studies conducted in Kenya, Ghana, and Nigeria show that women politicians are less featured on front pages not only because of policy directives but also because women rarely engage with the media and coverage is focused on a few powerful men (Osei-Appiah, 2019; Thuo, 2012). This finding likely reflects the differences in ownership and editorial policy between *HabariLeo* and *Mwananchi* (Fig. 2.1).

Most of the 414 news articles occupied less than a page (94% for *HabariLeo* and 69% for *Mwananchi*). Although HabariLeo provides higher front-page vis-ibility, it did not offer more in-depth coverage. Indeed, Spurk and Katunzi (2019) found that the government newspaper avoided in-depth stories and explained the root causes of an issue in only 20% of its articles as compared to 32% of articles in *Mwananchi*. This difference in reporting is also evident in the sources. On the one hand, the two *HabariLeo* articles that were longer than a page mainly sourced the president, with only a few paragraphs including opinions from officials, experts, and citizens. On the other hand, *Mwananchi*, which published 17 articles longer

Fig. 2.1.   Examples of Front-page Visibility in the Two Newspapers.
*Sources*: *HabariLeo* 11 October 2021 and *Mwananchi* 28 June 2021.

than one page, included more research-based and statistical information as well as quotes from experts and the opposition. As a state-owned media outlet, *HabariLeo* may have an editorial policy that focuses on routine promotion of the president and downplays critical analysis to control the narrative around her leadership.

### The Portrayal of President Hassan in News Articles

A count of the topics shows that leadership and politics dominate the articles about President Hassan in *HabariLeo* (39%) and *Mwananchi* (48%), followed by economics (18% vs 14%), diplomacy (14% vs 10%), and development (11% vs 14%). This diversity of topics enhances President Hassan's visibility around issues traditionally considered masculine. These findings contrast with studies elsewhere that suggest coverage of female politicians often focuses on soft and minor topics. For example, female politicians in the United States only received more coverage than their male counterparts in education and legislation, whereas male politicians dominated in stories about national security, economy, and technology (Andrich & Domahidi, 2024). Women leaders in Kenya were most visible in print media content about such topics as family, sexuality, and gender (Nduva, 2016).

President Hassan appeared as the main informant in most news articles (61% for *HabariLeo* and 69% for *Mwananchi*), followed by government officials and civil servants for the state-owned newspaper, and political parties and foreign political bodies for the private newspaper. Additional sources like citizens and health-care personnel had little to no coverage in either newspaper. Historically, women in positions of power have often faced marginalisation or the overshadowing of their voices in media coverage (Makulilo, 2020). Studies show that women in power are underrepresented, for example, across West African media (Osei-Appiah, 2019), but President Hassan's substantial presence as the main source in both the state-affiliated and independent newspaper underscores her as a key figure shaping the public agenda in Tanzania.

The vast majority of news articles, 96% in *HabariLeo* and 98% in *Mwananchi*, did not attach gender role traits to the president at all. Traits such as feminine, mother figure, and housewife were conveyed by only 2% of the articles. An even smaller proportion of the articles made use of adjectives like kind, caring, and compassionate. The few cases in *HabariLeo* and *Mwananchi* that did attach gender role traits to President Hassan were dominated by quotations by the president who referred to herself in gender terms:

> My people, I am a mother, and mother is a caregiver. However, there is a Swahili saying that a poor man is not fond of their child. It means that even if you want your child to look good, you will appear as if you do not love them, yet there is a way to make them look good. (*HabariLeo*, 2 May 2021, translated from Swahili)

This contrasts sharply with the coverage of Joyce Banda and Ellen Johnson Sirleaf, whose presidencies were framed as motherhood by both the local and international media (Sihvonen, 2016).

The count of attributives ascribed to President Hassan is demonstrative of this difference. Nearly 90% of the references to her by her name and official title employ the gender-neutral term 'president' (*Rais Samia*), and in only 3–4% of the stories is the title supplemented with the prefix 'female' ('female president'/*rais mwanamke*) that underlines the uncommonness of the president's gender. It is hard to imagine a newspaper article that would refer to 'male president' Magufuli, for example. The prefix 'female' brings attention to the personal side of the president in a way that a man would rarely experience, as does the newspapers' preference to refer to her by her first name, Samia. Importantly, the instances of 'female president' in the data set are all with positive connotations. What is more, 'mama' is occasionally used (comprising 6% of all attributions in *HabariLeo* and 10% in *Mwananchi*), a term that emphasises Samia's relatability and approachability as a leader. And again, the use of both 'mama' and 'female president' often came from President Hassan herself who referred to herself as 'mama' eight times and as 'female president' thrice. For example, when urging people to take the Covid-19 vaccine in July 2021, she appealed to the audience by pointing out that she is a mother ('mama') of four children, a wife, and a grandmother (*HabariLeo*, 29 July 2021). What we notice is that gender-specific attributes are used supportively in the studied material rather than as a means to frame the female gender negatively.

The data set included very few cases of articles that covered President Hassan's physical appearance and looks – only five articles among the 414. An article that appeared in *Mwananchi* on 9 December 2021 reads: 'President Samia, who was wearing a smart dress and a red scarf, did not speak much'. One could speculate whether her wardrobe would have been commented on had she been a male president, but, once more, it is interesting to note that two of these references to her appearance came from the president herself. In a statement in *HabariLeo* 2 April 2021, for example, Hassan underlined that she has 'real colours' for any who doubted that she is genuinely African. Although the statement alludes to physical appearance, it is hardly a strongly gendered use of figurative language. This almost non-existent reference to physical appearance in Tanzanian media coverage contrasts sharply with studies conducted elsewhere. For example, Anderson et al. (2011) found that after Johnson Sirleaf was elected president in Liberia, her style became newsworthy. An example they give is a 2006 article in the *Washington Post* which described the president's clothing style as 'royal', 'simple', and 'modest'.

### Visual Representation

We also analysed the visual representations of President Hassan in the data set of 414 articles by type (Table 2.1). Most articles in both newspapers included photos – 72% in *HabariLeo* and 83% in *Mwananchi*. The photos varied; some were close-ups, while others showed the president at a distance as part of a group. Most images portrayed President Hassan positively: as authoritative, decisive, and serious when giving speeches, or as friendly, happy, and calm when interacting with the general public. This contrasts with visuals in the Malawian press, where cartoons depicted former President Joyce Banda as indecisive, inefficient, and clueless, which Chikaipa (2019) argues reinforced gender stereotypes. The most common type of photograph in both newspapers was a shot of the president standing to give a public speech, either in the parliament or in another setting, but the president's formal and authoritative role is emphasised in the other types of photographs as well. The 'other' category comprised photographs of the president; for example, inspecting parades, visiting markets, or standing.

Table 2.1.   Photos of President Hassan by Context.

| Context | Percentage of Photos | |
|---|---|---|
| | *HabariLeo* | *Mwananchi* |
| Giving speeches | 31 | 36 |
| State visits, diplomacy | 14 | 13 |
| Social and cultural events | 7 | 6 |
| Project launch/visit | 5 | 2 |
| Official portraits | 4 | 1 |
| Press conference | 0 | 0 |
| Other | 11 | 25 |
| No photo | 28 | 17 |
| Total | 100 | 100 |

A closer look at each photo would be necessary to disentangle how the images visualise features that might empower or disempower female politicians and require more in-depth analysis of the many photos here than space constraints allow. Instead, we focus on two types of photographs that we identified as representative of the overall visuals published in the two newspapers. The first is taken during an administrative meeting, when President Hassan addresses government officials or similar groups. Her facial expression is serious and determined. Her sturdy posture expresses the president's high power and authority towards her audience. Hassan is also often represented using hand gestures actively in these photographs, apparently explaining a situation or elaborating on a viewpoint, and a speaker's activeness, rationality, and assertiveness signify masculinity (Gillian, 2001).

The other typical photo situation is of the president out in public and in a crowd. In these photographs, Hassan expresses calmness and happiness. These kinds of photographs include a wide range of expressions and gestures to display direct engagement with the crowd members, like thumbs ups, waving to the crowd, and meeting people with a smile. Friendly and humble gestures like these are traditionally linked to femininity (Gillian, 2001). We conclude that the photos of President Hassan contain both feminine and masculine expressions.

### Portrayal of Leadership Qualities

Most of the articles (84% in *HabariLeo* and 87% in *Mwananchi*) attributed no specific leadership style to President Hassan. When leadership qualities are mentioned, they were most likely to describe the president as transparent and inclusive and less frequently as a problem-solver, decisive, inspirational, visionary, or an effective communicator. Her leadership is described in negative terms in only two of the 414 articles in the data set, both of which were published in *Mwananchi*, as part of a longer quote from opposition candidates who accuse the president of being authoritarian and unaccountable. Almost 70% of the news articles portray the president as assertive (positive); for example, by describing her as accountable or quoting citizens who praise her work. No articles from *HabariLeo* portrayed President Hassan as passive (negative), and only 6% of the *Mwananchi* articles include claims that she is unassertive. Thus, in the majority of the news articles, President Hassan is portrayed as a state leader who keeps her promises, implements her policies, listens to others, and deserves praise for being strategic and innovative. Overall, however, we found that the media paid little attention to leadership qualities and focused instead on the president's regular activities such as official visits.

Our final research question asked to what extent the gender of the journalist had an impact on the reporting. Previous research from Argentina (Mitchelstein et al., 2020) and Central Europe (Shevchuck et al., 2022) suggests that female journalists covering politics are few because they are more often assigned to soft topics. Our findings indicate that when identifiable, there were nearly as many female journalists as male journalists covering presidential affairs in *HabariLeo* (19% vs 21%). Female journalists were fewer in *Mwananchi* (7% vs 16%). The gender ratio in the overall Tanzanian media favours men – 55% versus 45% (Josephi et al., 2019). The study coded eight different beats but found no systematic gender pattern. There were more male than female bylines among the stories focussing on leadership qualities, but the numbers were low and revealed no meaningful gender difference. Overall, the quantitative material indicates that the gender of the journalist did not have a significant impact on the portrayal of the president.

## Summary and Conclusion

This chapter examined the representation of Tanzania's first female president, Samia Suluhu Hassan, in a state-owned newspaper, *HabariLeo*, and a private outlet, *Mwananchi*. The president was featured more prominently by the government outlet, but the private outlet provided more in-depth analysis. The study found few cases of stereotypes directed towards President Hassan in terms of topics selected, gender role traits, titles, leadership qualities and focus on appearance and looks. Indeed, despite Hassan's status as the first female president of Tanzania, the coverage tended to downplay or overlook leadership attributes typically associated with gender, and the reporting prioritised such traditionally masculine topics as leadership, politics, and economics. In the few instances where the president was portrayed in female-stereotypical terms, for example, as feminine, a mother-figure, kind, and compassionate, the references most often came from the president herself. In other words, our findings suggest that her use of stereotypes is strategically deployed for the political advantage to be gained from how being a woman sets her apart from the previous presidents. The media themselves paid little attention to President Hassan's personal life.

The overall impression is that both newspapers portrayed Hassan as a capable leader and that the representation of the country's first female president is positive overall. The reporting focuses on leadership over personal characteristics and did not employ references to trivialise or degrade women's political activity. These findings contrast previous scholarship about how the efforts of women politicians are trivialised by the press (Falk, 2010), how female politicians are featured in soft-policy issues rather than in topics like national security and economy (Andrich & Domahidi, 2024) and that female politicians receive more attention for their physical appearance and personal life (Van der Pas & Aaldering, 2020). We are not, however, suggesting that the non-stereotypical portrayal of President Hassan in the Tanzanian media can be generalised to the coverage of all female politicians in Tanzania – Hassan is the nation's leader, and this exceptional role likely at least partially explains why she is treated professionally rather than stereotypically. Her age and decades of experience may also be a relevant factor. When Hassan was sworn in, she was 61 and already had a long, successful career in politics. The media representation could very well have been different had an unmarried woman in her 30s taken up the presidency. Consider, for example, how marriage and motherhood were prominent themes in the media's coverage of Finnish Prime Minister Sanna Marin (2019–2023), who was the youngest Prime Minister ever at 34 when the Social Democrat Party selected her to replace Prime Minister Antti Rinne (Kim, 2022). Nevertheless, the professional and largely non-gendered representation of Samia Suluhu Hassan by the Tanzanian media is a noteworthy finding that could potentially signal a new trend in African media coverage of their female leaders.

# References

Aalberg, T., & Strömbäck, J. (2010). Media-driven men and media-critical women? An empirical study of gender and MPs' relationships with the media in Norway and Sweden. *International Political Science Review*, *32*(2), 167–187. https://doi.org/10.1177/0192512110378902

Aaldering, L., & Van der Pas, D. (2020). Political leadership in the media: Gender bias in leader stereotypes during campaign and routine times. *British Journal of Political Science*, *50*(3), 911–931. https://doi.org/10.1017/S0007123417000795

Afrobarometer. (2024). *World Press Freedom Day: Africans strongly endorse media's role in holding governments accountable.* https://www.afrobarometer.org/wp-content/uploads/2024/05/News-release_World-Press-Freedom-Day-Africans-strongly-endorse-medias-role-in-holding-governments-accountable_30-April.pdf

Akpabio, E. (2017). Women in the Tanzanian media: A critical analysis. *Journal of Russian Media and Journalism Studies*, *9*(1), 168–183. http://worldofmedia.ru/WOMEN%20IN%20THE%20TANZANIAN%20MEDIA.pdf

Anderson, J. A., Diabah, G., & hMensa, P. A. (2011). Powerful women in powerless language: Media misrepresentation of African women in politics (the case of Liberia). *Journal of Pragmatics*, *43*(10), 2509–2518. https://doi.org/10.1016/j.pragma.2011.02.004

Andrich, A., & Domahidi, E. (2024). Still facing the 'paper ceiling'? Exploring gender differences in political news coverage of the last decade. *Journalism*, *25*(11), 2301–2319. https://doi.org/10.1177/14648849231215194

Cheeseman, N., Matfess, H., & Amani, A. (2021). Tanzania: The roots of repression. *Journal of Democracy*, *32*(2), 77–89. https://doi.org/10.1353/jod.2021.0020

Chikaipa, V. (2019). Caring mother or weak politician? A semiotic analysis of editorial cartoon representations of President Joyce Banda in Malawian newspapers. *Critical Arts*, *33*(2), 14–28. https://doi.org/10.1080/02560046.2019.1655583

Committee to Protect Journalists. (2024). *Tanzania's regulator bans media outlets as journalists harassed.* https://cpj.org/2024/10/tanzanias-regulator-bans-media-outlets-as-journalists-harassed/

Coulson, A. (2013). *Tanzania: A political economy* (2nd ed.). Oxford University Press.

Elias, S. (2018). *Constructing stereotypes in media: A critical analysis on the representation of women in Tanzanian newspapers* [Conference paper]. Proceedings of the international conference of communication science research (ICCSR, Surabaya, Indonesia 24–25 July 2018). https://doi.org/10.2991/iccsr-18.2018.68

Falk, E. (2010). *Women for president: Media bias in nine campaigns.* University of Illinois Press.

Garcia-Blanco, I., & Wahl-Jørgensen, K. (2012). The discursive construction of women politicians in the European Press. *Feminist Media Studies*, *12*(3), 422–441. https://doi.org/10.1080/14680777.2011.615636

Geertsema-Sligh, M. (2018). Gender issues in news coverage. *The International Encyclopedia of Journalism Studies*. Digital Commons @ Butler University. https://doi.org/10.1002/9781118841570.iejs0162

Geiger, S. (1987). Women in nationalist struggle: TANU activists in Dar es Salaam. *The International Journal of African Historical Studies*, *20*(1), 1–26. https://doi.org/10.2307/219275

Gillian, R. (2001). *Visual methodologies: An introduction to the interpretation of visual materials*. Sage.

Goswami, I., Balakrishnan, S., Vinotha, C., Chopra, R., Sivakumar, V., & Chetan, D. M. (2023). Gender and politics: Examining women's representation and empowerment. *Journal of Namibian Studies*, *33*(3), 1980–1994.

Holmén, L. (2023). *Media freedom in Tanzania today: A qualitative study on the freedom of press under President Samia Suluhu Hassan 2021–2023* [Bachelor thesis, Uppsala University]. DiVA Portal. https://urn.kb.se/resolve?urn=urn%3Anbn%3Ase%3Auu%3Adiva-511295

Johannessen, J. (2006). *Gender, media and development: The role of media in the cultural struggle of transformation in Tanzania* [Doctoral thesis, NTNU]. NTNU Open. http://hdl.handle.net/11250/268033

Josephi, B., Hanusch, F., Alonso, M. O., Shapiro, I., Andresen, K., de Beer, A. S., Hoxha, A., Moreira, S. V., Rafter, K., Skjerdal, T., Splendore, S., & Tandoc, E. C. (2019). Profiles of journalists: Demographic and employment patterns. In T. Hanitzsch, F. Hanusch, J. Ramaprasad, & A. de Beer (Eds.), *Worlds of journalism: Journalistic cultures around the globe* (pp. 67–102). Columbia University Press. https://doi.org/10.7312/hani18642-005

Juppi, P., Berege, S., & Yusuph, R. (2014). *Enhancing visibility and portrayal of women in Tanzanian media: Contrasting case study of Mwananchi Communications Limited against the Yellow Press*. Media Council of Tanzania. https://www.academia.edu/7046402/Enhancing_Visibility_and_Portrayal_of_Women_in_Tanzanian_Media

Kairuki, A. (2018). *The role of women in politics in Tanzania*. https://www.hss.de/download/publications/AMZ_90_Frauen_05.pdf

Kim, H. (2022). *International media representation of Finnish Prime Minister Sanna Marin* [Master's thesis, Tampere University]. https://urn.fi/URN:NBN:fi:tuni-202204273909

Lukanda, I. N. (2021). Female voices marginalised in media coverage of science in Uganda, both as authors and sources. *Journal of Science Communication*, *20*(2), A11. https://doi.org/10.22323/2.20020211

Makulilo, A. (2020). 'Where there is power, women are not': Rethinking women and politics in Tanzania. *The African Review*, *46*(2), 349–365. https://doi.org/10.1163/1821889X-12340005

Media Council of Tanzania. (2022). Print market in Tanzania. *Media Ownership Monitor 2018*. Media Council of Tanzania. https://tanzania.mom-gmr.org/en/media/print/

Meena, R., Rusimbi, M., & Israel, C. (2017). *Women and political leadership: Facilitating factors in Tanzania*. Uongozi Institute. https://uongozi.or.tz/newsite/wp-content/uploads/2022/12/Women-and-Political-Leadership_online.pdf

Mitchelstein, E., Boczkowski, P. J., Andelsman, V., Etenberg, P., Weinstein, M., & Bombau, T. (2020). Whose voices are heard? The byline gender gap on Argentine news sites. *Journalism*, *21*(3), 307–326. https://doi.org/10.1177/1464884919848183

Mushi, A. J. (2012). *Achieving gender parity in political participation in Tanzania*. National Women's Council of Ireland. https://nwci.ie/download/pdf/achieving_gender_parity_in_political_participationtanzanian_experience1.pdf

Nation Media Group. (2018). *Editorial policy guidelines & objectives*. http://www.nationmedia.com/wp-content/uploads/2018/02/Editorial-policy-online.pdf

Nduva, V. M. (2016). *Media portrayal of women leaders in Kenya: An intersection of female politicians and newspaper narratives* [Research project, University of Nairobi]. University of Nairobi Research Archive. http://hdl.handle.net/11295/99699

Osei-Appiah, S. (2019). *Media representations of women politicians: The cases of Ghana and Nigeria* [Doctoral thesis, University of Leeds]. White Rose eTheses Online. https://etheses.whiterose.ac.uk/26509/

Raicheva-Stover, M., & Ibroscheva, E. (2014). *Women in politics and media: Perspectives from nations in transition.* Bloomsbury.

Santoniccolo, F., Trombetta, T., Paradiso, M. N., & Rolle, L. (2023). Gender and media representations: A review of the literature on gender stereotypes, objectification and sexualization. *International Journal of Environmental Research and Public Health, 20*(10), 5770. https://doi.org/10.3390%2Fijerph20105770

Sheeler, K. H., & Anderson, K. V. (2013). *Woman president: Confronting postfeminist political culture.* Texas A&M University Press.

Shevchuck, S., Tithova, L., Talik, M., Biro, Z., Nemeckayova, N., Vanova, V., & Gubalova, V. (2022). *Women's voices in the media: A look at Central Europe.* GLOBSEC. https://globsec.org/what-we-do/publications/womens-voices-media-look-central-europe

Sihvonen, E. (2016). *The loving heart of a mother or a greedy politician? Media representations of female presidents in Liberia and Malawi.* University of Jyväskylä. http://urn.fi/URN:NBN:fi:jyu-201606153087

Solomon, E. (2023). Female gender stereotyping and President Samia Suluhu Hassan's political communication on Twitter: A blessing for female political leaders? *Information, Communication & Society, 26*(13), 2518–2543. https://doi.org/10.1080/1369118X.2023.2239889

Spurk, C., & Katunzi, A. (2019). *Yearbook on media quality in Tanzania 2018.* Media Council of Tanzania; Spurk Media Consulting. https://sjmc.udsm.ac.tz/yearbook/report-for-2018/

Sturmer, M., & Rioba, A. (1998). *The media history of Tanzania.* Ndanda Mission Press.

Thuo, W. J. (2012). *Media framing of women in politics: An analysis of print media coverage of women members of parliament in Kenya* [Doctoral thesis, University of Nairobi]. University of Nairobi Research Archive. http://erepository.uonbi.ac.ke:8080/xmlui/handle/123456789/8420

Van der Pas, D. J., & Aaldering, L. (2020). Gender differences in political media coverage: A meta-analysis. *Journal of Communication, 70*(1), 114–143. https://psycnet.apa.org/doi/10.1093/joc/jqz046

Who Makes the News? (2021). *6th global media monitoring project.* https://whomakesthenews.org/wp-content/uploads/2021/07/GMMP2020.ENG_.FINAL20210713.pdf

Zamfirache, I. (2010). Women and politics – The glass ceiling. *Journal of Comparative Research in Anthropology and Sociology, 1*(1), 175–185. https://doaj.org/article/be7c1a322fc84d168890a86d5e6e7a1e

Chapter 3

# Media Representations of Women Candidates in Kenya's 2022 General Elections

*Denis Ikachoi[a] and Joseph Njuguna[b]*

[a] *Maasai Mara University, Kenya*
[b] *Murang'a University of Technology, Kenya*

## Abstract

The media shape public opinion during elections by providing a lens through which voters assess their candidates. The media attention and discourse on such candidates have attracted increased scholarly interest, and this chapter explores how selected Kenyan print media covered and represented female candidates during the 2022 election campaigns. A content analysis of 52 news stories from the *Daily Nation* and *The Standard* newspapers drew insights from media agenda-setting, framing, and feminist theories. Eight 'popular' female candidates dominated coverage (especially those in gubernatorial and senatorial races), with most featuring on the hard news and a few on profile stories. The candidates were represented as electoral 'victims', self-effacing, coming of age, and as leaders. Despite some cases of humiliation and violence, media coverage generally portrayed Kenyan women leveraging their power to defeat age-old stereotypes of women's unfitness to lead as part of a gradual shift towards the one-third gender rule of women's political representation in Kenya. The study recommends all-inclusive coverage of different female candidates (i.e. that does not focus only on the most popular), balanced gender reporting of electoral issues, and a broader analysis of female candidates' campaigns involving different media formats.

*Keywords*: 2022 elections; Kenya; print media; female candidates; representation; feminist theories

## Introduction

As agents of education and socialisation, the media shape and reflect public opinion on issues like political participation of women and electoral politics. While media are expected to be fair arbiters and watchdogs in elections, they sometimes reinforce rather than curtail stereotypes and prejudices against women candidates (Llanos & Nina, 2011). Moreover, media are blamed for partisanship in their coverage of women candidates when they perpetuate conflicting narratives that oppose gender equality efforts (McRobbie, 2009). Thus, as more women run for higher political offices, gendered coverage of election matters has spiked scholarly interest.

One concern has been the amount of media attention given to candidates and how gender roles shape their representation. Biased coverage led to such international forums as the 1995 Beijing Platform for Action, which cited media as complicit in perpetuating gender inequality. Male-dominated media were accused of developing stories from patriarchal perspectives that foreground narratives about the 'unfitness' of women to lead and prop up the male candidates depicted with inborn leadership traits (Anaya, 2023). Female candidates are more often featured for superficial qualities, like physical appearance, than the substance of their campaigns. On the one hand, one study showed that the media's underreporting and biased coverage of female candidates makes them invisible, muted, and underdogs in the electoral process (Barasa & Gitau, 2021). Fair and balanced coverage, on the other hand, enables voters to make better judgements about the merits of each candidate. This study contributes to the literature by focusing on media coverage of Kenya's 2022 elections.

## Study Context

Kenya is a budding democracy characterised by a liberalised media space and heightened public awareness of citizen's rights and fundamental freedoms (BBC News, 2023). Elections are highly contested, and women are emerging as powerful disruptors to the traditionally male-dominated political space. Administratively, Kenya is divided into 47 counties, each led by a governor. Each county is also represented by one senator and a woman representative (a lady). In addition, there are 349 members of parliament representing constituencies. These are elected directly by the voters. Results released by the Independent Electoral and Boundaries Commission (2022) showed that seven women won governor positions, three were elected senators, while 26 took parliamentary seats. Forty-seven women representatives, including Linet Chepkorir, the youngest MP in Kenya's electoral history, were elected in the counties. Of the four male presidential candidates, three selected women as their running mates. Article 27 of Kenya's 2010 Constitution envisages gender equality through a gender quota: 'State shall take legislative and other measures to implement the principle that not more than two-thirds of the members of electoral or appointive bodies shall be of the same gender'. Implementation, however, has been slow, and women are still underrepresented in decision-making, especially in competitive politics. During the 2022 elections, women accounted for only 11% of all candidates for elective posts nationally (Independent Electoral and Boundaries Commission, 2022).

Kenyan media wielded significant influence in shaping public perceptions of the electoral process because they played an important role in constructing narratives around the candidates. Media coverage of elections in Kenya (especially from a gender perspective) has received mixed reviews. While some scholars (Anaya, 2023; Koin, 2023) applaud media's efforts at ensuring fairness and transparency, a report by the Media Council of Kenya (2022) showed that 2022 reporting fell short of being balanced and, in some cases, was leading to incitement. Because women play such significant roles in development, it is imperative that we investigate how media influences the political achievements of women through coverage of their campaigns. This chapter provides a case study of Kenya's 2022 elections to explore how female candidates were covered and represented by the media and what this means for the mediated struggle for gender equality in Kenya's political space.

## Empirical and Theoretical Framework

Voters get information about a candidate's electability from the media. Without such information, voters fall back on stereotypical perceptions of the candidate, which may lead to wrong choices. Biased media representation impedes efforts at gender parity during elections, especially when superficial traits are used to demonstrate female candidates' incompetence (Miller & Peake, 2013; van der Pas & Aaldering 2020). In his research, Markstedt (2007) illustrates this phenomenon through an analysis of the 2007 handbag debate in the UK, when a leader was accused of allegedly spending GBP 10,000 'on a handbag' at the expense of the struggling poor. After US Senator Elizabeth Warren declared her intention to run for president in 2019, the Independent magazine immediately commented on her 'unlikability' as the only hindrance to her goal (Zoellner, 2020).

Scholars argue that superficial traits like physical attractiveness form only a small fraction of the ability of a candidate. Although the way women present themselves can influence how media will tell their story, Krijnen (2020) argues that their issues are not as adequately captured as those of their male counterparts, and this makes women politicians more susceptible to gender biases that diminish their ability. Some progressive media outlets now evaluate their coverage in accord with established gender equality guidelines to create news environments more inclusive of women (Llanos & Nina, 2011).

Since low media coverage of a candidate can impact for whom a ballot is cast, studies on the relationship between gender and the amount of media coverage have become more prevalent. The focus has been on the prominence of coverage as well how candidates are represented as suitable or not for the positions (Mpofu, 2017). Media representation often reinforces traditional gender roles, depicting women in subordinate roles and objects of sexual aggrandisement (Santoniccolo et al., 2023), while portraying men as dominant, aggressive, and authoritative (Krijnen, 2020). Such representations perpetuate masculine supremacy and the subjugation of women by confirming misplaced perceptions about women's leadership abilities (Seluman et al., 2024).

Merouani (2019) argued that media has a powerful influence on voter attitudes based on the balance of coverage given to candidates and their stories. Ruiz Vidales and Muniz (2017) demonstrated the pervasive use of stereotypes against women running for elective posts in Mexico. While van der Pas and Aaldering (2020) found no differences in the political coverage of gender issues in the American and Canadian elections, research in Sweden and Norway showed lower media visibility for female politicians despite these countries' strong promotion of gender equality in media. China, Japan, and South Korea receive a mix of gender portrayals, where women politicians with steady careers receive more favourable media coverage (van der Pas & Aaderling, 2022). Media often reflect deeply entrenched patriarchal values in India, Pakistan, and Bangladesh, where women (especially in Bollywood films) feature in more peripheral roles, like beauty icons, rather than in politics (Ul Huda & Ali, 2015).

Research conducted by CFi Media Development (2022) on sexist media stereotypes in Ghana, Côte d'Ivoire, the Democratic Republic of Congo, and Niger revealed that female politicians were often portrayed as mere tokens of gender equality. In Ghana, an intimidating environment of male dominance in the press discouraged women from participating in electoral interviews. In Côte d'Ivoire and Niger, media usually highlight the marital status of female political candidates alongside their names. By foregrounding marital status, the women are considered 'real and eligible' for leadership positions. Koin's study (2023) of television coverage of women politicians in the run-up to the 2022 general elections in Kenya showed that women politicians received 65% of the total coverage, with seasoned politicians more visible than newcomers. About 56% of the women politicians were framed under the economic empowerment narrative.

The current study draws on agenda-setting, media framing, and feminist media theories. By giving prominence to certain issues, the media shapes audience perceptions and what people consider a priority (Entman, 2007). Thus, the more attention a candidate receives, the more the media will influence how voters perceive them. In addition, the media selects and emphasises certain attributes of an issue to make these attributes more salient than others – a process called framing (Entman, 2007). Frames employed by the media influence how audiences interpret the issue. If the media gives little attention to female candidates' issues or portrays them through a parochial lens, then society is likely to adopt these media cues and judge them unfit for leadership. Thus, gendered differences in election coverage can not only shape voter opinions about candidates but also hinder certain candidates from achieving their political goals.

Feminist media theorists explore how media portrayals of women can perpetuate gender inequalities. They argue that excluding women from the news creates power imbalances within male-dominated political systems that largely ignore women's issues (Hawkesworth, 1989). Feminists claim that the media tends to focus on the superficial rather than the substantive when covering women, but they also position media as key to supporting feminist causes and disrupting patriarchy. Given that media coverage can sway voters, this study is a timely contribution to the academic debates about media representation of female candidates based on Kenya's 2022 elections.

## Methodology

The data set for this content analysis was drawn from two Kenyan daily newspapers: *The Daily Nation* and *The Standard*. Content analysis provides a systematic and objective means to make valid inferences from verbal, visual, or written data to describe and/or quantify specific phenomena (Berelson, 1952; Gallagher, 2014). The newspapers were selected for their depth of coverage and wide circulation (Media Council of Kenya, 2024). Stories included in the analysis were published between May 29 and 6 August 2022, the gazetted campaign period for elections that occurred on 9 August 2022. The stories were identified from the print versions of the newspapers, readily accessible as part of the Maasai Mara University library collection. The unit of analysis was the individual article.

A total of 52 stories were identified for analysis. Stories were read and coded for the female candidates' story placement, news genre, and frequency of coverage. Open coding was employed, meaning that each of the stories were read several times to identify themes as they emerged from text that represented different aspects of how the female candidates were represented in print media.

## Results and Discussion

### Media Attention to Female Candidates

Out of the 52 stories about the upcoming elections and candidates that were analysed, 31 stories (60%) from the *Daily Nation* and 22 stories (40%) from *The Standard* covered female candidates. Out of the three women who were running mates on the presidential ticket, Martha Karua dominated with 78% headline mentions in both newspapers. Other candidates with considerable frontpage exposure included a candidate for a county woman representative seat, Linet Chepkorir, and county governor hopefuls Cecily Mbarire, Ann Waiguru, and Kawira Mwangaza. Most of the candidates for county woman representative and member of parliament featured in the middle sections of newspapers as passing mentions, in electoral disputes, and in association with popular male candidates. This supports prior findings that media tends to negatively portray and deprioritise women candidates (Padovani et al., 2022).

The frequency of coverage of the female candidates was erratic, and only 'popular' candidates like Martha Karua, Susan Kihika, Kawira Mwangaza, and Anne Waiguru received almost daily coverage. Male candidates (especially the presidential candidates) were more frequently covered (by more than 60%) in the front pages and editorials than the female candidates. Martha Karua, the opposition candidate's running mate, had media space in 45% of the stories, followed by Susan Kihika (38%), and Anne Waiguru (35%). Among gubernatorial candidates, Cecile Mbarire received the fewest mentions (12%). Most candidates were discussed in hard news presenting factual stories of the candidates' campaign events. A few, like Cecile Mbarire, Susan Kihika, and Gladys Wanga, received profile coverage. Some, like Kawira Mwangaza, were featured in editorials after allegations of forged academic documents and misappropriation of funds.

Most of the female candidate's stories were presented in a broader narrative about women in leadership and the implementation of Article 27 of the Constitution's one-third gender quota rather than on specific examples or profiles of the individual candidates. Profiled candidates gave episodic accounts of their experiences and achievements that had motivated them to seek elective positions. Although some candidates suffered character assassination from rivals, the content was mainly issue-based. Such story contents have been seen to minimise women's underrepresentation especially where media systems drop their male-oriented interpretations of female issues (Santoniccolo et al., 2023).

Statistical analysis of the campaign coverage by gender reveals a significant difference in how male and female candidates were covered ($M = 3.7$, $SD = 2.4$; $t = 0.834$, $p = 0.001$). Male candidates were more likely to be prominently covered than the female candidates, which supports prior findings that media relegates women to the political periphery as voters and not voices during campaigns (Mpofu, 2017; van der Pas & Aaldering, 2020). When media obscures women in the political arena, the candidates' lack of visibility compromises the likelihood of their election to office.

### Representations of the Female Candidates

#### Victims of the Political Game

Electoral campaigns in Kenya have repeatedly reflected a disregard for the laws prohibiting women's fair accessibility to political positions (Media Council of Kenya, 2022). Candidates (especially men) employ verbal abuse and physical assault to demean and intimidate women into abandoning the electoral race as victims of a male-orchestrated scheme to shunt their voices from political representation (Media Council of Kenya, 2022). The 52 stories illustrate several narratives of such victimhood. For example, stories had demeaning allusions of Martha Karua as a divorcée, Cecily Mbarire as an 'outsider' for having married outside her community (Mugo, 2022), Martha Wangari as a 'prostitute' for being a single mother of children with different fathers and Mary Mugure as a 'sexual worker' (see Gaitho, 2022a; Ndonye, 2022). This extent to which women candidates went to address stereotypes against them was captured in a BBC news article by Musambi (2022) which indicated that the candidates had decided to take the sexist bullies by their horns. In the story, one female candidate castigated men's unfair targeting of women with foreign spouses, which did not count when male candidates married from outside their communities.

Candidates were also disparaged for allegedly presenting fake academic credentials (see Wangui, 2022; Wanyoro, 2022). For example, Kawira Mwangaza,

Aisha Jumwa, and Wavinya Ndeti were considered not fit to be nominated by their parties, despite having been cleared to vie by relevant government organs (like Ethics and Anti-corruption Commission and the Commission for Higher Education) which are charged with verifying the credentials of candidates before they submit nominations. While Ndeti considered the resulting petitions against her nomination a witch hunt only meant to discredit them as women, Mwangaza credited God for survival from a barrage of similar media attacks on her childless status and conflicting roles as bishop and aspiring politician.

Umra Omar, a CNN Hero of the Year in 2016 (see CNN, 2016) and the founder of Safari Doctors, who was running for county governor in Lamu, was once framed as sympathetic to the LGBTQ course and potentially dealing in drugs for working with an organisation that rehabilitated youth and promoted gender equality (Kazungu, 2022). The source further suggested that Umra had seemingly punched above her weight by running for the governorship position (Praxides, 2022). In another story, one male opposition leader sarcastically questioned Martha Karua's ability to succeed Raila as president in 2027 instead of experienced men like himself (Maundu, 2022). A Muslim candidate for governor position, Fatuma Achani, suffered religious bigotry where opponents promoted the narrative that Muslim women could not lead (see Maundu, 2022). Charity Ngilu, a seasoned politician, was coerced to resign from the race for governor of Kitui in favour of a male candidate in exchange for the promise of a government appointment should he win (Mutua, 2022). These examples demonstrate a male-dominated discourse that legitimises male hegemony and women's tokenism in politics consistent with the findings of Llanos and Nina (2011).

Stereotyping abounds in the data set. Female candidates depict men as 'envious' of their progress (e.g. Muiruri, 2022; Otieno, 2022), while male candidates mostly dwell on personal and character attacks – claims about dysfunctional homes, questionable morals, weak personalities, and inexperience. Experienced female candidates consider the men's approach an old gimmick to intimidate female candidates, blaming the culture of negotiated male-led 'democracy' where elders determine who runs to the disadvantage of qualified and competent women (see Muiruri, 2022). A June 7 *Standard* article, 'The raw deal for women in Kenya Kwanza and glaring contradictions', explicitly covered how veteran male politicians imposed sanctions on candidates whom they found incompatible with their ideals (Maritim, 2022). From a feminist theoretical point of view (see Krijnen, 2020), the media's prioritisation of a candidate's gender over capability perpetuates and legitimises patriarchal values. This bias is evident among male journalists who cover women from a perspective of male dominance. These stereotypes may be ingrained in journalists' subconscious and enacted with time rather than intentional acts of discrimination (Ruiz Vidales & Muniz, 2017).

### Female Candidates as Self-effacing

Despite media debates portraying men as barriers to women's political emancipation, some female candidates attributed their political careers to their spouses' support. This self-effacing technique deflects attention away from the candidates themselves and highlights instead such social qualities as 'humility', 'people-centredness', 'shared responsibility' and 'regard for shared success' (Hawkesworth, 1989). Female candidates' reliance on men has been associated both with indecisiveness and with strong social bonds and shared values that endear them to voters.

Consider, for example, Kawira Mwangaza's description of her husband as her 'campaign champion' to the extent that she attributed half her campaign success to his guitar performances for her audiences (Mutembei, 2022). Fatuma Achani of Kwale County similarly acknowledged that her campaigns would not have succeeded without her husband's support (Nation Team, 2022). Martha Karua credited Raila Odinga's selection of her as his presidential candidate running mate with her impeccable record of fighting human rights abuses and inefficient governance. She described them as a safe pair of hands to fight corruption (Njaaga, 2022). Other candidates used self-effacing language to shore up commonality of purpose too. Susan Kihika considered her voters 'great' for seeing the good leadership potential in her (Mureithi, 2022). Gladys Wanga considered her impending triumph in the elections as belonging to the electorate (Odhiambo, 2022b), and Mwangaza delivered a clarion call for 'respect for the people of Meru' among the male candidates (Mutembei, 2022).

While backing formidable male candidates may seem like taking on the role of spectator, scholars argue that female candidates who support strong male candidates and their manifestos gain voter approval when they decide to run for office (Barasa & Gitau, 2021). These examples underscore the female candidates' awareness of the need to deflect voter attention from them as women to the supporting mechanisms that resonate with the electorate. Winning an election is not an individual feat and acknowledgement of the role of external stakeholders like family, social groups and the media shores up a candidate's support base. Critics, however, advocate for media space portrayals of women candidates as decisive and independent, not as men's supporters (Anaya, 2023).

*Women with Appeal*

The media used different labels to characterise the personality and appearance of the candidates. Such labels were associated with their physical appearance, and nurturing traits. For instance, A *Daily Nation* story described Martha Karua's 'good sense of style and sartorial finesse' as an evolution from power suits to tastefully designed 'African attire' (Chege, 2022a). Studies show the media's preference for using traits-based appeals to promote candidates (Padovani et al., 2022) that focus on physical traits like dress risk stereotyping female politicians through their appearance. The media also portrayed her as the 'iron lady' of Kenya's political landscape due to her long-standing frontline fight against gender imbalance in power in the male-dominated political space in Kenya. However, in a CNN interview, Karua sought to dissociate herself from the 'iron lady' moniker, considering it misogynistic because it portrays women's power as given by men (see Ambani, 2022; Madowo & Feleke, 2022).

Anne Waiguru adopted the campaign slogan *Minji* (Kikuyu for 'green peas') to appeal to the voters in Kirinyaga County by associating herself with the 'soft and sweet' delicacy in central Kenya (see Omulo, 2022; Sanga & Inyanji, 2022). Her youthful, brown complexion added to her *minji minji* appeal, especially among her male constituency who might prioritise 'beauty' and 'tenderness' when choosing a candidate (Omulo, 2022). What is more, Waiguru described her political rival, Martha Karua, as 'green grams', which are more difficult to cook and less tasty (Sanga & Inyanji, 2022). In other words, name-calling is common in political campaigns among both men and women. An incumbent woman candidate for MP, Mary Waithera, adopted the slogan *Wa Mahua* (Kikuyu for 'the flowery one') a reference both to her flower business and to the degree of her appeal ('beauty') to the voters (Muiruri, 2022).

During the campaigns, female candidates used gendered slogans in their campaign materials in order to gain leverage over male candidates in themes such as 'development-oriented', action-oriented and 'motherliness' to their advantage. Although media mainly frame mothers through the cultural lens of domesticity such as housekeeping and family care, candidates leveraged a mother's compassionate, nurturing and productive nature to position themselves as pillars of society (Obwogi, 2022). For example, the women candidates appealed to voters with such slogans as *Kaba maathe* (better a mother) for Ms Gathoni wa Muchomba who was vying for a member of parliament position in Githunguri constituency. M/s Millicent Omanga, who vied for Nairobi women county representative position used the slogan *Mama miradi* (mother of development projects). M/s Aisha Jumwa used the slogan *Shangazi wa taifa* (the nation's aunt) while vying for Kilifi County governor position. In Kirinyaga County, Wanguri Ngirici used the slogan *Mama wa kazi* (Mother of tasks) and Faith Lukosi used the slogan *Mama sanitizer*, a term that she was accorded by the youth in informal settlements when she donated sanitisers during the COVID-19 pandemic (Obiria & Maichuhie, 2022). The candidates positioned themselves as the face and cornerstone of the nation and promised to be leaders who would prioritise voter interests as they would their children's.

Despite some stories that used 'woman' as a derogatory term in headlines like 'Women defying odds in bid to run counties' (Beja, 2022), the female candidates chose to leverage their womanliness to appeal to the electorate to vote for change from the male-dominated politics. *The Standard* newspaper portrayed Linet Chepkorir, a county gubernatorial candidate, as so small and young as to have shocked 'the old politicians in the party primaries' (Kimutai, 2022). Such descriptions perpetuate the stereotype of the 'normal' woman leader as tall and mature (Mwaura & Oiruria, 2017) even as they appear to celebrate Chepkorir's youthful vigour and gumption. Using feminised traits of appearance, personality, and familial background to describe female candidates reinforces how women's deviation from traditionally ascribed roles is frowned upon and can hurt their campaigns (Van der Pas & Aaldering, 2020). What is more, traits-based appeals may reduce candidates' accountability since voters find it more difficult to remove from office those with good traits who later fail to meet expectations (Mpofu, 2017).

### Women as History Makers in Electoral Politics

Media coverage during the period of political campaigns up to general elections was perceived as a positive shift and time for reflection and awakening for not only the

voters but also the respective female candidates (UN Women, 2022). Veteran politicians took to the media to advise and position upcoming female candidates as the
needed changes agents. In one story, Fatuma Achani, the current Governor of Kwale
County, narrated how she overcame various hurdles in a male-dominated society
and won as a result of the new-found political space anchored in the 2010 constitution that is progressive (Muiruri, 2024). Mary Wangari, the incumbent for Gilgil MP,
also encouraged candidates to leverage the one-third gender rule as the entry point
in the fight for their inclusion (Parliament of Kenya, 2022). Linet Chepkorir, who
was on the ticket for Bomet County, said she was too resilient and had to overcome
those who laughed and scoffed at her, almost making her lose focus (Chege, 2022b).

By focussing on issues rather than personalities, most female candidates
presented themselves as hands-on, tried-and-tested agents of change. Fatuma
Achani campaigned on her experience as the first deputy governor and promised to solidify her legacy (Muiruri, 2024). Kawira Mwangaza appealed to voters
by talking about her philanthropic initiative, *Operation Okolea* (Operation Save)
which distributed free cows to poor households in her county, and positioning
herself as a prudent manager who could be 'trusted with a bigger county budget
of 12 billion' (Muchui, 2022). Gladys Wanga presented herself as forward-think-
ing and a planner by campaigning on the several agreements she had signed with
professionals for the development of Homa Bay should she become governor
(Maombo, 2022). By taking strong, political positions, women dismantle their
exclusion from decision-making (Seluman et al., 2024).

The media ran headlines that confirmed women's onslaught on the male political space. Examples include 'Game on! Women candidates in epic poll contest'
(K'onyango, 2022); 'Why 2022 election could be the defining moment for women
leadership' (Odhiambo, 2022a); 'Gachagua vs Karua will make for a riveting debate'
(Gaitho, 2022a); 'Take-homes from Rigathi Gachagua, Martha Karua "deputies"
debate' (Gaitho, 2022b) where Martha Karua and Rigathi Gachagua as female and
male running mates, respectively, were to engage in a live media debate. These stories represented the candidates as 'history-makers': Karua as the first female deputy
president, Susan Kihika as the first female governor of Nakuru County, Tabitha
Karanja as the first female senator for Nakuru, and Liza Chelule as a re-elected
female MP for Nakuru. Indeed, Nakuru County was positioned as the model of
a safe space for women's leadership, where women would seize six elective posts.

## Conclusion

Media portrayed the new generation of women candidates as both a product of
the affirmative action enshrined in Section 27 of the 2010 Constitution and as
sincere, passionate challengers to the patriarchal mindset that relegated women to
political periphery. Some candidates saw the August 2022 election as 'a moment
of women vindication', when the country would witness women leading the much-
desired change in Kenya (UN Women, 2022). While feminists extol the breaking
of the glass ceiling of power and historic 'firsts' in Kenya's political leadership,
critics argue that voters may not necessarily regard the candidates as qualified to
hold office given the structural barriers that reinforce women as outliers in the

struggle for leadership (CFi Media Development, 2022). It is crucial to observe that when media emphasises women's achievements, experiences, and abilities, it can raise these issues on the public agenda and improve female candidates' polling (Anaya, 2023). By giving voice to the candidates (e.g. through profile stories), the media provides a platform from which voters get to know and can evaluate the candidates. Such spaces also support policy efforts aimed at eradicating gender inequalities and socio-economic and political emancipation of women.

Results of this content analysis of mainstream media coverage and representation of female candidates in Kenya's 2022 elections show that popular candidates like Martha Karua, Anne Waiguru, Kawira Mwangaza, and Susan Kihika received more media coverage and more frontpage coverage than newcomers. Although a few newcomers were given profile coverage (e.g. Linet Chepkorir), most of their coverage was hard news and editorial opinions rather than feature-length stories. Only a handful of high-profile female candidates were given extensive coverage by the media, which supports the marginalisation discourse on the media attention given exclusively to known and popular news sources (Barasa & Gitau, 2021). Moreover, scant attention to women's issues on the front pages while prioritising male candidates reinforces women's issues as peripheral. It was evident that Martha Karua gained top media coverage as a running mate (an unelected position) to a male presidential candidate, which may portray women as unable to stand and fight on their own. A gendered analysis showed that male candidates received more issue-based coverage than their female counterparts, whose coverage instead focussed on proving their ability and fighting stereotypes about their place in politics.

The media portrayed women candidates as victims of a political system intent on marginalising their political voices and representation. Other stories presented female politicians as victims arising from the ashes of gender discrimination, courtesy of seasoned political role models, who are broadening the recognition of women's rights among a growing, critical mass of electorate who desire and believe in socio-economic and political change that female political leadership will bring. The media also represented the candidates with physical and character traits that emphasised their struggles to overcome misogyny. Some candidates used campaign slogans to represent themselves as both womanly and as worthy competitors. Labels that underscore the physical characteristics of the candidate may pander to the male stereotypes that judge women as 'political ornaments' (Mpofu, 2017, p. 43).

While Kenya saw a surge in elected female politicians in 2022, the media coverage of only a handful was a disservice to many 'ordinary' candidates who may have lost elections due to their lack of visibility. From an agenda-setting perspective, the issues raised by a few prominent candidates seemed to shape the narrative for the rest of the women candidates and undermined the media's duty to provide balanced coverage. Although the media aligned with feminist views by giving attention to female candidates and highlighting their role in nation-building, the extent to which it dismantled patriarchal tendencies remains debatable. To gain deeper insight into the media's role in shaping gender empowerment during the campaigns, further research is needed. This should include an analysis of how various media formats (broadcast, online, and print) represented the candidates, which issues were prioritised, and how coverage influenced candidates' performance. Additionally, an in-depth study of gendered media coverage during elections would help uncover disparities in media access, messaging, and representation, guiding future media practices during elections.

# References

Ambani, S. (2022, August 5). Why Martha Karua doesn't like the nickname 'Iron Lady'. *The Daily Nation.* https://nation.africa/kenya/news/why-martha-karua-doesn-t-like-the-nickname-iron-lady-3904300

Anaya, E. R. (2023). Exploring the paradox of gender preferred leadership in Kenya: A globe study on gender egalitarianism and women in leadership. *Gender in Management, 38*(7), 855–876. https://doi.org/10.1108/GM-03-2022-0107

Barasa, M. N., & Gitau, M. (2021). Media representations of women politicians in Kenya: Lesson from 2017 general elections. *Kenya Studies Review, 9*(2), 42–45. https://kessa.org/volume-9-issue-2-2021/

BBC News. (2023). *Kenya media guide.* Kenya Scholars and Studies Association. https://www.bbc.com/news/world-africa-13681344

Beja, P. (2022, July 8). Women defying odds in bid to run counties. *The Standard.* https://standardmedia.co.ke/health/politics/article/2001447428

Berelson, B. (1952). *Content analysis in communications research. Free Press.*

CFi Media Development. (2022). *Gender equality in the media and media content.* https://cfi.fr/en/dossier/gender-equality-media-and-media-content

Chege, N. (2022a, June 10). Ode to Karua's sense of style, sartorial finesse. *The Daily Nation.* https://nation.africa/kenya/blogs-opinion/opinion/ode-to-karua-s-sense-of-style-sartorial-finesse-3844734

Chege, N. (2022b, April 22). 'Toto' epitomises girl power in a very cruel world. *The Daily Nation.* https://nation.africa/kenya/blogs-opinion/opinion/-toto-epitomises-girl-power-in-very-cruel-world-3791554

CNN. (2016, December 13). *CNN heroes tribute.* https://www.cnn.com/videos/world/2016/12/13/cnn-heroes-umra-omar-tribute-show-pkg.cnn

Entman, R. M. (2007). Framing bias: Media in the distribution of power. *Journal of Communication, 57*(1), 163–173. https://doi.org/10.1111/j.1460-2466.2006.00336.x

Gaitho, M. (2022a, July 19). Gachagua vs Karua will make for a riveting debate. *The Daily Nation.* https://nation.africa/kenya/news/politics/3884284

Gaitho, M. (2022b, July 21). Take-homes from Rigathi Gachagua, Martha Karua 'deputies' debate. *The Daily Nation.* https://nation.africa/kenya/news/politics/take-homes-from-gachagua-karua-deputies-debate-3886900

Gallagher, M. (2014). Media and the representation of gender. In C. Carter, L. Steiner, & S. McLaughlin (Eds.), *The Routledge companion to media and gender* (pp. 332–341). Routledge.

Hawkesworth, M. E. (1989). Knowers, knowing, known: Feminist theory and claims of truth. *Signs, 14*(3), 533–557. https://psycnet.apa.org/doi/10.1086/494523

Independent Electoral and Boundaries Commission. (2022). *Statutory timelines towards the 9th August 2022 general elections.* https://www.iebc.or.ke/uploads/resources/sH0oLFfhUV.pdf

Kazungu, K. (2022, May 16). Ethnicity, coalition politics to play major roles in Lamu gubernatorial race. *The Daily Nation.* https://nation.africa/kenya/counties/lamu/ethnicity-coalition-politics-to-play-major-roles-in-lamu-gubernatorial-race-3816338

Kimutai, G. (2022, July 16). *Toto, 24, shocks old politicians in UDA primaries for woman rep.* https://standardmedia.co.ke/srticle/2001443305

Koin, I. S. (2023). *Television coverage of women politicians in the run-up to the 2022 general elections in Kenya* [Unpublished Master's dissertation]. Aga Khan University, East Africa. https://ecommons.aku.edu/theses_dissertations/2098/

K'Onyango, O. (2022, July 1). Game on: Women candidates in epic poll contest. *The Daily Nation.* https://nation.africa/kenya/news/gender/3865750

Krijnen, T. (2020). Gender and media. In *International encyclopedia of gender, media and communication.* John Wiley & Sons, Inc. https://doi.org/10.1002/9781119429128.iegmc016

Llanos, B., & Nina, J. (2011). *Election coverage from a gender perspective: A media monitoring manual.* International IDEA & UN Women. https://www.idea.int/publications/catalogue/election-coverage-gender-perspective-media-monitoring-manual

Madowo, L., & Feleke, B. (2022). *A record number of women are running in Kenya's elections but many face harassment and abuse.* CNN. https://edition.cnn.com/2022/08/06/africa/kenya-elections-women-candidates-intl/index.html

Maombo, S. (2022, February 13). Gladys Wanga launches Homa Bay gubernatorial bid. *The Star.* https://the-star.co.ke/news/2022-02-13

Maritim, D. (2022, June 7). The raw deal for women in Kenya Kwanza and glaring contradictions. *The Standard.* https://www.standardmedia.co.ke/counties/article/2001447723/the-raw-deal-for-women-in-kenya-kwanza-and-glaring-contradictions

Markstedt, H. (2007). *Political handbags. The representation of women politicians. A case study of the websites and newspaper coverage of the women candidates in the Labour Party Deputy Leadership election* [Unpublished master's thesis]. London School of Economics. https://www.lse.ac.uk/media-and-communications/assets/documents/research/msc-dissertations/2007/Markstedt-final.pdf

Maundu, P. (2022, June 4). I should succeed Raila in 2027, says Kalonzo Musyoka. *The Daily Nation.* https://nation.africa/kenya/news/politics/i-should-succeed-raila-in-2027-says-kalonzo-musyoka-3838006

McRobbie, A. (2009). *The aftermath of feminism: Gender, culture and social change.* Sage.

Media Council of Kenya. (2022). *MCK pushes for women representation in the media.* https://mediacouncil.or.ke/~mediaco7/index.php/media-center/mck-newsroom/news/mck-pushes-women-representation-media

Media Council of Kenya. (2024). *State of the media report (2023–2024).* https://mediacouncil.or.ke/sites/default/files/downloads/MCK_%20State%20of%20the%20Media%202023%20Survey%20Report.pdf

Merouani, W. (2019). *The impact of mass media on voting behaviour: The cross-country evidence.* https://erf.org.eg/publications/the-impact-of-mass-media-on-voting-behavior-the-cross-country-evidence-2/

Miller, M. K., & Peake, J. S. (2013). Press effects, public opinion, and gender: Coverage of Sarah Palin's Vice-Presidential Campaign. *International Journal of Press/Politics, 18*(4), 482–507. https://doi.org/10.1177/1940161213495456

Mpofu, J. (2017). Media representation of women in politics and media in southern Africa. *European Journal of Social Sciences Studies, 2*(7), 32–47. https://oapub.org/soc/index.php/EJSSS/article/view/172

Muchui, D. (2022, August 14). Kawira Mwangaza: How I floored Meru Governor Kiraitu Murungi. *The Daily Nation.* https://nation.africa/kenya/counties/meru/3914568

Muiruri, M. (2022, June 3). DP promises half Cabinet to women to counter Karua effect. *The Daily Nation.* https://nation.africa/kenya/news/gender/dp-promises-half-cabinet-to-women-to-counter-karua-effect-3837000

Muiruri, F. (2024, August 13). How Achani beat the odds to secure Kwale governorship. *The Daily Nation.* https://nation.africa/kenya/news/gender/4723130

Musambi, E. (2022, July 18). *Kenya election: Taking on the sexist bullies to stand.* https://www.bbc.com/news/world-africa-61801282

Mutembei, F. (2022, July 15). Meru governor Kawira appoints husband Baichu hustler ambassador. *The Standard*. https://www.standardmedia.co.ke/eastern/article/2001457058/meru-governor-appoints-husband-hustler-ambassador

Mutua, K. (2022, June 17). Ngilu: Polished political schemer or lucky opportunist? *The Daily Nation*. https://nation.africa/kenya/news/politics/ngilu-polished-political-schemer-or-lucky-opportunist-3851268

Mureithi, F. (2022, July 2). Ghost of Nakuru City status returns to haunt Susan Kihika in gubernatorial race. *The Daily Nation*. https://nation.africa/kenya/news/politics/ghost-of-nakuru-city-status-returns-to-haunt-susan-kihika-in-gubernatorial-race-3867050

Mwaura, J., & Oiruria, C. (2017). Representation of femininity and masculinity in televised advertisements: The paradigm shift. *International Journal of Innovative Research and Development*, 6(4), 3–9. https://www.internationaljournalcorner.com/index.php/ijird_ojs/article/view/136837

Mugo, M. (2022, June 15). Party popularity, tribe dynamics dominate Embu governor battle. *The Standard*. https://www.standardmedia.co.ke/counties/article/2001447214/party-popularity-tribe-dynamics-dominate-embu-governor-battle

Muiruri, F. (2022). Fatuma Achani: Here's how I plan to change Kwale. *The Daily Nation*. www.https://nation.africa/kenya/news/gender/fatuma-achani-here-s-how-i-plan-to-change-kwale-3894980

Nation Team. (2022, October 28). The men behind powerful women on county thrones. *The Daily Nation*. https://nation.africa/kenya/news/politics/the-men-behind-powerful-women-on-county-thrones-3927872

Ndonye, M. (2022, July 17). Women will surely steal men's thunder in August elections. *The Standard*. https://www.standardmedia.co.ke/article/2001446454/women-will-surely-steal-mens-thunder-in-august-elections#

Njaaga, D. (2022, June 29). Raila agrees to attend the 2022 Presidential Debate, wants opponents to turn up. *The Standard*. https://www.standardmedia.co.ke/sports/amp/politics/article/2001449106/raila-agrees-to-attend-the-2022-presidential-debate-wants-opponents-to-turn-up

Obiria, M., & Maichuhie, K. (2022, June 6). Mama sanitizer, mama miradi; Of women's campaign slogans. *The Daily Nation*. https://nation.africa/kenya/news/gender/mama-sanitizer-mama-miradi-of-women-s-campaign-slogans-3840000

Obwogi, P. K. (2022). *Women in politics: Gender dynamics in Kenyan national politics*. https://nmbu.brage.unit.no

Odhiambo, H. (2022a, June 10). Why 2022 election could be the defining moment for women leadership. *The Standard*. https://standardmedia.co.ke/article/2001431131

Odhiambo, H. (2022b, July 18). Gladys Wanga: We are not scared of chauvinistic and misogynistic men. *The Standard*. https://www.standardmedia.co.ke/article/2001448465/gladys-wanga-to-political-detractors-i-am-unbwogable

Omulo, C. (2022, May 4). I'm uniquely qualified: Waiguru on race to be Kenya's number two. *The Daily Nation*. https://nation.africa/kenya/news/politics/i-m-uniquely-qualified-waiguru-on-race-to-be-kenya-s-number-two-3803802

Otieno, B. (2022, July 20). Karua: Is the daring second liberation leader just days away from making history? *The Standard*. https://www.standardmedia.co.ke/article/2001450768/karua-is-second-liberation-leader-days-away-from-making-history

Padovani, C., Belluati, M., Karadimitriou, A., Horz-Ishak, C., & Baroni, A. (2022). Chapter 4: Gender inequalities in and through the media: Comparing gender inequalities in the media across countries. In J. Trappel & T. Tomaz (Eds.), *Success and failure in news media performance: Comparative analysis in the Media for Democracy Monitor 2021* (pp. 79–100). https://doi.org/10.48335/9789188855589-4

Parliament of Kenya. (2022). *We will work to achieve two-third gender rule: House debate*. https://parliament.go.ke

Praxides, C. (2022, June 7). Umra set to make history after IEBC clearance for Lamu governor. *The Star.* https://www.the-star.co.ke/counties/coast/2022-06-07-umra-set-to-make-history-after-iebc-clearance-for-lamu-governor

Ruiz Vidales, P., & Muniz, C. (2017). Estereotipación de la mujer en la publicidad política. Análisis de los estereotipos de género presentes en los spots electorales de la campaña 2015 en Nuevo León. *Communicacion Y Sociedad, 29,* 69–91. https://doi.org/10.32870/cys.v0i29.6289

Sanga, B., & Inyanji, J. (2022, July 15). Political insults that will go down memory lane. *The Standard.* https://www.standardmedia.co.ke/sports/features/article/2001450354/www.digger.co.ke

Santoniccolo, F., Trombetta, T., Paradiso M. N., & Rollè, L. (2023). Gender and media representations: A review of the literature on gender stereotypes, objectification and sexualization. *International Journal of Environmental Research and Public Health, 20*(10), 5770. https://doi.org/10.3390%2Fijerph20105770

Seluman, I., Eguono, A., Gbemga, A. P., & Aimiomode, A. (2024). Stereotypical portrayal and gender mainstream media and its effects on societal norms: A theoretical perspective. *International Journal of Multidisciplinary Research and Growth Evaluation, 5*(1), 743–749. https://www.allmultidisciplinaryjournal.com/archives/year-2024.vol-5.issue-1?page=11

UN Women. (2022). *A summary analysis of women's performance in Kenya's 2022 election.* https://Africa.unwomen.org/sites/default/files/2023-01/womens%27s%20performance%20

Ul Huda, A. R., & Ali, R. A. (2015). Portrayal of women in Pakistani media. *International Journal of Research and Reflection, 3*(1), 12–13. https://www.idpublications.org/ijarr-vol-3-no-1-2015/

Van der Pas, D. J., & Aaldering, L. (2020). Gender differences in political media coverage: A meta-analysis. *Journal of Communication, 70*(1), 114–143. https://psycnet.apa.org/doi/10.1093/joc/jqz046

Wangui, J. (2022, June 14). Petitioners: Wavinya Ndeti's computer science degree is fake. *The Daily Nation.* https://nation.africa/kenya/news/politics/petitioners-wavinya-ndeti-s-computer-science-degree-is-fake-3847642

Wanyoro, C. (2022, June 16). Linturi, Mwangaza win petitions challenging their degrees. *The Daily Nation.* https://nation.africa/kenya/counties/meru/linturi-mwangaza-win-petitions-challenging-their-degrees-3882130

Zoellner, D. (2020, March 5). 'I need some space': Elizabeth Warrren says she won't immediately endorse anyone as she quits Democratic race. *The Independent.* https://www.independent.co.uk/news/world/americas/us-election/elizabeth-warren-drops-out-bernie-sanders-joe-biden-endorsement-democratic-nomination-a9379871.html

Chapter 4

# Critiquing Language and Discourse in 'Rwanda 20 Years on: The Tragic Testimony of the Children of Rape' Newspaper Article

*Margaret Jjuuko*

*University of Rwanda, Rwanda*

## Abstract

This chapter draws on media ethics and the social responsibility of the media perspectives to critique discourse and language in a media report about women and children in conflict situations. The focus is on a news article published in the *Guardian*'s online newspaper in 2014 entitled 'Rwanda 20 years on: The tragic testimony of the children of rape' and in which the victims of rape (women) during the 1994 Genocide in Rwanda and the children born as a result narrate their ordeals. The critical analysis of the discourse and the linguistic features in the news article draws on such selected linguistic tools as lexicons, transitivities, grammar, and syntaxes to show that while the article highlights the consequences of sexual violence, notably the destruction of women's dignity and will to live, it falls short in safeguarding the rights and the dignity of both women and children. These discoveries, evidenced by the discursive strategies deployed in representing and constructing these events, support the literature on the unprincipled approaches deployed in foreign media narratives in the representation of conflict. I posit that reporting

Gender and Media Representation: Perspectives from Sub-Saharan Africa, 57–70

doi:10.1108/978-1-83608-406-820251005

such issues requires sensitivity and heedfulness of the negative implications of journalistic decisions.

*Keywords*: Rwanda; 1994 Genocide; *The Guardian*; news discourse; discourse analysis; language; journalism ethics; social responsibility

## Introduction

*The Guardian* is a daily international newspaper that publishes hardcopy and electronic online news that operates in 25 countries. It covers both local and international breaking news and current affairs. As do many other foreign news organisations, *The Guardian* has actively covered social, political, and cultural conflicts in Sub-Saharan Africa. On 8 June 2014, *The Guardian* published a news article entitled, 'Rwanda 20 years on: the tragic testimony of the children of rape'. The 1779-word text depicts the tragic testimonies of women raped during the 1994 Rwanda Genocide and the children born as a result. The article was part of a series of events to commemorate the 20th anniversary of the infamous genocide against the Tutsi that claimed close to a million people's lives and displaced thousands, and its publication coincided with the Global Summit to End Sexual Violence in Conflict, hosted by the British foreign secretary, William Hague, and actress Angelina Jolie in June 2014. A decade has elapsed since the publication of the news article, but its significance cannot be underestimated, particularly in the digital age, when the articles of daily newspapers are easily accessible long after print and digital and social media platforms have increased not only free speech but also hate speech (Melck, 2024). Media's continued loyalty to ethics and to their civic roles in society – including as a watchdog, a mirror, as information transmitter and as educator – remains important. Indeed, this year's International Day for Countering Hate Speech (18 June 2024) foregrounded the role of the media, media scholars, and civil society organisations in the fight against hate speech.

While women and children are priority groups in many societies, they are often the most vulnerable population in Africa. Reporting that sensitises media audiences to their plight has often been scant and quite often misconstrued. *The Guardian*'s news article, thus, provided valuable space for women to share their dreadful experiences during 1994 and highlighted not only the consequences of rape as an integral part of the Rwandan genocide but also how sexual violence was used as a weapon against the Tutsi. I accessed the article in October 2020 during preparations for a training workshop on ethical reporting of gender issues for Rwandan journalists that I conducted under Fojo Rwanda Programme. Several print news articles and stories on women and children were downloaded from both local and international news agencies and platforms for review and discussion, and the participant-journalists were asked to analyse the framing of gender- and children-related issues (prominent topics/foci, selections, recurrences, news sources, use of photographs, naming, referencing, etc.). This particular news article drew substantial concern and sparked much debate. The disagreements lay in the approaches used to represent and construct events and people, particularly language deployment and the treatment of photos.

The analysis is theoretically positioned within critical media studies as an engagement with media production discourse (Fairclough, 2015), what Fortner and Fackler (2011) refer to as the 'social responsibility' of the media and the journalistic ethics of reporting on women and children's issues. News media production discourse is a system of guidelines that specifies journalistic practices embodied in both institutional and professional norms (Fairclough, 2015). As a branch of linguistics, discourse analysis is concerned with how and why certain texts affect readers and listeners in certain ways (Fairclough, 2013; Jones, 2024). Media are assumed to shape the public's knowledge and understanding of a given conflict, as well as the rights and needs of children, thereby changing people's perceptions on these issues. These practices include the roles of journalists in society, media laws, policy and regulations, media production processes, and the professional code of conduct among others. This chapter focuses on the social responsibility of the media in relation to the specific guidelines of the Society of Professional Journalists' (SPJ, 2014) Code and the Code of Deontology and Ethics (Rwanda Media Commission (RMC), 2014) for journalists and other media professionals in Rwanda. One of the SPJ clauses cautions journalists to 'show compassion for those who may be affected by news coverage; use heightened sensitivity when dealing with juveniles, victims of sex crimes, and inexperienced sources' (RMC, 2014, p. 37).

Article 8 of the Code of Deontology and Ethics for media professionals in Rwanda also guides journalists on the protection of minors and victims of rape:

> The journalist shall show sensitivity and exercise caution while handling information relating to rape victims and minors less than 18 years of age. He/she shall be careful not to identify the names of victims of rape weather minors or otherwise, take care not to publish their pictures and photos or details likely to lead to their identification, except is this serves the child's interests. (RMC, 2014, Art. 8)

Taking off from these perspectives, this chapter critically analyses the deployment of language and discourse in the representation and construction of the events, particularly the victims of rape, that is, women and the children born as a result. The investigation seeks to uncover the linguistic strategies drawn on to report the events, particularly the grammatical and syntactic choices.

## Literature Review

### *Social Responsibility and Media Ethics*

Social responsibility theory in media studies provides a philosophical framework for journalists to ethically authenticate their judgements and actions before reporting a story (Fortner & Fackler, 2011). The Ethical Journalism Network (2024) emphasises five core values of journalism, namely accuracy, independence, impartiality, humanity, and accountability. Although getting the facts and getting them right is fundamental to journalists, they are further cautioned to act independently of such special interests as political, corporate, and cultural and to declare any potential conflicts of interest. Objectivity and balance are crucial elements of journalism practice, and they obligate journalists to present both sides of the issue in addition to context (Fortner & Fackler, 2011). While objectivity may not always be attainable and desirable (e.g. in brutal or inhumane cases), impartial reporting builds trust and confidence. The principle of accountability as an undisputable hallmark of professionalism and responsible journalism compels journalists to own up to their errors, correct them with regret and sincerity, and provide remedies to unfair actions (Aiden Adam in Ethical Journalism Network, 2024). Since news media content may hurt people, the principle of 'humanity' cautions journalists to avoid harm or minimise it and to be cognisant of the impact of their words or images on the lives of others (Fortner & Fackler, 2011).

Of the above principles, humanity is the most disregarded in news and social media, particularly in the 21st century when citizen journalists, digital activists, and other non-professionals produce and share news on social media platforms. The dizzying speed of information dissemination means that editors have come to accept these unauthenticated sources as active players in the news business. I therefore posit that in news media production processes, the social responsibility and ethical principles should be incorporated into journalists' daily actions and decisions, particularly those affecting their sources and audiences.

In the news media professional code of ethics (e.g. the social responsibility code), journalists have a responsibility to recognise the rights of vulnerable categories and reflect them in their reports. This responsibility requires a form of reporting that includes an orientation towards safeguarding the rights and dignity of these groups (Jempson, n.d.). Both women and children should be treated as human beings with a distinct set of rights as opposed to passive objects of care or charity. Despite media's presumed roles and potential, they have often disappointed the people whom they are supposed to serve. Media in Sub-Saharan Africa have not effectively responded to children's and women's issues, and, in most cases, such stories only appear in the media in cases of gender-based violence, child abuse, or exploitation, with the reports likely to be blown out of proportion or highly sensationalised (UNICEF, 2015).

The foreign media, in particular, have been criticised for exploiting children through dehumanising and controversial descriptions and the unethical treatment of children's images and photographs (Unite for Sight, 2000–2015). Unite for Sight (2000–2015), a not-for-profit and pioneer of responsible healthcare delivery that serves, empowers, and mentors organisations and individuals to provide high-quality outcomes, cautions Western photojournalists working abroad to be ethically responsible, preserve the dignity of their subjects and provide a faithful, comprehensive visual depiction of their surroundings to avoid public misperceptions. In many ways, the foreign media coverage of conflicts has generally done more harm than good. For example, Tyrrell (2015) found that the western media's coverage of the 1994 genocide in Rwanda aggravated countless issues concerning the relationship between the West and Africa. Her master's thesis analysed *Le Monde* and *L'Express* (French), *The Times* and *The Economist* (British), and *The New York Times* (US) daily newspapers and established that these publications perpetuated 'Western superiority over Africa by utilizing racism to preserve colonial ideologies and stereotypes of Africans' (Tyrrell, 2015, p. iii). She further contends that 'the inherent Western racism frustrated the enactment of human rights legislation that might have saved many Tutsis' lives' (Tyrrell, 2015, p. iii), and her study contextualises the foreign media coverage of the Rwandan genocide within a larger historiographical Western-African dichotomy. While these media organisations publicised the genocide, to think of them as monolithic and consistent in their reporting is problematic. Their different political affiliations, national influences, targeted objectives, and institutional news production discourses merit consideration.

### The Discourse of News Production

Media products (texts) are conventionally characterised in relation to their genre, which refers primarily to the formats of texts, and this categorisation signals to the audience the nature of the content that they are about to read (Jjuuko, 2023). News is only one of a wide range of genres in journalism, which also includes features, opinion columns, photojournalism, letters to the editor, and so on. The concept of discourse in news production applies to, among other things, the 'values and identities encouraged, contained or prevented by journalistic practices (often unspoken) as well as rules of a particular discourse' (Durant & Lambrou, 2009, p. 152). It also refers to 'interactions that take place through a text, whether spoken or written, in which the discourse is oriented to a non-present reader, listener or viewer' (O'Keeffe, 2011, p. 441). Journalistic discourse has specific textual characteristics and methods of textual production and consumption (Durant & Lambrou, 2009, p. 154). These are defined by a particular set of relationships between the text (itself) and other agencies of symbolic and material power. These three sets of characteristics (the language of journalists, production, and consumption), and the relation of a journalist to social ideas and institutions are also clearly related and sometimes difficult to disentangle (Fairclough, 2013).

Discourse as well as the concepts of 'discursive practices' and 'discursive formations' is important for our understanding of how media represents public issues. I use 'representation' here and elsewhere to refer to how meaning is given to things through language, how people make sense of these things, people, and events, and the communication of ideas and description of events to audiences through a language understood by the recipients (Hall, 1997; Jjuuko, 2023). News media products (radio, television, and newspapers) in their various formats, whether newspaper articles, photographs, or radio and television programmes, are sets of representations and, for some, they can be understood as realistic. O'Keeffe (2011), however, argued that language as a system of representation does not reflect reality but constructs it for people to conceptualise social life. In other words, meaning cannot be restricted to single words, sentences, or particular texts but is a consequence of the relationships between different texts and their production and reception contexts. Discourse analysts have looked at a wide variety of spoken and written texts to demonstrate how text producers use language (wittingly or not) in a way that could be ideologically significant, and 'given the power of the written and spoken word, DA [discourse analysis] is necessary for describing, interpreting, analyzing and critiquing social life reflected in a text' (Jones, 2024, p. 98).

These theoretical perspectives guide the following critique of the discourse and the linguistic features of 'Rwanda 20 years on the tragic testimony of the children of rape'. By analysing grammar, I seek to, among other things, uncover the concealed dogmata that can influence a reader's view of these events.

## Method

The linguistic tools used in media production have four facets examined here. First, the sentences, choice of words, and types of actions (in the text) – who does them and to whom they are done (syntax and transitivity). Second, the choice and meaning of words and phrases connoted and denoted (lexicons). Third, the naming of and references to people. Fourth, the choice of words to value or assign qualities to people, events, actions, times, and places (predications) and the likely presupposed meanings (hidden) in the text and other sets of language characteristics. Discourse is viewed here as a process, and therefore words, phrases, and sentences in a particular news text are tools actively employed by a journalist to present events to readers and can influence a reader's interpretation of those events.

The analysis was eclectically executed to investigate the structural features and the representation of discourse content with a focus on language that considered the interaction between the reporter and information sources (addressers), and the reader/audience (addressees), particularly the way in which the addressee understands the addresser's intended meaning in a particular situation and in the way the requirements of a particular addressee determine the organisation of a discourse. A pragmatic approach that focussed on 'the speaker's meaning at the level of utterances situated in a context' and the potential of the receiver/reader to actively participate in the process of communication by supplementing the 'missing link' was deployed (Buja, 2010, p. 260).

## Findings

### The Structure

The 2014 *Guardian* news article comprises 22 paragraphs, 1,779 words, 4 photographs (Table 4.1), and 20 direct quotations. Most of the words used are English, and the few Kinyarwanda words are either names of people and places or references to the children. Only two individual Kinyarwanda words appear in this article: *Kibirizi* (an administrative unit in southern Rwanda) and *Interahamwe* (the militiamen implicated in the 1994 murders). There are eight key *addressors*: three assaulted women, three children born as a result, one therapist who is also a genocide survivor, and the journalist, Lindsey Hilsum, who is best known for her work as international editor with *Channel 4 News*. For ethical considerations, the codes *A*, *A1*, *B*, *B1*, *C*, *C1*, and *X* were adopted to replace the real names of all information sources, and these codes reflect the familial relationships between the sources: *A* and *A1* are mother and son; *B* and *B1* are mother and daughter; and *C* and *C1* are mother and daughter. *X* is a genocide survivor and a therapist for 22 raped women and 12 children. Other sources of information in the article include the International Criminal Tribunal, the United Nations (UN), Survivors Fund (a British charitable organisation), and a Kibirizi court verdict.

### Overview of Language and Discourse Content

The construction of the events in 'Rwanda 20 years on: The tragic testimony of the children of rape' combines stylistic features of both print and broadcast media writing. Hilsum's article emphasises simplicity, description/colour (of the key actors), and active verbs to illuminate the actions and utterances and to whom they are addressees. There are many active verbal processes that bring to light the violence encountered by the mothers (raped women) and their children (the result) and the disequilibrium between the mothers and their children. Overall, the article establishes and demonstrates how these conflicts have persisted from conception and throughout the lives of the children. The women narrate their emotional challenges raising children conceived out of tribulations and living with the reality that their fathers are the same people who murdered their families. The children seem to understand the rejection and cruelty of their mothers, but still, the journalist narrates, 'things are not clear as there has never been an open discussion with their mothers – most of them learned about their dark past from their neighbours' (Hilsum, 2014).

Consistent with the conventional structure of a newspaper feature (Jones, 2024), the narrative is weaved together by the main addressor, the journalist. News is produced with a target or intended audience (addressees), so although it is a fair assumption that the article targets its predominantly British audience, its readership by other addressees and readers is likely (Watson, 2021). It is also possible that some readers have a personal connection or knowledge of the background of these events. The article is filled with hints to historical events and is about the sociological and psychological aspects related to post-genocide Rwanda (the origin of these events), so a consideration of the social values and existing prejudices in post-genocide Rwanda is as critical as the need for sensitive and constructive journalism.

## Language and Discourse: A Critical Analysis and Discussion

### The Title

'Rwanda 20 years on: The tragic testimony of the children of rape', in linguistic terms, is positioned as a 'discourse topic'. In other words, the title is a proposition about the claims being made in the article. Here, the title informs the reader that

Table 4.1.    A Description of Photographs in the Text.

| Description | | Captions |
|---|---|---|
| Photo 1 | Source A1 sitting with his mother (A) facing the camera that captured their full faces | [A1, 19], and his mother, [A, 44], outside their home … The *son of rape*, he is her only close surviving relative, after her families were killed in the genocide |
| Photo 2 | B1 (teenager) in her school uniform is facing the camera with both her eyes in view. Her mother B is leaning on her daughter on the right in a profile view to the camera | B, right, has now made peace with her teenage daughter B1, left, having *tried for an abortion* after being raped in the genocide |
| Photo 3 | Two militiamen facing the camera; one is wielding a gun on his shoulders and the other a machete | A *Hutu Interahamwe* militiaman in central Rwanda in June 1994 |
| Photo 4 | In a medium closeup, C1 is facing the camera with both eyes in view | [C1] was born after her mother was repeatedly raped. Withdrawn and nervous, she is now her mother's sole care taker |

*Source*: Hilsum (2014).

the issues being presented are as much in the past as they are in the present and will be in the future.

- *Rwanda* (the Rwanda of yesterday, today and tomorrow).
- *20 years on* (past, present, and future).
- *Tragic* (happened in the past).
- *Testimony* (constructed on present and past events).
- *Children* (past, present, and future).
- Rape (committed to women in the past).

The title of any journalistic text has been equated to the topic, and it concisely and accurately expresses what is being discoursed in the following verbal presentation either written or spoken. Buja (2010, p. 263) viewed the topic [title] as an 'intuitively satisfactory way of describing the unifying principle which makes one stretch of discourse about something and the next stretch about something else'. In this case, the title illuminates the progression of events from the tragedies of 1994 (20 years have passed) to the present lives of the children born of it. Viewed from the social responsibility code of journalism ethics, the label 'Children of rape' in the title is not constructive and conveys insensitivity towards the mentioned subjects. As one of my 2023 workshop participants opined:

such expressions can lead to isolation or exclusion of a child from society if they are identified or identify themselves with heightened sin .... a sin beyond humanity; can you ever feel confident in whatever you do in your life, among your people and friends? (Rwandan journalist, Kigali, 2023)

As this Rwandan journalist suggests, the use of such labels can influence people's view of reality and make children feel or be seen as outcasts of society and feel ashamed of not only their very beings but also their mothers. Language implicitly classifies experience and influences a person's view of reality, and there are various ways of presenting this topic that would have conveyed the same understanding of what the article is written about. To illustrate, in the first paragraph of the article, the author exercises rationality and not an appeal to pathos when they use 'children born as a result'. Even though the narrator's words are purposed to critique the media for their lack of sensitivity towards genocide victims, their choice of words in reference to the children entrenches the stigma. Such descriptions, often made by reporters, reinforce dehumanisation and can deepen the wounds that make them feel less human and unworthy of humane treatment. This behoves journalists to be more constructive, limit destructive statements (even from sources), and circumvent journalistic analyses that may lead to feelings of intense hatred and alienation among people involved in conflict situations and their aftermaths.

### Illustrations (Quotes and Photos)

In the article's construction of the narrative, all voices (quotes) of the addressors are flagged off (lead-ins) to speak by their real names. This contradicts the ethical principles of reporting victims of sexual abuse and minors. Three of the four photographs expose the children's faces and names and, consequently, their identities (Table 4.1). This is despite the journalist's explicit acknowledgement that the subjects are 'teenagers'.

### Narrative Construction – Diction and Syntax

The narrative sets off with deictic expressions that reference the time span: 'Two decades after the 1994 genocide', the television-journalist author is back in Rwanda to witness the 'extraordinary' stories of women raped during the violence and the children 'born as a result'. Unlike in the title, here the addresser is sensitive in the way she uses language by replacing the earlier reference 'children of rape' with 'born as a result'. The detail that the journalist has been in Rwanda before is an important element of the discourse for it demonstrates her competent knowledge of the historical events in focus and their context and credibility.

The first paragraph is proceeded by a photograph and introduces A1 and A using both their real names and their facial features (Table 4.1). In addition to revealing the identity of the victim, the journalist refers to him as 'the son of rape'.

In news narratives, the manner in which a journalist names those involved in the story or conflict is likely to influence a negative view and have an ideological effect on the audience about those being referred to (Jones, 2024). Paragraphs 2–5 set the narrative in motion by introducing characters B1 and B. The reader learns that when she was 12, B1 'sneaked' out of school to see her father (for the first time) at a trial where her mother (B) was testifying against him for rape. B1 had discovered from the neighbours that she was conceived in a banana plantation in 1994, after the Interahamwe (Hutu militia) gang-raped her mother (and other women) and massacred others. To add colour, B is introduced with unnecessary predications: 'a delicate woman like a brightly coloured bird'. She is quoted as saying that she had 'hated' her daughter to the extent of 'wanting to kill her' because her father killed her family. The persistent conflicts between the women and their children that resulted from their father's offenses are revealed to the addressee.

The journalist (main addresser) uses the caption under the second photograph (which appears before the fifth paragraph) to inform readers (addressees) that this woman had to accept her daughter against all odds for peace to prevail: 'B, right, has now made *peace* with her teenage daughter B1 (left), after having *tried for an abortion* after *being raped* in the genocide' (Table 4.1, my emphasis). That the subject in the second photograph is wearing her school uniform denotes that she is of school-going age, but still the image has both her eyes in view. Her mother, however, was photographed in a profile view. The caption highlights the conflict between mother and daughter through the reference to the action of having 'tried to abort' her daughter after discovering she was pregnant.

A cohesion within the text and language manipulation is revealed here in a retrospective sequence to create harmony; from peace to rape, from rape to attempted abortion, attempted murder, hate, mistreatment, and then, acceptance and peace. The verbal processes and descriptions (in syntax) used (through language) to convey the women's actions (and to some extent the children's) seem to depict the living children as their mothers' failures to kill them either by attempting to terminate the pregnancies or, in other circumstances, as babies, toddlers, and children. These actions include 'had hated', 'wanted to kill', 'tried to abort', 'throwing her out of the house' and 'beating her all night long'. Such verbal processes facilitate how the children make sense of positions and social relations within the communication spheres they inhabit. As Jones (2024) contends, principles of language broadly constitute the underlying associations of ways of speaking with social meanings and vice versa.

Consistent with the conventions of news article writing, paragraphs 6–9 contextualise the narrative and gives it depth. The journalist reflects on the incidents of 1994 and provides the statistic (attributed to the UN and Survivors Fund) that sexual violence against women resulted into the birth of 'approximately 20,000 children'. The addressee learns further on that the Rwandan government and aid programmes have neglected the children and concentrated on the raped women. Consequently, many of these children live in poverty and grew up 'feeling rejected by their mothers and stigmatized by the wider community' (Hilsum, 2014). While the issue of child neglect and the reasons behind it are of great importance to the reader too, they are not explored and left for the reader to fill in the dots. Instead, the journalist dwells on ethnicity and pedigree, drawing more on negative naming and referencing strategies used by informers – particularly to describe the children's associations with their fathers, 'since in the Rwandan context, children belong to their father's line' such that the children are also labelled by their own mothers as Interahamwe (i.e. killers and rapists) and the 'child of a snake'. Comparing children to criminals has the potential to inspire many different interpretations and quite likely reinforces stigma that has an impact on women and children in their community and society.

The representation of the militia men posing triumphantly in the third photograph may seem natural to the main addresser (the journalist), but to many addressees, particularly in Rwanda, 'the image triggers memories of the painful past' (workshop participant, 2023). In terms of intertextuality, or that which interconnects similar or related items or aspects in a given text (O'Keeffe, 2011), this photo treatment can easily influence interpretations that relate other subjects in the story to the militia men/killers.

Paragraphs 10–15 are devoted to X, A1, A, and C and share their experiences. The therapist, X, had been counselling the women and children to help them 'express themselves' and 'overcome their anger and grief' since 2007. Her attributions and quotes describe the children as having 'behavioural problems'. Whereas girls are 'ashamed' and often take on the suffering of their mothers, boys have 'explosive fits of temper' and are 'sullen and aggressive'. The journalist introduces sources A and A1 and locates the latter's given name within the conflict. After several attempts to 'abort her son', A named her son with a metaphor that connotes 'he belongs to them', 'them' here implying his mother's tormentors, the Interahamwe.

While metaphors enable addressors to poetically describe things, people, and places, they can also be harmful and damaging when applied to people. As Jones (2024) explains, the manner in which things or people are named can inform the readers/addressees about a lot of the way the world is viewed and can generate many different ideological perceptions, ranging from negative to neutral and positive, about that person. The ideological aspect here is established because when a noun phrase is applied to something, a label is immediately formed, the existence of which is presupposed. For instance, referring to children with such negative adjectives as 'Interahamwe', 'ashamed', 'explosive and temperamental', 'sullen', and 'aggressive' presupposes that these personalities exist and that raping, killing, temperamentality, and aggressivity are part of their being.

The addressee learns further on that A 'refused' to breastfeed A1 and 'attempted to kill' him when he was a baby. The son is represented as having 'reconciled' with his mother's 'hatred' and cruelty though he remains '*haunted* by the father he cannot bring himself to *hate*' (my emphasis). It is apparent that rape is downplayed by A1's words when obscures 'rape' with 'sexual consent':

> Sometimes I blame him because he raped my mother ... but maybe they were going to kill her and my father told her, 'If you let us have sex with you, we won't kill you', so mum had to agree. (Hilsum, 2014)

This misunderstanding is interpreted by the journalist as 'confused', since A1 not only acknowledges rape as a bad thing, but also posits it as a strategy used by his father to save his mother. The journalist reports further that while A1 acknowledges that rape is 'wrong', he is troubled by his own 'confused identity' and 'feels embarrassed and angry every time he's asked his father's name' (Hilsum, 2014). The choice of the phrase 'confused identity' brings to light the ongoing challenges genocide survivors in Rwanda deal with individually in the context of reconciliation.

More depth to the story is provided in paragraphs 16–18, which describe the socio-economic statuses of these women and their reflections on their past: they are subsistence farmers, poor and desperate, who are constantly stigmatised by their dark history. The journalist draws on the discourse strategies of colour to paint a vivid picture of poverty in the lives of C and C1: 'The two live in a one-room house. The mud floor floods in the rain, and a battered old bus seat with springs protruding through the plastic serves as a sofa' (Hilsum, 2014). The current efforts in Rwanda to address the socio-economic statuses of the women as part of the programme for genocide survivors (e.g., the Survivors Fund (SURF), Genocide Survivors Support and Assistance Fund (FARG), are left out of the report despite their significance.

The discourse shifts in paragraph 18, when the journalist deploys predications to assign C1 with the qualities of 'a smart girl', who has 'dreams' of travelling to Europe or 'getting a job in a bank'. These predications, however, change direction, and suddenly the same subject is reported as having 'fallen behind' in school and as speaking in 'monosyllables' at a volume that is 'scarcely audible', all details that denote lack of confidence. Apparently, the journalist is no longer sure of this young woman's intellectual abilities or that she has the confidence to work in a bank. The technical features of the fourth photograph (between paragraphs 19 and 20) are similar to photographs 1 and 2 and represent another example of unprincipled journalistic actions reinforced by negative lexicons in the caption: 'withdrawn' and 'nervous' to refer to the teenager, and they are accompanied by predications that assign her the qualities of being responsible: she is 'her mother's sole care taker'. As is the convention for the genre of a news article, paragraphs 19 and 20 present the events retrospectively by linking the present to the past and transporting the addressee back to the events of 1994.

The main addresser concludes the narrative in paragraphs 21 and 22 by drawing and building on X's quote: 'rape is devastating as it affects mental, physical [and] social statuses of women [...]. What a great misfortune to be a child of rape!' (Hilsum, 2014). The author combines two kinds of contrasting predicates to make predictions here, the one to flag the inescapable situations for women and the other to posit promise for children. Women have 'little hope of happiness', whereas the children can 'forge their own lives if they complete their education'. Of course, word choice can propose a different understanding than that which the addresser intended to convey. The verb 'hope', insignificant as it may sound, is still confirmatory. By using it in this context, the addresser is predicting the potential, if slim, of a bright future for the women, yet the children's future is conditional and depends on the completion of their education. Considering X's statement that it is 'a great misfortune [...] to be a child of rape', this is ambiguous. From a contemporary news discourse perspective, where reporters need to go beyond the 5Ws and H in certain contexts, this conclusion is lacking because it ignores the details and complexities.

## Conclusion

This chapter has critiqued discourse and language use in 'Rwanda 20 years on: The tragic testimony of the children of rape' (Hilsum, 2014) from the social responsibility of the media and the news discourse theoretical perspectives to uncover concealed meanings that can influence a reader's interpretation of events. The analysis has revealed language and lexical forms used to present facts and events that vary from very straightforward to very esoteric – including idiomatic expressions, naming and referencing, and lexical items that are insensitive, unconstructive, and generally unethical. From a professional ethics standpoint, the article generally falls short in safeguarding the rights and dignity of women and children. Three major flaws are identified: the unethical use and treatment of images and names that identify sources; the stigmatising language in reference to the subjects while constructing the testimonials for readers; and disregard of the social values and the ongoing prejudice within the context of the origin of the events reported to international audiences.

As 'symbolic elites' who control the production mode of articulation with power and freedom to select the discourse genres within and determine topics, style, or presentation of discourse (Van Dijk, 2016), journalists should be mindful that this emblematic power is not restricted to articulation but encompasses the mode of influence. This critique demonstrates how the mode in which media represent events and subjects in conflict situations is likely to shape negative or positive views and ideological effects about those who are being represented. Since matters related to such vulnerable groups as women and children are sensitive in nature, reporting these issues requires greater responsibility and ethical procedures.

## References

Buja, E. (2010). The discourse analysis of a newspaper article. *Acta Universitatis Sapientiae, Philologica, 2*(2), 259–227.

Durant, A., & Lambrou, M. (2009). *Language and media: A resource book for students.* Routledge.

Ethical Journalism Network. (2024, May 24). *Ethics 101: The five core values of journalism. A video by Aiden White.* Retrieved May 24, 2024, from https://ethicaljournalismnetwork.org/5-core-values-of-journalism

Fairclough, N. (2013). *Critical discourse analysis—The critical study of language* (2nd ed.). Routledge.

Fairclough, N. (2015). *Language and power.* Routledge.

Fortner, R. S. P., & Fackler, M. (Eds.). (2011). *The handbook of global communication and media ethics* (Vol. 1). Wiley-Blackwell.

Hall, S. (1997). (Ed.). *The work of representation. Cultural representation and signifying practices.* Sage.

Hilsum, L. (2014, June 7). Rwanda 20 years on: The tragic testimony of the children of rape. *The Guardian.* https://www.theguardian.com/world/2014/jun/08/rwanda-20-years-genocide-rape-children

Jempson, M. (n.d.). *Children and the media*. The Press Wise Trust. Retrieved March 10, 2018, from https://www.unicef.org/magic/briefing/childmedia.html

Jjuuko, M. (2023). Cultural studies and construction of developmental discourses in indigenous African language media. In P. Mpofu, I. A. Fadipe, & T. Tshabangu (Eds.), *African language media* (pp. 23–35). Routledge, Taylor and Francis Group. https://doi.org/10.4324/9781003350194-4

Jones, R. H. (2024). *Discourse analysis. A resource book for students*. Routledge.

Melck, M. (2024). *Freedom of expression and hate speech: The legalities for social media users*. https://www.dmllaw.co.za/freedom-of-expression-and-hate-speech-the-legalities-for-social-media-users/#:~:text=Freedom%20of%20Expression%20and%20Hate%20Speech%3A%20The%20Legalities%20for%20Social%20Media%20Users

O'Keeffe, A. (2011). Media and discourse analysis. In J. Gee & M. Handford (Eds.), *The Routledge handbook of discourse analysis* (pp. 44–54). Routledge.

Rwanda Media Commission (RMC). (2014). *Code of Deontology and Ethics. Kigali*. https://rmc.org.rw/wp-content/uploads/2022/03/Code-of-Ethics-final-copy.pdf

Society of Professional Journalists (SPJ). (2014). *Code of ethics*. Retrieved May 24, 2024, from https://www.spj.org/ethicscode.asp

Tyrrell, C. (2015). *The Rwandan genocide and Western media: French, British, and American press coverage of the genocide between April and July 1994* [MA thesis, University of Central Florida]. Retrieved May 24, 2024, from https://stars.library.ucf.edu/cgi/viewcontent.cgi?article=2187&context=etd

UNICEF. (2015). *Annual report*. https://www.unicef.org/media/50046/file/UNICEF_Annual_Report_2015_ENG.pdf

Unite for Sight. (2000–2015). *Ethics and photography in developing countries*. Retrieved March 12, 2018, from http://www.uniteforsight.org/global-health-university/photography-ethics_ftnref1

Van Dijk, T. A. (2016). Structures of discourse and structures of power. *Annals of the International Communication Association, 12*(1), 18–59. https://doi.org/10.1080/23808985.1989.11678711

Watson, A. (2021). Circulation in the United Kingdom (UK) 2003–2016. *The Guardian*. Retrieved August 10, 2023, from https://www.statista.com/statistics/288278/circulation-trend-of-the-guardian-newspaper-uk/

Chapter 5

# Unveiling Voices and Visibility: Women's Engagement and Representation in Three Morning Prime-time Radio Shows in Accra, Ghana

*Theodora Dame Adjin-Tettey[a], Manfred Kofi Antwi Asuman[b] and Mary Selikem Ayim-Segbefia[c]*

[a]*Durban University of Technology, South Africa*
[b]*The University of Western Ontario, Canada*
[c]*University of Media, Arts and Communication, Ghana*

## Abstract

While women's status in Ghanaian media has improved in terms of the beats they cover, it is important to identify how this trend is reflected in such prime-time programmes as morning shows and how it has influenced gender sensitivity in content programming. This study investigates the engagement and participation of women in the three most popular morning radio shows in Accra, Ghana. We employed qualitative content analysis and systematically monitored and analysed the three shows over four weeks in terms of gender roles, issue representation, and the frequency and prominence of women's participation. The results showed that there were more men than women participating in the morning shows as hosts/journalists or guests on a daily basis. Female co-hosts hardly ever filled in as programme hosts in the absence of male hosts. The study further established that men are more often the participants in political discussions on prime-time radio as both hosts and resource persons. We recommend that media organisations establish a culture that guarantees gender-transformative

Gender and Media Representation: Perspectives from Sub-Saharan Africa, 71–84 and gender-sensitive programming and representation to increase women's participation and engagement in media projects.

*Keywords*: Media representation; women in news; media experts; morning shows; news sources; prime-time programmes; FM radio; Ghana

## Introduction

Women's empowerment and development are closely related in theory and practice (Asuman & Moodley, 2023). Women's empowerment is crucial for the growth of every society as it frequently leads to positive outcomes (Anyamesem, 2017), and a McKinsey's (2019) Power of Parity Report found that the continuing gender gap in Africa is a potential barrier to women's development (Moodley et al., 2019). Egbetayo (2019) asserted that one of the greatest threats to Africa's future is gender inequality because women fall short in terms of basic amenities that support economic opportunity, political voice and legal protection, physical security, and autonomy (cited in Moodley et al., 2019). Indeed, the African continent's Inclusive and Sustainable Development Goals (SDG) framework (particularly Goal 5) emphasise gender equality and the balancing of the socio-economic and environmental needs of women (African Union, 2013).

A global study on the causes and effects of gender equality in news media that sampled 123 nations showed that the representation of women in the news as subjects or sources only increased from 17% to 24% between 1995 and 2015 (Macharia, 2020). Based on this analysis, Djerf-Pierre and Edström (2020) predicted that gender parity in the news media would not be achieved for another 70 years. The Media Ownership Monitor report on Ghana (Media Foundation for West Africa, 2017) and the Status of Women in the Ghanaian Media Report (Yeboah-Banin et al., 2020) also found that men dominated the ownership of media institutions. For gender representation, coverage, and programming, only 24% of the people represented in the media are women (WACC, 2020). Such popular programmes as political and morning shows on radio and television are mostly hosted by men, and when women are included, their roles are likened to tokenism (Chavranski et al., 2022).

## Problem Statement

There have been some significant improvements concerning the representation and participation of women in African media, and South Africa was considered a global leader for women's leadership in the media in 2020, ranking higher than the United States and the United Kingdom (Andi et al., 2020). A study on the status of women in the Ghanaian media found that despite the gender gaps in the media, women were covering more beats, including those traditionally reserved for men, like politics and business (Yeboah-Banin et al., 2020). It is important to ascertain how that trend has been reflected in prime-time programmes like morning shows and how it has informed gender sensitivity in content programming and empanelling.

This study delivers valuable insights about the status of gender representation and women's engagement in prime morning radio shows and ultimately contributes to a more inclusive and informed society, using three radio morning shows as a case. The specific objectives are two-fold: (a) to analyse the frequency and prominence of women's participation, including hosts, guests, and contributors in prime morning radio shows; (b) to analyse the topics and issues related to women as discussed on these shows. Our research was guided by the question: how are females represented and engaged in the top-three morning shows in Accra, Ghana?

## Literature Review

### Radio and Empowerment

The African Union uses 'women's empowerment' to describe strategies to increase women's agency in Africa by, among other efforts, maximising possibilities, acknowledging the rights of women and girls to security, dignity, and physical and mental integrity, and providing women a voice and visibility (African Union, 2024). This, as is well argued in Asuman and Diedong (2019), is not something that can be conferred on women but requires active engagement. This study examines radio as a medium that can strategically unite women through the two-way exchange of ideas and through participatory programming that enables them to form partnerships that facilitate changes within their lives and environment. Through educational programmes, for example, radio motivates women to understand and transform new knowledge into action and support community development outcomes (Cornwall, 2016).

Peak-time radio programmes present women with the opportunity to discuss issues salient to women's livelihoods with change agents and elected officials (Asuman & Moodley, 2023). 'Peak-' or 'prime-' time radio programming refers to the period that broadcast channels' content is consumed by the greatest number of viewers or listeners (newsclip, 2024), and it can contribute significantly to women's empowerment in Ghana and generally in sub-Saharan Africa. Peak-time radio programmes are sources of knowledge for empowerment efforts because they provide information and education on sensitive community development issues (Asuman & Moodley, 2023). Prime-time broadcasts are when such participatory channels as phone-ins and text messages are utilised, and they provide an appropriate channel for women to discuss and freely share their thoughts on matters with which they cannot publicly participate in traditional settings (Heywood, 2020). In other words, commercial radio presents a new form of media – different from traditional state-controlled broadcast media – that offers an unadulterated public sphere for the advancement of women's voices and the improvement of gender relations in patriarchal and traditional societies (JOR, 2014). What is more, commercial radio broadcasts have the power to raise the political consciousness of women in such orally based cultures and traditions as Ghana, where the average woman is less educated than the average man (Anyamesem, 2017). Chingwell

(2009) argues that radio empowers women through women-focussed programmes and women-related initiatives, as well as through talk shows, political debates, and phone-in contributions. Through engagement with radio media, women contribute to building a strong public sphere, hence improving the democratisation process.

Women's empowerment helps women to maximise agency by reflecting on the knowledge and choices available to them (Rifkin, 2009). Here, agency is a critical step in helping women to free themselves from the grips of patriarchy in traditional societies, where patriarchy perpetuates poverty, lack of mobility, and the overall powerlessness of women (Morgan, 2001). Asuman and Moodley (2023) argue that barriers to women empowerment can be reduced through women's representation in the media and more prominence of issues that affect the lives of women.

### *Importance of Women's Representation and Participation in Radio*

The inclusion and involvement of women and girls in discussions about meeting the SDGs optimise the effects of behavioural change and developmental initiatives (Asuman, 2022). Women's representation, participation, and access to the media have remained low in such sub-Saharan African countries as Ghana for varied reasons: poor conditions of services, institutional barriers, poverty, and other workplace conditions unfavourable to women (Adjin-Tettey et al., 2023; Yeboah-Banin et al., 2020). Participatory development communication has been recognised as a means of including and improving the representation of women in the media (Asuman & Moodley, 2023). The integration of participatory development communication approaches into media practices has enabled the acquisition of audience feedback by centralising the participation and representation of marginalised groups like women and girls. Participatory methods have been applied in a variety of contexts and sectors in independent commercial broadcasting and shown to improve the diffusion of agricultural innovations, public health promotion, water and sanitation, and gender awareness and relations (Ross & Byerly, 2014).

The theoretical support for the participation and representation of women and girls in radio broadcasting is that it enhances access to media and access to information, which promotes the welfare of women and girls by safeguarding their human rights (Sharma & Kumar, 2010). Even with the new opportunities for women and girls' representation in the media at the turn of the 21st century, Opoku-Mensah (2001) contended that professional journalism has never welcomed women and that they face structural problems that stifle their employability in mostly male-dominated newsrooms. Little has changed in the past 20 years: Asuman and Moodley (2023) reported that of the five radio stations they studied in northern Ghana, not only did none have women as on-air hosts of prime-time programmes but also did few have women employees at all, and, where there was a woman employed at the radio station, she was in administration (Asuman & Moodley, 2023). Adjin-Tettey et al. (2023, p. 141) confirm that structural and traditional challenges make it impossible for women to have successful journalism careers in Ghana and contend that despite private media in certain communities, various traditions, cultural norms, and perceptions that view women journalists as 'promiscuous and unfaithful in their personal relationships' make it difficult for women to enter journalism and have successful careers as on-air personalities.

## Method

The study used qualitative content analysis to explore gender representation on the three most popular radio morning shows in Accra. Qualitative content analysis is 'an approach of empirical, methodological controlled analysis of texts within their context of communication, following content analytic rules and step-by-step models, without rash quantification' (Mayring, 2000, para 4). The initial coding was informed by theory and pertinent research findings, and we immersed ourselves in the data to let themes emerge throughout data analysis.

We monitored and analysed three prominent morning radio shows (Kokrokoo, Citi Breakfast Show (CBS), Super Morning Show) on three different radio stations (Peace FM, Citi FM, Joy FM) in Accra for a four-week span between 16 October and 17 November 2023. The first stage of data collection was monitoring and tracking the output of the three morning shows using a monitoring guide that enabled the documentation of information on the host(s)' gender, the primary topics discussed each day, the frequency of a female host's contribution to the discussions, the segments that females handled, topics that female host(s) addressed in comparison to male hosts, topics discussed that were related to women, the women resource persons participating in the shows, the issues those women covered, and whether the listener was given the impression that women were well-represented in the content. A total of 60 shows were monitored over the four weeks, 95% of which were monitored live.

The thematic data analysis was guided by the research objectives and the literature and focussed on three main themes: gender parity of resource persons chosen to discuss issues; representation of gender in programme hosting/journalistic roles; and the gender parity of issues chosen for discussion.

### *Rationale for the Selection of Radio Stations and Programmes*

Radio was selected because it is the most reliable and trusted source of information on such developmental issues as agriculture, education, health, and the environment – especially among people living in rural areas (Antwi-Boateng et al., 2023). In Ghana, morning radio shows typically address pertinent political, social, economic, and environmental issues facing the country.

A survey conducted by Safiyo (2022) established that most radio listeners in Accra listen to radio in the early hours of the day, and it is thus presumed that gender-sensitive radio programming can impact many areas of society. The three most popular radio stations in Accra, according to the same audience survey, were Peace FM, Citi FM, and Joy FM (Safiyo, 2022). Although Peace FM's Kokrokoo was the most popular, the Super Morning Show on Joy FM (Joy SMS) was the Chartered Institute of Marketing Ghana's radio programme of the year in 2022. The three selected morning shows were deemed appropriate units of analysis for the study because they are the flagship shows of these networks.

# Results

## Content of Issues Covered in the Morning Shows

In the presentation of results, 'female' and 'woman' are used synonymously. The content on all three morning shows within the four weeks of monitoring ranged from politics, disaster management, media freedom, health, and social issues such as family life, education, effects of small-scale mining, entrepreneurship, leadership, the energy sector, the Akosombo Dam spillage, and the economy. Much of the political conversations across the three morning shows focussed on the New Patriotic Party's (NPP) impending presidential candidate primary poll.[1]

## Representation Parity in Programme Hosting

Joy SMS was consistently co-hosted by a female journalist, Mamavi Owusu Aboagye, and three male journalists. Citi FM's CBS was usually hosted by four male journalists and sometimes the managing director of the station. The show did not have a regular female host, and in the absence of the main host, another male journalist served as a replacement. Similarly, the morning show on Peace FM was also regularly hosted by a male who, in his absence, would also be replaced by a male journalist and news anchor. Even though presenters of certain segments of the show were occasionally pulled into the day's big discussions, female presenters of business news on Citi FM were not engaged in any of the topical discussions on the shows.

Female journalists never filled in as programme hosts in the absence of regular hosts. Peace FM's morning show had female representation as news readers, particularly of the newspaper review segment and the reading of live presenter mentions (LPMs), but women journalists neither engaged in any of the topical discussions on the show nor moderated discussions. The few female hosts of the various segments of morning shows showed a mastery of the typical duties they performed, like reading the news articles and tidbits featured in the broadcasts, and they hence projected a strong sense of confidence. The female host for Joy SMS was able to demonstrate her intelligence and competency as well as strong viewpoints in a way that encouraged personal growth and knowledge acquisition on topical issues. The data generally demonstrate that women can perform exceptionally well when given the chance to host morning shows. As it stands now, women are unable to demonstrate their competence due to exclusion.

## Gender Representation of Issues on Morning Shows and the Female (Woman) Factor

All the representatives of the NPP flagbearers who spoke on the issues of their presidential candidacy race as well as the experts who participated in conversations about the NPP primaries were men. Throughout most of the monitoring and analysis, the only female host (on Joy SMS) mainly participated in the

---

[1]New Patriotic Party (NPP) was the ruling party at the time of writing.

newspaper reviews, read adverts, and presented the LPMs, while the male hosts took charge of the topical issues. The situation changed when the topic of discussion was the Akosombo Hydroelectric Dam (or Volta Dam) spillage, when the Volta River Authority raised water levels that led to floods in low-lying areas. During this event, discussions centred around the socio-economic effects of the Akosombo Dam spill, and the female host on Joy SMS effectively drove the conversations and efficiently analysed the situation. This ultimately brought a different dynamic to the show. For instance, on 19 October 2023, the newspaper review segment on Joy SMS included a debate about how the Akosombo Dam affects people's livelihoods. Voices from men and women whose businesses were impacted by the dam spill were included in the discussion. The female fishmongers were heard complaining that their fish products were being ignored by customers who thought the water was contaminated. The female co-host contributed to the conversation and recommended that these women and other traders needed financial support and advocacy to help recover their businesses and sustain employees.

The issue of dam spillage remained at the centre of attention in subsequent broadcasts of Joy SMS. In the few other instances when women's voices were heard, they spoke as representatives of organisations donating relief items to the victims of the Akosombo dam spillage disaster. The female guests showed empathy and sensitivity for the suffering of the victims, and by doing so, they garnered support for a course of action and the development of long-lasting solutions. Female guests offered an out-of-the-norm viewpoint when they expressed worries about how the flood would affect women and children and the need for more corporate intervention. Male resource persons from the National Disaster Management Organisation, the member of parliament (MP) for the affected areas, the Volta regional minister, and journalists working for affiliate radio stations in the affected areas participated in the discussion of dam spillage on 26 October 2023.

Another discussion on the dam spillage was moderated by the host of the Kokrokoo morning show on Peace FM, Kwame Sefa Kayi on 19 October 2023. He hosted the Deputy CEO, Engineering and Operations, of the Volta River Authority for an extensive historical and technical discussion about why water is spilled from the Akosombo Dam, in a bid to provide context for the spillage. The conversation was expanded to such other dams as Bagre and Weija and how they are connected to the spillage. The engineer also discussed how the water can be used for other purposes and how future engineering endeavours can assist in eliminating the need to spill water when dams reach their limits. The next section of the programme was a panel discussion about how the general public might assist those affected by the dam disaster and the kinds of institutional and structural support that can be provided in such cases and to avert it totally. The panel consisted entirely of men and included an MP, a professor, and a lecturer from two Ghanaian universities who are frequent panellists on the programme. During the show, listener messages were read. However, the majority of the messages came from male listeners, indicating either the minimal active engagement of women in terms of sending messages or a bias (unconscious or conscious) towards the selection of messages by men. This absence of female representation also occurred on 14 November 2023, when

Joy SMS took phone call-ins during the energy crisis talks, and only male voices were heard, including the four hosted experts.

The CBS broadcast on 17 October 2023 included a discussion of the utilisation of filtration bottles as a potential health-promotion intervention during pregnancy. Although the issue was especially pertinent to women, the resource person was male. This is not to say that the issue was not adequately dealt with, but we argue the incorporation of a female voice, whether as a host or resource person, would have made a significant difference. It should also be noted that this conversation on the CBS was a rare instance of airtime allocated to a problem that affects women.

The female co-host's unique perspective on the Joy SMS discussions was particularly evident when 'Poisoned for Gold', a documentary produced by Erastus Asare Donkor, aired on October 16 and 30 October 2023. This documentary highlights the devastating effects of illegal mining and its particular effects on pregnant women and their unborn babies. The resource person in the documentary was a male medical expert, and he cited the birth of a baby with one limb and without genitalia. The female co-host, Mamavi Owusu Aboagye, reinforced strong arguments against illegal mining by pointing out the dangers of cyanide and its effects on pregnant women and their unborn babies. Her voice and experiences not only brought clarity and deeper insights into the discussion, but also provided a perspective and energy to the show that would not have been achieved with an all-male panel. Additionally, that day saw an improvement in the program's participation that was fuelled by discussions in which the female co-host took a prominent role.

Joy SMS's regular female co-host often drew attention to topics that raised socially relevant issues the male hosts might have easily overlooked. For example, on 9 November 2023, while addressing what Ghanaians desire in a leader, she hosted a discussion on the good and bad qualities of a leader. She also contributed to discussions on the Drive Safe Campaign, infrastructure to support tourism sites, inappropriate TV content, and marital property ownership and its division in the event of divorce. In contrast, the male co-hosts focussed on newspaper reviews.

Some other instances when women's voices and perspectives were heard on Joy SMS include a broadcast aired on 16 October 2023, during which Joy SMS hosted a female and a male resource person from the Ghana Education Service for a discussion of the Senior High School Renewable Energy Challenge[2] moderated by Mamavi Owusu Aboagye. The female resource person competently presented arguments for students' creativity and in support of the efforts of the Ministry of Education to enhance the students' creativity. The next day, on 17 October 2023, the Joy SMS broadcast included a discussion of real estate with a female resource person who was serving as the deputy country head of Apolonia

---

[2]Launched in 2019, the Senior High Schools Renewable Energy Challenge (Schools Challenge) is a joint project of the Ghana Education Service and the Energy Commission of Ghana. The effort intends to create interest in renewable energy and energy efficiency among students in Ghana's second-cycle institutions as well as to educate and raise awareness of these topics in senior high schools and technical institutions around the nation.

City, an urban housing developer, and her male colleague. She shared insights about how girls can take advantage of and benefit from real estate development, a predominantly male-dominated space. Her contributions sharply contrasted with the male resource person's more general approach.

On all three morning shows, the resource persons on political issues were usually male, including the hosted representatives of presidential candidates. Political figures and leaders interviewed on non-political issues like the Akosombo Dam spillage were also mostly male and included assembly members whose communities had been affected by the floods, MPs, a regional minister, community leaders, and heads of public and private agencies and organisations. A discussion about Ghana's democracy and the duration of office for lawmakers on CBS on 16 November 2023 hosted two men, including an MP and the chairperson of a political party, the National Democratic Congress. A discussion about the activities of the constitution review committee was steered by Joy SMS's female host on 13 November 2023, and voices from another programme that addressed the subject – including a female academic and lawyer – were replayed. Two male resource persons, however, were called in live when more explanation on some of the issues raised was required.

On 16 November, the female co-host of Joy SMS engaged in an 'informal' conversation with the hosting panel over the finance minister's presentation of the budget to Parliament, but when it came to interviewing experts, a male co-host took charge. Nonetheless, the female host's contributions demonstrated her understanding of the budget's economic consequences as she made clear connections between some of the budget's input and its effects on the economy. Another woman, a senior lecturer and economist, was also hosted on the show on 16 November, and she too spoke about the economic implications of the budget with competence and confidence.

Other female resource persons heard on Joy SMS included the director of an education unit, who spoke about the Senior High School Renewable Energy Challenge 2023 on 13 November 2023, and a strategy, digital, and data executive with Old Mutual Group, who was on the show on 10 November to discuss Old Mutual's 10th anniversary. The deputy country head of Apolonia City was on the Joy SMS to discuss real estate development in Ghana on 17 October. Some women affected by the dam spillage were featured on the show on 19 October, while on 13 November, the project lead of the National Science, Technology, Engineering and Mathematics Project competition was part of the team hosted. She exhibited mastery of the topics and complemented her male colleague when he had left out some important details. On 15 November, a discussion on the closure of the road tolls in Ghana included a physically disabled woman, who shared the challenges she was facing due to the closure of road tolls across the country. On 14 November 2023, brand ambassador and media personality 'Nana Ama' also came on the show to talk about MiWay Insurance's offerings. She was accompanied by two male MiWay Insurance executives who also spoke on the same subject.

Apart from the female journalist who read the business news on CBS, the other female voices included a representative of organisation donating money to those who had been affected by the Akosombo Dam spillage and former students of the Aburi Girls Senior High School who discussed the various programmes concerning an event at their alma mater. During the four weeks of monitoring, the only occasion on which CBS hosted a female politician was 17 November 2023, when Betty Krosbi Mensah, then-MP for Afram Plains North, spoke about people in her constituency who had been impacted by the dam spillage with three male journalists who formed the hosting panel. Thus, it is impossible to ignore the male predominance on CBS.

On Peace FM, the only female resource persons hosted included the head of corporate affairs of the National Lotteries Authority, whose contribution was via a telephone interview; two women (in addition to two men) from a credit union, former students from Aburi Girls Senior High School; and Afia Foriwa Boafo, who was promoting a food (*Angwamo*) festival. A deputy minister of information was on the show on 17 November 2023 to talk about the media fund to support mainstream media. It should be mentioned that on 16 November 2023, the Peace FM host revealed that a female deputy finance minister was scheduled to appear on the programme to engage in post-budget discussions, but she later declined owing to other personal engagements, an action that upset some of the show's regular panellists. The female deputy minister and expert, unfortunately, passed up the chance to guarantee female representation on a crucial national issue. Peace FM appeared to provide more room for female politicians to make appearances than other Joy FM or Citi.

## Discussion

The findings of this study are consistent with other findings that demonstrated the poor representation and limited engagement pertaining to women in the media. A study conducted across the Ghanaian news media between February and June 2021, for example, found that men dominated radio and television shows in terms of presenters, journalists, interviewees, and invited experts (Franks, 2021). This study has shown that this trend has not changed for morning shows, but it was generally observed that whenever the perspectives of women surfaced, either in the form of resource persons or a female host (particularly on Joy FM) contributing to the discussion or asking questions, their engagements influenced the focus and the direction of discourse. This is clear from the differences in the topics and directions of conversations chosen by Joy FM's female host, Mamavi Owusu Aboagye. As a member of the hosting panel and, by extension, the production team, her role in the selection of resource persons likely accounts for the relatively more female resource persons on Joy SMS as compared to CBS and Kokrokoo.

Although some have argued that female journalists and presenters are typically pigeon-holed to cover the bulk of the soft news areas of features, the arts, education, and health (North, 2016), Yeboah-Banin et al. (2020) found that women were covering more beats, including those traditionally preserved for men, like politics and business. This study's data included a female journalist who read the business news on Citi FM's CBS, a domain formerly exclusively for men. However, because she only read the news and was not included discussions about current business and economic topics, she did not address the underrepresentation of female voices (as a host or as part of the panel) on the prominent morning programme. The other female journalists on Kokrokoo also fell short because they only read the news and newspaper reviews.

Recent reports indicate that female resource persons shy away from appearing in the media (ACME, 2019), and this could have been a factor in their exclusion as much as selection bias. By including gender-sensitive and gender-transformative content, the media can play a significant role in establishing gender equality (Adjin-Tettey, 2020), so when women's interests are piqued to contribute to gender-sensitive and transformative issues, they are more likely to join in more general conversations pertaining to other socially, politically, and economically significant issues.

In addition to structural challenges (Adjin-Tettey et al., 2023; Asuman & Moodley, 2023), and technological barriers (Gadzekpo, 2009; Opoku-Mensah, 2001), editorial decisions also contribute to the minimal participation of women in the media. Some producers and journalists are more comfortable with resource persons with whom they have established relationships and rapport than unfamiliar sources who are riskier and less reliable (Barnoy & Reich, 2023). This, we argue, may disproportionally impact newer entrants who are women when familiar sources have historically been men. What is more, studies indicate that although professional women gained their position on merit, many are fearful of coming across as unqualified imposters when they are not given adequate time to prepare for media engagements (Howell & Singer, 2017).

Factors like lack of confidence and trust in the media – by not recognising the impact women make when they consent to interviews – account for women's reluctance to engage in public discourse in the media (ACME, 2019). The dam spill and its effects on communities downstream, for example, was a good opportunity to flag the challenges women and children face. The vulnerability of these demographic categories makes it important to shed light on these issues and find ways to address them. There were reports of women and girls exposed to rape and other forms of sexual assault and abuse when communities were displaced by the Akosombo Dam spillage. These incidents, however, did not feature prominently on the morning radio shows monitored – even though they should have been a springboard for women resource persons and other advocacy groups to champion the cause of the victims.

## Conclusion

Studying women's participation in primetime radio is crucial not only to the advancement of gender equality and women's empowerment but also for the improvement of media discourse. This study has yielded significant empirical data and nuanced insights regarding the representation of women in prime-time media and the potential benefits of positive representation for women's advancement and media diversity. Further research can contribute to a more inclusive media environment and society at large by pointing out areas for improvement and modelling similar studies in other areas. Gender representation requires awareness and deliberate effort, so gender-sensitive and gender-transformative content and representation, as well as the dismantling of gender stereotypes, are crucial to the establishment of a newsroom culture that prioritises gender. Media organisations should also be constantly evaluating their decisions' and actions' alignment with the ideals of positive gender portrayal and engage in regular roll out staff education and training programmes that consider the perspectives of women media specialists. Allowing women journalists more time to participate in media interactions and highlighting them as primary sources for media content are two cultural attitudes that media organisations can cultivate during the newsgathering process, news output, and programme planning stages. We also recommend the recruitment of more women practitioners in newsrooms and in production. This, we argue, can ensure that topics that significantly impact women are brought up for editorial consideration.

This study used data from a relatively small timeframe and examined only three current affairs morning shows. Literature could benefit from other studies that employ larger, more diverse samples and relevant conceptual frameworks to enable more sophisticated statistical and theoretical analysis and facilitate generalisation. Future researchers may consider broadening their foci to encompass other similar shows, diverse programme formats, and gender representation in radio news sound bites.

# References

ACME. (2019, March 7). *Barriers to gender equality in the news*. African Centre for Media Excellence. https://acme-ug.org/2019/03/07/barriers-to-gender-equality-in-the-news/

Adjin-Tettey, T. D. (2020, October 16). *The media have muted the voices of women during COVID-19: Can the tide be turned?* The Conversation. https://theconversation.com/the-media-have-muted-the-voices-of-women-during-covid-19-can-the-tide-be-turned-148010

Adjin-Tettey, T. D., Asuman, M. A., & Ayim-Segbefia, M. S. (2023). Safety of journalists from a gendered perspective: Evidence from female journalists in Ghana's rural and peri-urban media. *Communitas, 28*, 133–150. https://doi.org/10.38140/com.v28i.7599

African Union. (2013). *Agenda 2063: The Africa we want*. Addis Ababa.

African Union. (2024). *AU strategy for gender equality and women's empowerment*. https://au.int/en/articles/au-strategy-gender-equality-and-womens-empowerment

Andi, S., Selva, M., & Nielsen, R. K. (2020). *Women and leadership in the news media 2020: Evidence from ten markets*. Reuters. https://reutersinstitute.politics.ox.ac.uk/women-and-leadership-news-media-2020-evidence-ten-markets

Antwi-Boateng, O., Musa, M. D., & Andani, M. A. I. (2023). Audience listenership of FM radio: A case study of rural development in Northern Ghana. *Cogent Arts & Humanities, 10*(1), 2184750. https://doi.org/10.1080/23311983.2023.2184750

Anyamesem, D. (2017). Women and the rugged road to political office in Ghana (1992–2010). In E. Aryeetey, B. Sackey, & S. Afranie (Eds.), *Contemporary social policy issues in Ghana* (pp. 96–109). South Saharan Publishers.

Asuman, M. K. (2022). *Participatory communications as a tool for women's empowerment* [Unpublished Ph.D. thesis, Nelson Mandela University].

Asuman, M. K., & Diedong, A. L. (2019). Multiplicity of voices in community development through radio in Fanteakwa district, Ghana. *Ghana Journal of Development Studies, 16*(2), 178–198.

Asuman, M. K. A., & Moodley, S. (2023). Livelihood improvement through participatory mass communications: A study on community radio and the lives of women in northern Ghana. In P. Mpofu, I. A. Dasipe, & T. Tshabangu (Eds.), *Indigenous African language media: Practices and processes* (pp. 381–399). Springer Nature Singapore.

Barnoy, A., & Reich, Z. (2023). The familiarity paradox: Why has digital sourcing not democratized the news? *Digital Journalism, 11*(6), 1084–1103. https://doi.org/10.1080/21670811.2021.1937254

Chavranski, N., Mélanie, C. M., & Lebret, M.-C. (2022). *Gender equality in media and media content.* https://cfi.fr/fr/dossier/egalite-des-genres-dans-les-medias-et-les-contenus-mediatiques

Chingwell, S. (2009). *Community radio as a tool for development amongst rural farmers in the Rift Valley Region of Kenya* [Unpublished Master's thesis]. Daystar University.

Cornwall, A. (2016). Women's empowerment: What works? *Journal of International Development, 28*(3), 342–359.

Djerf-Pierre, M., & Edström, M. (Eds.). (2020). *Comparing gender and media equality across the globe: A cross-national study of the qualities, causes, and consequences of gender equality in and through the news media.* Nordicom. https://www.nordicom. gu.se/en/publications/comparing-gender-and-media-equality-across-globe

Egbetayo, V. (2019). *One of the greatest threats to Africa's future: Gender inequality.* Global Partnership for Education. https://www.globalpartnership.org/blog/one-greatest-threats-africas-future-gender-inequality#:~:text=Women%20and%20 girls%20still%20lag%20far%20behind&text=In%20Africa%2C%2070%25%20 of%20women,1%20would%20be%20full%20parity

Franks, S. (2021, October 19). *Male experts outnumber females by 10 to 1 on Ghana media programmes. We found out why.* The Conversation. https://theconversation.com/ male-experts-outnumber-females-by-10-to-1-on-ghana-media-programmes-we-found-out-why-169684

Gadzekpo, A. (2009). Missing links: African media studies and feminist concerns. *Journal of African Media Studies, 1*(1), 69–80.

Heywood, E. (2020). Radio journalism and women's empowerment in Niger. *Journalism Studies, 21*(10), 1344–1362.

Howell, L., & Singer, J. B. (2017). Pushy or a princess? Women experts and British broadcast news. *Journalism Practice, 11*(9), 1062–1078.

JOR (Joy of Resistance). (2014). *Multicultural feminist radio.* WBAI.

Macharia, S. M. (2020). *Who makes the news? 6th global media monitoring project.* World Association for Christian Communication (WACC). https://whomakesthenews.org/ wp-content/uploads/2021/07/GMMP2020.ENG_.FINAL20210713.pdf

Mayring, P. (2000). Qualitative content analysis. *Forum Qualitative Sozialforschung / Forum: Qualitative Social Research, 1*(2), Art. 20. http://nbn-resolving.de/urn:nbn:de:0114-fqs0002204

Media Foundation for West Africa. (2017). *Media ownership monitor Ghana 2017.* https:// ghana.mom-gmr.org/en/

Moodley, L., Kuyoro, M., Holt, T., Leke, A., Madgavkar, A., Krishan, M., & Akintayo, F. (2019). *The power of parity: Advancing women's equality in Africa.* Mckinsey Global Institute. https://www.mckinsey.com/featured-insights/gender-equality/the-power-of-parity-advancing-womens-equality-in-africa

Morgan, L. M. (2001). Community participation in health: Perpetual allure, persistent challenge. *Health Policy and Planning, 16*(3), 221–230.

newsclip. (2024). *Utilising peak time slots in media monitoring.* https://www.newsclip.co.za/ news/utilising-peak-time-slots-in-media-monitoring

North, L. (2016). The gender of "soft" and "hard" news: Female journalists' views on gendered story allocations. *Journalism Studies, 17*(3), 356–373. https://doi.org/10.1080/1461670X.2014.987551

Opoku-Mensah, A. (2001). Marching on: African feminist media studies. *Feminist Media Studies, 1*(1), 25–34.

Rifkin, S. B. (2009). Lessons from community participation in health programmes: A review of the post Alma-Ata experience. *International Health, 1*(1), 31–36.

Ross, K., & Byerly, C. (2014). *Women and media: International perspectives.* Wiley-Blackwell.

Safiyo. (2022, February 8). *These are the top radio stations in Accra.* https://www.linkedin.com/pulse/according-our-survey-top-radio-stations-accra-survey54/

Sharma, A., & Kumar, B. (2010). Audience profile of women community radio listeners. *Journal of Communication Studies, 28*, 50–59.

WACC. (2020). *Who makes the news? 6th Global Media Monitoring Project.* https://whomakesthenews.org/wpcontent/uploads/2021/07/GMMP2020.ENG_.FINAL20210713.pdf

Yeboah-Banin, A. A., Fofie, I. M., & Gadzekpo, A. (2020). *Status of women in the Ghanaian media: Providing evidence for gender equality and advocacy project.* Alliance for Women in Media Africa (AWMA) and School of Information and Communication Studies, University of Ghana. https://sics.ug.edu.gh/sites/sics.ug.edu.gh/files/Status%20of%20Women%20in%20Ghanaian%20Media%20Report%20opt1.pdf

Chapter 6

# Exploring the Affordance of Equality and Equal Opportunities to Female Journalists in Rwanda's Media

*Margaret Jjuuko[a] and Solveig Omland[b]*

[a]*University of Rwanda, Rwanda*
[b]*NLA University College, Norway*

## Abstract

Rwanda's media industry has expanded in diversity and plurality. Various reforms and efforts to professionalise and enable media contribute to national socio-economic development efforts. Media have gradually been liberalised and transformed into free and independent communication platforms and spaces for dialogue consistent with the principles of democracy and the protection of civil and political human rights. A major area of concern in most media development endeavours in Rwanda has been the creation of appropriate work environments where gender is mainstreamed in all media activities – from education to practice. This chapter examines the state of current gender equality in the Rwandan media to understand how issues of equality and equal opportunities are afforded to female journalists. A mixed-methods approach reveals an inequitable allocation of journalistic roles between male and female journalists and claims of biased coverage of women's issues, salary discrepancies, a general misunderstanding of the concept of gender equality and its implications, and modest approaches in the implementation of gender-related policies. The authors argue that continued focus on gender mainstreaming in the Rwandan

*Gender and Media Representation: Perspectives from Sub-Saharan Africa*, 85–98

doi:10.1108/978-1-83608-406-820251007

media should foster gender equality and develop capacity, inclusiveness, and non-discriminatory work environments.

*Keywords*: Rwanda; Rwandan media; gender equality; women journalists; gender policy

## Introduction

Gender equality comprises equal rights, responses, and opportunities for women and men and girls and boys (UNESCO, 2014–2021). This conceptualisation implies that the interests, needs, and priorities of women and men are taken into consideration and their diversity recognised. The United Nations' (2015) *2030 Agenda for Sustainable Development* conceives of gender equality as a crucial element in policy development that engages the international community and a plurality of stakeholders. Goal 5 envisions a world of 'universal respect for human rights and human dignity' where 'every woman and girl [can] enjoy full gender equality without any legal, social, and economic barrier to their empowerment' and further declares gender equality as a fundamental human right and a necessary foundation for a peaceful, prosperous, and sustainable world (United Nations, 2015). The principles of gender equality and non-discrimination have been sanctified in numerous international treaties, including the European Convention on Human Rights (Council of Europe, 1950, article 14), the governing treaties of the European Union (Treaty on European Union, 2009, articles 2 and 3), the European Charter of Fundamental Rights (Treaty on European Union, 2000, article 21), the Protocol to the African Charter on Human and Peoples' Rights (African Union, 2004), the Protocol to the African Charter on Human and Peoples' Rights on the Rights of Women in Africa (African Union, 2015), the Inter-American Convention on the Prevention, Punishment, and Eradication of Violence against Women (Organization of American States, 1994), and the SADC Protocol on Gender and Development (Southern African Development Community, 2008) among very many others.

These international frameworks have informed Rwanda's engagements with gender equality, and the country is now a signatory to several conventions. Subsequently, a legal and policy enabling environment has been created to facilitate the realisation of gender equality and empowerment of women across different sectors. The national constitution (Republic of Rwanda, 2015a), for example, provides a minimum quota of 30% women in all decision-making organs. The Ministry of Gender and Family Promotion's (2010) *National Gender Policy* underlines the urgency with which the national government seeks to remove all forms of gender-based discrimination and create an environment where both men and women equally contribute to the country's development. Gender empowerment is also a key, cross-cutting aspect of the socio-economic transformation outlined in Republic of Rwanda's (2015b) *Vision 2050*.

The Rwandan Ministry of Gender and Family Promotion (2021) reports that efforts have been made to cascade gender empowerment efforts at local and national governance levels. The Inter-Parliamentary Union Report (2021) ranked Rwanda ninth globally in women's political representation at 61.3%. The World Economic Forum's (2019) *Global Gender Gap Report 2020* also indicates substantial progress in women's participation in the labour force at 83.9%. The report also identified Rwanda's good progress in women's empowerment. But not all reports agree. The African Union's (2015) *Agenda 2063* and Moodley et al.'s (2019) report indicate contrasting findings that show little progress in addressing gender inequality across different sectors of the economy, including the media.

A growing issue of concern within the Rwandan media is the absence of gender mainstreaming in most news media institutions and media training/education institutions. Various stakeholders underscore the need to professionalise the media sector in ways that strengthen a balanced, fair, and equal gender representation in training and practice (e.g. Akinbobola, 2020; Media High Council, 2019; Wood, 2015). Such proposed efforts align with Rwanda's policies of gender empowerment as laid out in frameworks like the Republic of Rwanda's (2017) *National Strategy for Transformation 2017–2024 (NSTI)*, the formerly Media High Council's *Rwanda Media Policy* (2011) as well as in such mechanisms as the United Nations' (2015) *2030 Agenda for Sustainable Development*, which especially addresses Sustainable Development Goal 5.

### Study Purpose and Questions

This study examines the current status of gender in the Rwandan media to comprehend how issues of equality and equal opportunities are afforded to female journalists such that they can equally participate in media work by answering these questions:

1. What is the current gender composition in the media industry in Rwanda?
2. What are the existing gender roles and how do women journalists participate in media work?
3. How is the professional performance of female journalists perceived by their male counterparts?
4. Are there gender equality policies and guidelines in Rwanda's media institutions, and, if so, are they fairly applied?

## Literature Review

Studies on gender issues in news media contexts have been weighted towards gender balance in job segregation; representation and portrayal in media content, including who makes news (Steiner, 2009; Wood, 2009); and audiences in their access to and use of media, among other issues. Gender inequalities in the media are often related to conflict in the newsrooms about who should perform which roles, salary discrepancies, sexual harassment, and limited or stereotyped representations of women in media discourses (Akinbobola, 2020; Santonic-colo et al., 2023) – even where gender equality policies exist. Despite the increase in women beat reporters covering politics and business, women are typically assigned to stories in arts, education, and health that consequently impact their progression up the organisational ladder (North, 2014).

Santoniccolo et al. (2023) have defined 'gender wage gap' as the difference between the remuneration offered to men and women for doing the same work. It is also described as the 'percentage difference between the annual earnings for women compared to the annual earnings for men in work fields' (Pires, 2017, p. 3). Salary discrepancies are a reoccurring financial issue in all aspects of the media business and most career paths worldwide. In the United States, for example, women earn around 80% of men's salaries for the same work in the same position (Pires, 2017).

In addition to gender inequality in sub-Saharan Africa, sexual harassment also is raising concern among media and gender researchers. The World Association of News Publishers (WAN-IFRA, 2022) reports that one in four women has faced sexual harassment at work, about 35% have experienced verbal harassment, and 17% have experienced physical harassment. WAN-IFRA further reported that African media has the highest number of sexual harassment problems. Yet most of the time, cases of physical and verbal sexual harassment go unreported because of fear of further victimisation and a lack of confidence in management systems and interventions.

The *6th Global Media Monitoring Project* report by Who Makes the News? (2021) revealed that women make up 25% of the persons heard, read about, or seen in newspaper, television, and radio news, which is only a single percentage increase since 2010. Suppressing women's voices in the media violates the principle of 'leaving no one behind' espoused in the SDGs. Underrepresentation and misrepresentation of women in news stories significantly distort the way women view themselves because, of the many influences on how men and women are viewed, media are the most pervasive and most powerful (Wood, 1994, 2009). All media 'forms are purveyors of communicating images of the sexes', many of which 'perpetuate unrealistic, stereotypical, and limiting perceptions' (Wood, 1994, p. 31). The stereotypical portrayal of men and women in media content both reflects and sustains socially endorsed views of gender that falsely imply that men are the cultural standard and women are invisible and less important (Steiner, 2009). Despite the empowering effect of technology, the ordinary woman is often portrayed by the Rwandan media as passive and disinterested in public participation-related issues (Jjuuko & Njuguna, 2019). Such depictions and/or images sustain and reinforce socially constructed views of the genders among audiences and at the workplace (media institutions, in this case) and normalises the mistreatment and sexual harassment of women as well as rape and gender-based violence.

### Gender Equality in the Rwandan Media

Women are critically underrepresented in Rwandan newsrooms, television and radio stations, film production houses, and journalism and media training institutions

(Akinbobola, 2020; Media High Council, 2013, 2019; Wood, 2015). Women media owners are few, over 70% of journalists operating in 2011 were men, and less than 10% of the women working in the media were in management positions as directors, media managers, and chief editors (Media High Council, 2012; Rwanda Governance Board, 2016). About 40% of female journalists report on social and legal issues rather than economic, politics, and business (Media High Council, 2019). The latest statistics from the Rwanda Media Commission (2019) indicate little change in the past decade: of the 1,611 accredited journalists[1] in Rwanda, 1,129 (70%) were men and more men than women are in media management positions.

Reports also indicate that Rwandan female journalists suffer various forms of discrimination and sexual harassment. According to Akinbobola (2020), most female journalists in Rwanda, as in several other countries in sub-Saharan Africa, decry discrimination in salaries, sexual harassment, and male chauvinism as hindering their performance in media houses. They also cited a lack of editors' trust in their ability (as women) to independently cover news stories from the field. Yet most women respondents (80%) chose journalism out of passion, talent for the career, and the opportunity to empower others through news.

An online survey by WAN-IFRA that polled 103 journalists in 2021 indicated that about 41% of women journalists in Rwanda had experienced verbal sexual harassment at the workplace that was most often committed by male editors and programme managers. The report established that most victims chose to remain silent to keep their jobs and preserve their reputations with colleagues who considered these offences trivial. Others were not aware that they had been sexually harassed since this concept was not clear to them. According to the report, the offenders were merely warned. It is important to note that about 24% of male journalists had also experienced verbal sexual harassment and about 12 were physically harassed. A February 2021 editorial in *The New Times*, a national daily newspaper, reminded Rwandan media of their duty to respond to and act on such sexual harassment reports.

Gender-based corruption has been implicated in the recruitment process as well as in the working conditions for female media practitioners. For example, student admission into journalism and communication training institutions reflects gender imbalance, and approximately 30% of students at the University of Rwanda were women between 2013 and 2015 (Media High Council, 2018; Wood, 2015). What is worse, of the few female students who study journalism, only 15% end up employed in the media industry for either lack of interest, opportunities, or inadequate investment opportunities in the media sector, and those who proceed into journalism and related work are frustrated by the looming gender inequalities in media institutions (Akinbobola, 2020).

The studies highlighted in this brief literature review emphasise the need for gender mainstreaming in institutions not only in Rwanda but also other countries, particularly in Sub-Saharan media contexts. This will tackle gender-related issues within media and society as a whole. Despite the excellent studies on media

---

[1]There are no reliable estimates of the number of unaccredited journalists in Rwanda.

in Rwanda, we must continuously update the literature and systematically analyse the status quo. This study re-examines the current gender situation in Rwandan media to comprehend how issues of equality and equal opportunities are
afforded to female journalists and investigates other issues of gender discrimination in the workplace.

## Method and Approach

The study used a mixed methods approach comprising an online survey, focus-
group discussions (FGDs), and key informant interviews to gather quantitative
and qualitative data in a complementary way that would provide an overview of
the issue and more in-depth insight. We also chose different categories of respondents (journalists, managers, and editors) to get different perspectives. The survey
respondents were accredited journalists in print, broadcast, and online media,
media managers, and editors selected from official lists of accredited journalists
provided by the Rwanda Media Commission. The online survey included both
closed- and open-ended questions and was customised for the various categories
of respondents. Two hundred accredited journalists responded (42% women and
58% men). We also conducted two face-to-face FGDs. In each focus group FGD1
(including male journalists) and FGD2 (including female journalists), eight practising journalists of the same gender randomly selected from the pool of survey
respondents participated. The Key Informant Interviews targeted media managers.

All the respondents gave informed consent to participate in the study. They
were anonymised and given the option to complete the questionnaire if they
wanted. The data were analysed as a whole to answer the four research questions.
Both qualitative and quantitative data are presented in a complementary manner.

## Findings

The findings presented below answer the research questions about the current
gender composition in the media, gender roles and participation of women in
media work, male journalists' perceptions about women's professional performance, the impediments female journalists face while performing their duties,
and the existence and implementation of gender equality policies in news media
institutions.

### Gender Composition in Rwanda's Media

Women are underrepresented in both professional journalism practice and leadership positions like news and production managers and editors. Of the 200 journalists surveyed, 6% of women compared to 23% of men occupied these positions.
The findings were confirmed and elaborated on in the FGDs with eight women.
One female respondent argued that gender disparities arise from 'discrimination
against women in hiring' and what she called 'sexist stereotypes on the capabilities
of women journalists', such that 'some men are considered and treated as supe-
rior [to] women during recruitment' (FGD2-F5). Another added that recruiters

are 'blinded by gender stereotypes that women are not brave as men' and do not therefore consider their professional capacity during recruitment (FGD2-F3).

A related finding was that employers are also concerned about female journalists' responsibilities as both wives and mothers, which can divert women's attention from their professions and career paths, such that they are categorically denied recruitment opportunities. One of the senior managers interviewed stated that even though gender is considered an important aspect of the media house, gender equality is yet to be attained. He affirmed that only 30% of his staff are women, and men dominate most leadership positions with just a few 'talented females in positions of responsibility' (interview, July 2021). He was, however, concerned about the general conflation of 'gender' with 'women's emancipation'. He argued, in this regard, that this misunderstanding goes against the need to balance men and women in different roles and added that, 'empowering women is empowering the nation'.

### *Gender Roles and Female Journalists' Participation and Work Confidence in Media*

Assessing the roles played by media professionals was crucial to this study's goal of understanding the contribution of women journalists to the news production process. More male journalists have reporting, production, and editorial roles (singly or in combination) than female journalists. Men are overrepresented as editors, photographers, and graphic designers. Both, however, are equally freelancing. The high number of female journalists who own media houses (mostly online media) was a remarkable finding: of the 22 media house owners surveyed (who are also accredited journalists), 86% are female. Among participants with management positions, women also dominate as owners of media houses, especially online news sites. Some of the women media owners who participated in the FGDs observed that an online media business start-up is less complex than venturing into the mainstream, which motivates more women to take up the ventures.

The data from the FGDs also gave us insights into the journalistic focus of female and male journalists. The findings imply that some media institutions, particularly those with religious affiliations, consider women incapable of 'perform[ing] certain journalistic tasks as men do' (FGD2-F6). Typically, women are not given such assignments as 'presidential conferences, working during night shifts, or reporting stories outside the country – simply because women are considered unable to withstand the pressures and expectations of such work' (FGD2-F6). Female FGD participants also criticised their supervisors for considering soft news stories easier to report and therefore fit for women: 'Supervisors should be aware that reporting social or soft news stories is as complex as reporting hard news, and should value this section of news' (FGD2-F1).

The subject of women's participation in media work raised another crucial concern: women journalists' levels of professional confidence in their ability to satisfactorily perform journalistic tasks or work in the industry in general. Survey respondents were asked to rate their levels of confidence on a Likert-type scale. Fig. 6.1 visualises those results disaggregated by gender.

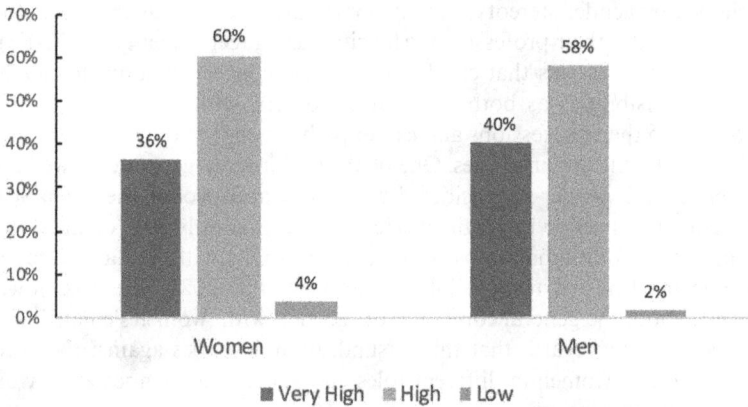

Fig. 6.1.    Journalists' Level of Professional Confidence.

The results indicate a substantial level of professional self-confidence among both male and female journalists. Of the 77 respondents (47 male and 30 female) who evaluated their level of confidence as 'very high', 40% were men and 36% were women. In total, 115 male journalists rated their confidence either 'high' (58%) and 'very high' (40%), whereas 80 female journalists self-reported the same confidence bracket (60% and 36%, respectively). Only five journalists (2% of male and 4% of female respondents) indicated a low confidence in performing journalistic tasks. In other words, the disparities in the levels of confidence between the men and women were minor.

Professional confidence was followed up in the FGDs. A male participant opined that women generally 'lack confidence and fear to perform certain journalistic tasks' (FGD1-M4). He, however, explained this phenomenon as the result of workplace gender discrimination: men, who are usually the managers, 'don't give women opportunities to exhibit their potential' (FGD1-M4). His colleague was more explicit:

> Female journalists are competent, but they lose their confidence because they are considered as simple helpers [assistants] to their male colleagues. The biases and gender stereotypes against them also prevent them from filling the same tasks with male journalists. (FGD1-M7)

One of the female participants stated that since confidence is built over time, colleagues should be given an opportunity to cover hard news stories to develop and increase their knowledge and experience (FGD2-F6).

### *Male Journalists' Perceptions of Female Journalists' Professional Performance*

Gender roles in the media industry may be determined by stakeholders' perceptions of who performs better. Previous studies have shown a strong bias towards male journalists as more capable of effectively performing journalistic tasks than their female counterparts (Rwanda Media Commission, 2019; Wood, 2015). This

Table 6.1. Professional Performance of Female Journalists and Male Media Practitioners.

| Are Male Journalists Better Performers? | Journalists | | Editors/Managers/Directors | |
|---|---|---|---|---|
| | **Male** | **Female** | **Male** | **Female** |
| Yes (%) | 36 | 13 | 73 | 22 |
| No (%) | 37 | 59 | 27 | 78 |
| Not sure (%) | 27 | 28 | 0 | 0 |
| Total | 117 | 83 | 11 | 18 |

study sought to confirm this finding in the Rwandan context, and the results are shown in Table 6.1.

Most male media managers (73%) affirmed the ability of male journalists to outperform female journalists, whereas the majority (59%) of female journalists and female media managers did not. Perhaps more striking was the finding that more than 25% of men and women journalists were not sure. One male survey respondent noted in an open-ended question that female journalists are 'sometimes naïve about certain areas and get trepidant to report on topics like politics and economics [which] require critical thinking skills'. This thinking described as 'disrespectful' by a female participant in an FGD: 'such are perceptions and stereotypes that media managers (and society) use to frame women as "weak" and "incompetent"' (FGD2-F6). A male FGD participant shared a similar view and argued against such frames that view women as incompetent:

> Many women journalists work with men journalists and have the same responsibilities with the same capacity to carry out all related journalistic assignments. We all can do research and write news and have the same knowledge and expertise [...]. We are all the same and deserve equal treatment. (FGD1-F7)

Some of the participants in FGD2-F acknowledged not always working towards their emancipation and recognition as equal partners in media work. These reported that often times they 'don't try to go an extra mile' (FGD2-F3). As women, however, they felt an obligation to do their 'best and not wait for favours from our supervisors owing to our gender' (FGD2-F5). Another participant (FGD2-F7) reiterated the need for self-help by 'becoming relevant' and building up the confidence to speak out about the discrimination against women journalists.

## Gender Equality Policies in Media Houses

A gender policy in an institution designates the resolve of management to address any gender imbalances and conflicts that may arise among the organisation's male and female members. This study thus sought to explore whether such policies

Table 6.2.    Existence of Gender Policies in Media Institutions.

| Our Institution Has a Gender Policy | Journalists | | Editors/Managers/Directors | |
|---|---|---|---|---|
| | Male | Female | Male | Female |
| Yes (%) | 77 | 65 | 91 | 65 |
| No (%) | 12 | 12 | 9 | 12 |
| Not sure (%) | 11 | 22 | 0 | 23 |
| Total | 117 | 83 | 11 | 18 |

exist in media organisations and whether the respondents were aware of them. Table 6.2 shows the quantitative results.

The findings indicate that institutions in Rwanda have policies on gender equality, with gender sensitisation, which aims to create equality among male and female members of the organisations, as a priority. Both quantitative and qualitative data revealed that some staff members, albeit few, were unaware of the existence of such policies in their workplaces. Of the 117 male journalists surveyed, the majority (77%) confirmed the existence of gender policies at their media organisations. A small percentage (12%) indicated that their media houses lacked the policy, and 11% did not know. About 65% of the female journalists reported being aware of gender policies in their media houses, whereas 22% were unsure and 12% confirmed the lack of such a policy in their institutions. The majority of the 11 male managers (91%) and 18 women managers (83%) confirmed the existence of gender policies in their media institutions.

This finding points to the need to raise awareness among staff not only about the existence and substance of the policies but also about their implementation and enforcement. For example, an FGD respondent voiced a concern that some media houses lacked the financial means to operate professionally, 'making such policies irrelevant' (FGD1-M5,7). The study further sought to assess if the policies (where they exist) are applied in a non-discriminatory manner and to the satisfaction of all stakeholders. Results are shown in Table 6.3.

While most male respondents (in both categories of journalists and managers) considered the gender policies of their organisation non-discriminatory, their female counterparts were less likely to agree. Indeed, of the 200 journalists studied, 60% of female journalists affirmed that the existing gender policies were being applied discriminatively against them. Specific examples of this discrimination were discussed in the FGDs, including limited recruitment opportunities and that story assignments. Whereas 73% of male media managers believed that policies were applied justly, almost as high a percentage of female media managers (61%) opined that the application of the policies was discriminatory. A small number of journalists in both categories were not sure about the effectiveness of the gender policies in their institutions. The respondents who did not know of such policies (Table 6.2) support the inference that the policy development process may not have been participatory. Participatory approaches in policy development are a useful

Table 6.3.    Are Gender Policies Effectively Applied Without Discrimination?

| There Is No Discrimination at the Workplace | Journalists | | Editors/Managers/Directors | |
|---|---|---|---|---|
| | **Male** | **Female** | **Male** | **Female** |
| Yes (%) | 70 | 35 | 73 | 39 |
| No (%) | 20 | 60 | 18 | 61 |
| Not sure (%) | 10 | 5 | 9 | 0 |
| Total | 117 | 83 | 11 | 18 |

way to ensure that the critical issues pertaining to all stakeholders are captured in a knowledge base that guides the policy and what it represents (Poole et al., 2019).

Adherence to the gender policy has been lacklustre in some Rwandan media institutions for different reasons. A female FGD participant declared, 'There are some media managers who don't agree with gender perspectives, and they choose not to adopt gender guidelines in their newsrooms' (FGD2-F4). One of the media managers described the broadcaster's adherence rate to the gender policy as average, stating that they are working to achieve a '1:1 ratio of male and female staff in the next five years' (interview July 2021). The qualitative data gathered during the FGDs and interviews demonstrated that although the current gender laws and policies clearly stipulate the importance of gender policies, they are not implemented because the staff do not generally understand them. The need for awareness creation on the notions of gender, gender balance/equality, and all related issues in the entire industry is still great.

## Discussion

The results from this study have confirmed gender discrepancies in professional journalism practice and in leadership positions. The dominance of male practitioners in the Rwandan media industry is not a new phenomenon. A Media High Council (2019) study that sampled 355 journalists established that men outnumbered women in the media sector due to business decisions that did not favour women (36.6%), the nature of the profession (28.6%), and perceived low self-esteem and ability among women regarding the profession (18.6%). The same study revealed that only 19 (12.8%) female journalists occupied leadership or editorial positions. Our findings are also consistent with the Rwanda Media Commission (2019) study that revealed that of the 1,611 accredited journalists in Rwanda, 1,129 (70%) were men.

Our findings from the Key Informant Interviews show that there is a general misunderstanding, particularly among male managers, that women are incapable of performing certain journalistic tasks and that female journalists (e.g. at the Rwanda Broadcasting Agency) are more talented than journalists. These findings flag the need for recruitment policies that encourage and motivate qualified female candidates to apply for jobs to address the existing gender gaps. At the time of writing, more male journalists (possibly explained by their bigger population, generally) eventually apply for media jobs and get hired, thereby reinforcing the discrepancy.

The high number of female owners of (mostly online) media was an interesting and remarkable finding. Of the 22 media house owners (who are accredited journalists), 14 were female, and they comprised the bulk of female respondents with management positions. FGD participants attributed this trend to the comparative ease of online business start-ups as compared to ventures into mainstream media. One interpretation of these data is that since women are given fewer opportunities in leadership roles in traditional media, the launch of an online start-up could be a sign of resilience. Further research into these women's motivations is warranted.

A gender policy in an organisation is just the first stride towards the achievement of gender equity and equality among the members of the organisation. The actual challenge lies in effective implementation and enforcement. The results on media policy can be interpreted as highlighting how FGD respondents perceived the centrality of a gender policy in ensuring equitable treatment of male and female journalists as they pursue and realise their career dreams. The survey and FGDs showed that media industry stakeholders are generally aware of gender equality as a critical debate in the industry. Although gender debates are not prominent in the newsrooms, some journalists indicated that when issues like sexual harassment arise, the managers remind the journalists about the existing gender policies and the need for policy adherence. Whether these discussions comprise most of the situations when the gender policies are thematised also merits further investigation. If so, how does this limited context of engagement with these policies impact how they are perceived?

## Conclusion

Before considering how issues affecting women and men in the wider society are represented or portrayed in media content, we should start with news media institutions and newsrooms themselves. Gender mainstreaming as a way of addressing the concerns raised in this study should seek to foster gender equality and should be reinforced by inclusivity, non-discriminatory work environments, and professional, equal treatment for all categories of journalists. Potential outcomes from these efforts may include women journalists who are well-mentored to face the industry, media owners and managers who are sensitised on the rationale of gender equality in the success of the media industry, and professionals who are gender-sensitive in all aspects of their work.

## References

African Union. (2004). *Protocol to the African Charter on Human and Peoples' Rights on the Establishment of an African Court on Human and Peoples' Rights*. https://au.int/en/treaties/protocol-african-charter-human-and-peoples-rights-establishment-african-court-human-and

African Union. (2015). *Agenda 2063: The Africa we want*. https://au.int/en/document/36204-doc-agenda2063popularversionenpdf

Akinbobola, Y. (2020). *Barriers to women journalists in sub-Saharan Africa*. FOJO: Media Institute, Linnaeus University; Africa Women in Media. https://urn.kb.se/resolve?urn=urn%3Anbn%3Ase%3Alnu%3Adiva-101111

Council of Europe. (1950). *European Convention on Human Rights (Article 14)*. https://www.echr.coe.int/Documents/Convention_ENG.pdf

Inter-Parliamentary Union. (2021). *Women in Parliament in 2020*. https://www.ipu.org/women-in-parliament-2020

Jjuuko, M., & Njuguna, J. (2019). The discourse of digital inclusion of women in Rwanda: A thematic frame analysis of *Imvaho Nshya* and *The New Times* dailies. In B. Musvairo & R. Massimo (Eds.), *Mapping the digital divide in Africa: A mediated analysis* (pp. 131–150). Amsterdam University Press. https://doi.org/10.2307/j.ctvh4zj72.11

Media High Council Gender Mainstreaming Strategy. (2013). *Promoting freedom, responsibility and professionalism of the media*. https://www.igihe.com/IMG/pdf/mhc_gms___m_e.pdf

Media High Council. (2018). *Media High Council 5-years activity report in line with media capacity building: 2013–2018*. https://erc.undp.org/api/download?filePath=%2Fdocuments%2F6891%2Fmgmtresponse%2Fkeyaction%2Fdoc_239762768312025959FinalReportonGenderAssessmentinmediasector.pdf

Media High Council. (2019). *Assessment of gender status in Rwanda media sector*. https://erc.undp.org/api/download?filePath=%2Fdocuments%2F6891%2Fmgmtresponse%2Fkeyaction%2Fdoc_7471570627579583346PROGRESSREPORTOCT-DEC2019.pdf

Ministry of Gender and Family Promotion, Republic of Rwanda. (2010). *National gender policy*. https://www.migeprof.gov.rw/fileadmin/user_upload/Migeprof/Publications/Guidelines/National_Gender_Policy-July_2010.pdf

Ministry of Gender and Family Promotion, Republic of Rwanda. (2021). *Revised national gender policy*. https://migeprof.gov.rw/fileadmin/user_upload/Migeprof/Publications/Guidelines/Revised_National_Gender_Policy-2021.pdf

Moodley, L., Kuyoro, M., Holt, T., Leke, A., Madgavkar, A., Krishnan, M., & Akintayo, F. (2019). *The power of parity: Advancing women's equality in Africa*. McKinsey Global Institute. https://www.mckinsey.com/featured-insights/gender-equality/the-power-of-parity-advancing-womens-equality-in-africa

North, L. (2014). The gender of 'soft' and 'hard' news: Female journalists' views on gendered story allocations. *Journalism Studies, 17*(3), 356–373.

Organization of American States. (1994). *Inter-American convention on the prevention, punishment, and eradication of violence against women*. https://oas.org/juridico/english/treaties/a-61.html

Pires, C. (2017). *The gender wage gap in the film industry: A review of literature* [Senior thesis, Dominican University of California]. https://doi.org/10.33015/dominican.edu/2017.CMS.ST.04

Poole, M., Vargas, M., Hoyuelos, M., Byerly, C., Lemma, M., Suriaga, E., Desai, M., Nunez-Gomez, P., Zurian, F., Garcia-Ramoz, F., Mencia-Ripley, A., & Díaz, S. (2019). *Gender, media & ICTs: New approaches for research, education, and training in UNESCO*. UNESCO Series on Journalism Education.

Republic of Rwanda. (2015a). *Rwanda's constitution of 2003 with amendments through 2015*. https://faolex.fao.org/docs/pdf/rwa128551.pdf

Republic of Rwanda. (2015b). *Vision 2050*. https://www.minaloc.gov.rw/fileadmin/user_upload/Minaloc/Publications/Useful_Documents/English-Vision_2050_full_version_WEB_Final.pdf

Republic of Rwanda. (2017). *National strategy for transformation 2017–2024 (NST1)*. https://vision2050.minecofin.gov.rw/root/nst/nst1

Rwanda Governance Board. (2016). *Rwanda media barometer 2016*. https://www.rgb.rw/fileadmin/user_upload/RGB/Publications/RWANDA_MEDIA_BAROMETER-RMB/RWANDA_MEDIA_BAROMETER_2016.pdf

Rwanda Media Commission. (2019). *Content analysis of gender based harassment in media 'The case of online media.'* Rwanda Media Commission Media Self-Regulatory Body. https://rmc.org.rw/wp-content/uploads/2019/10/Content-Analysis-gender-based-harrasment-in-online-media.pdf

Santoniccolo, F., Trombetta, T., Paradiso, M. N., & Rollè, L. (2023). Gender and media representations: A review of the literature on gender stereotypes, objectification and sexualization. *International Journal of Environmental Research and Public Health*, *20*(10), 5770. https://doi.org/10.3390/ijerph20105770; https://www.ncbi.nlm.nih.gov/pmc/articles/PMC10218532/

Steiner, L. (2009). Gender in the newsroom. In K. Wahl-Jorgensen & T. Hanitzsch (Eds.), *The Handbook of Journalism Studies* (pp. 116–129). Routledge.

UNESCO. (2014–2021). *UNESCO education strategy 2014–2021.* https://unesdoc.unesco.org/ark:/48223/pf0000231288

United Nations. (2015). *Transforming our world: The 2030 agenda for sustainable development.* https://sdgs.un.org/2030agenda

United Nations. (2021). *The sustainable development goals report.* United Nations Statistics Division. https://unstats.un.org/sdgs/report/2021/

WAN-IFRA. (2021). *New research shows extent of sexual harassment in African Media.* https://wan-ifra.org/2021/07/new-research-shows-extent-of-sexual-harassment-in-african-media/

WAN-IFRA. (2022). *Women in news research confirms extent of gender gap at top levels of media.* https://wan-ifra.org/2022/12/women-in-news-research-confirms-extent-of-gender-gap-at-top-levels-of-media/

Who Makes the News? (2021). *6th global media monitoring project.* https://whomakesthenews.org/wp-content/uploads/2021/07/GMMP2020.ENG_.FINAL20210713.pdf

Wood, A. (2015). *Baseline study: Fojo Media Institute Project Capacity Building of the School of Journalism and Communication.* University of Rwanda. https://urn.kb.se/resolve?urn=urn%3Anbn%3Ase%3Alnu%3Adiva-119300

Wood, J. T. (1994). Gendered media: The influence of media on views of gender. In J. T. Wood (Ed.), *Gendered lives: Communication, gender, and culture* (pp. 231–259). Wadsworth Publishing Company.

Wood, J. T. (2009). Feminist standpoint theory. In S. W. Littlejohn & K. A. Foss (Eds.), *Encyclopedia of communication theory* (Vol. 2, pp. 397–398). SAGE. https://doi.org/10.4135/9781412959384

World Economic Forum. (2019). *Global gender gap report 2020.* https://www.weforum.org/reports/gender-gap-2020-report-100-years-pay-equality

Chapter 7

# Communicating Abortion in the Mass Media: A Literature Review of the Challenges and Possibilities

*Jeanne d'Arc Mukamana[a,b], Emma Durden[b] and Sarah Gibson[b]*

[a] *University of Rwanda, Rwanda*
[b] *University of KwaZulu-Natal, South Africa*

## Abstract

Abortion is among the recognised services for sexual reproductive health and rights (SRHR), and respecting women's rights to safe abortion and their SRHR is linked with respecting women's right to life (African Union, 2003; Durojaye et al., 2021; Starrs et al., 2018; WHO, 2022). Research indicates significant gaps in protecting and respecting SRHR in Africa, specifically in Sub-Saharan countries (Durojaye et al., 2021; Poku, 2020; Starrs et al., 2018). This may be a result of restrictive laws and policies as well as prevailing religious and cultural beliefs and attitudes related to SRHR. The media has a key role to play in shaping public discourse and impacts attitudes towards abortion and its access as a health service and a right of pregnant girls and women (Fraile & Hernández, 2024). This chapter explores some of the available literature on mass media's potential to share information and open up global debate about abortion in the Sub-Saharan African region, where legal access to abortion is restricted. It draws not only on the literature examining how mass media serve as effective tools for the public sphere to discuss issues regarding abortion but also about how what is communicated can either create a sense of moral panic by highlighting deviance from social norms and values or foster change of those social norms to create a more favourable environment for safe abortion.

*Keywords*: Abortion; mass media; representations; moral panic; public sphere

Gender and Media Representation: Perspectives from Sub-Saharan Africa, 99–108

doi:10.1108/978-1-83608-406-820251008

## Introduction and Background

Safe abortion care is among the nine recognised essential services for sexual reproductive health and rights (SRHR; African Union, 2003; Durojaye et al., 2021; Starrs et al., 2018; WHO, 2022). Since the International Conference on Population Development held in Cairo in 1994 and the Beijing Declaration and Platform for Action in 1995, respecting and protecting SRHR have been considered an important responsibility for governments across the world (Durojaye et al., 2021). The UN sustainable development goals link SRHR to goals and targets and commit governments to ensuring access to SRHR and promoting gender equality (goal 5.6) and to healthy lives and well-being for all (goal 3.7) by 2030 (Munyati, 2018; Starrs et al., 2018; UNFPA, 2023). Respecting women's rights to safe abortion is linked with respecting women's right to life (African Union, 2003; UNFPA, 2023; WHO, 2022). However, many countries are falling behind in their provision of this essential SRHR service (Starrs et al., 2018).

The Maputo Protocol (2003) is recognised as the first African document on human rights that specifically mentions access to safe abortion as a woman's right. More than 15 years later, research shows that there are significant gaps in protecting and respecting SRHR in Africa, specifically in Sub-Saharan countries (Durojaye et al., 2021; Poku, 2020; Starrs et al., 2018). As a key source of political and social information, the media has an important role to play in shaping public discourse and can impact on how SRHR are advanced or restricted (Feldman & Zmerli, 2019). This chapter aims to explore how mass media coverage facilitates the public sphere's engagement in discussion about abortion as a social issue and how its framing of abortion issues can create or dilute a sense of moral panic among audiences.

This chapter uses the term 'mass media' to refer to all those forms of media facilitating communication to a large and dispersed audience, including newspapers, radio, television, and online media (McQuail & Deuze, 2020). It employs the concept of the 'public sphere' to describe the domain of social life where public opinion can be formed and where citizens can freely share their opinions (Habermas, 1989, p. 398). 'Moral panic' as explored in the chapter refers to media coverage that exaggerates an event represented as a threat to societal values and interests (Cohen, 2002, p. 1).

## Mass Media as a Source of Information and Influence

Mass media in its varied forms can reach a wide audience and offer the space to discuss issues affecting their societies in a 'public sphere' (Habermas, 1989; McQuail & Deuze, 2020). Indeed, mass media is seen as possibly the most credible and effective source of information on SRHR generally, and abortion specifically, and plays a key role in influencing the formation of public opinion about abortion (Fraile & Hernández, 2024). How media frames and represents abortion depends largely on the countries' context in terms of religious beliefs, social and cultural values, and legislation as well as current scientific justifications and international human rights conventions (Davis Kempton, 2024; Fraile & Hernández, 2024; Hadley, 2023; McDonnell & Murphy, 2019; Nyathi & Ndhlovu, 2021).

The recent increase in coverage of abortion issues and the negative representations of abortion in the media can result in amplified moral panic in societies (Goode & Ben-Yehuda, 2009; Jewkes & Linnemann, 2018). The creation or reinforcement of negative representations and stereotypes among audiences can promote misconceptions and abortion stigma among the public (Jewkes & Linnemann, 2018; Purcell et al., 2014), whereas the increased coverage of abortion that advocates for women's rights to abortion as a human right can not only change social-cultural attitudes to be more accepting of women and girls' need for and right to abortion but also impact legislation (Davis Kempton, 2024; McDonnell & Murphy, 2019).

## Four Factors Impacting Media Coverage of Abortion

Several factors influence how much and what kind of coverage abortion receives in the mass media. The reviewed literature focuses predominantly on four: the newsworthiness of the topic, the political and social context, media freedom, and media ownership.

Successful journalists know what interests their audience, and when issues are considered important and interesting to the public, mass media can increase the coverage of a topic by changing the way those issues are communicated to better meet the audiences' appetite and boost sales by abiding by the 'rule of newsworthiness':

> Editors and journalists select, produce, and present news according to a range of professional criteria that are used as benchmarks to determine a story's newsworthiness [...] if a story does not contain at least some of the characteristics deemed newsworthy, it will not appear on the news agenda. News values, then, are the value judgments journalists and editors make about the public appeal of a story as well as whether it is in the public interest. (Jewkes & Linnemann, 2018, p. 67)

This suggests that before journalists choose to cover issues related to abortion, they consider criteria to identify what is relevant, two of which include a new subject or a subject interesting to the public. Decisions about whether to cover the topic of abortion may be influenced by this concept of newsworthiness.

A country's political and social context and level of freedom of the press also impact how mass media covers abortion. South Africa provides a strong example of how these contexts impact the media coverage of abortion: there is a marked difference between newsprint media representation of abortion by commentators in South Africa before 1990, when there were restrictive laws and media freedom was limited, and after 1990, after democratic reform, the liberalisation of abortion laws, increased gender activism, and the establishment of an environment of greater media freedom (Feltham-King & Macleod, 2015).

Media ownership status (i.e. whether an organisation is government-controlled or privately owned) also affects how media houses represent abortion issues (Nyathi & Ndhlovu, 2021). On the one hand, media houses owned by interest groups that oppose the right to abortion are more likely to emphasise anti-abortion perspectives, frame abortion rights arguments negatively, and potentially limit the diversity of viewpoints available to the public (Feltham-King and Macleod, 2015; Nyathi & Ndhlovu, 2021). On the other hand, pro-rights media ownership is more likely to provide coverage of abortion-related issues that support and normalise such perspectives and highlight the importance of reproductive rights (Nyathi & Ndhlovu, 2021). In other words, privately owned media houses can either contribute to a sense of moral panic about abortion or facilitate the informed rational discourse envisioned in Habermas' public sphere by providing factual information on the topic.

A recent case study of media coverage in Zimbabwe reveals that government-controlled media houses also suffer from bias. Nyathi and Ndhlovu (2021) found that the government-owned newspaper tends to criminalise abortion and promote restrictive laws on abortion, which is consistent with the current legislation in Zimbabwe, where abortion is illegal except in limited circumstances. Most of *The Chronicle*'s coverage of abortion frames the women who seek abortion services as criminals and killers. What is more, the study found that the government-owned newspaper draws readers' attention to the dangerous consequences of abortion for women, without clarifying the difference between safe abortion and unsafe abortion. The three privately owned and independent newspapers examined, however, participate in debate about abortion and advocate for decriminalisation. Articles that discuss the consequences of unsafe abortion on women's health, advocate for women's rights to abortion, criticise the restrictive abortion law in Zimbabwe, and call for review of the laws to provide access to legal and safe abortion and prevent the consequences of unsafe abortions were prominent in the private media's coverage. Nyathi and Ndhlovu (2021) argue that how the government-owned newspaper in Zimbabwe criminalises abortion not only spreads fear about the risks of having an abortion and discourages women from seeking medical assistance to terminate an unwanted pregnancy safely but also discourages abortion supporters' movements and increases stigma for women who have an abortion.

## Abortion as Controversy and the Amplification of Moral Panic

As women are the population most impacted by abortion, the framing, language, and focus of abortion-related media coverage often demonstrate underlying biases and power dynamics and reveal how media narratives can reinforce or challenge traditional gender norms and the social status of women. How mass media frames abortion can add to or reduce stigma and a sense of moral panic around abortion. More often than not, media coverage of abortion is not advocacy for human rights but the presentation of a controversial topic related to what women's bodies are expected to be and how they are intended to work (Jewkes & Linnemann, 2018; Lagos & Antezana, 2018; Purcell et al., 2014). For example, a 2014 study of newspaper coverage of abortion in Great Britain found that only a few newspapers framed abortion positively, advocated for the right of women to abortion services, and challenged the stigmatising and negative discourse surrounding abortion and women who decide to terminate their pregnancies (Purcell et al., 2014). A much larger number of the analysed newspapers presented abortion as a criminal act and portrayed women who terminate their pregnancies as 'incompetent' or 'unnatural' women who are unable to deal with motherhood. This deviation from the 'norm' of womanhood and motherhood can be exaggerated in the media and result in moral panic. The study also indicated that British newspapers tended to associate abortion with post-abortion complications and health risks, which discourages women from seeking abortion services.

The framing of abortion in South American mass media operating online also condemns or stigmatises women who have or seek abortions. Lagos and Antezana (2018, p. 136) criticise the online media public sphere 'as a male domain', where men's voices are seen to encourage gender-based violence with their violent discourses. Lagos and Antezana further contend that even if mass media is a good space for the public to express freely their opinions, what is said in that sphere and how it is said can contain elements that lead to moral panic. Their study indicates that in the context of South American countries, online public opinion often propagates a distorted picture of abortion and holds the survivors of rape and sexual assaults accountable for the pregnancies that result from these crimes. The impact of this media coverage has serious consequences; increased negative portrayals and representations of abortion and those who seek them reinforce stigmatisation, discourage women from seeking abortion services, and pose a barrier to the activists engaged in advocating for women's rights to abortion (Lagos & Antezana, 2018).

Men's voices are more often heard in the media's discussion and representation of the topic of abortion. As Davis Kempton's (2024) assessment of the coverage of the change in abortion laws in the United States of America (USA) indicates, mass media privileges men's voices because men hold more political power and more actively participate in the decision-making processes. Women's voices claiming their reproductive health rights are not boosted in the same way as the voices of men opposing legal access to abortion are. Many other studies also argue that the mass media coverage of the legalisation of abortion is more politicised than any other health issue (Davis Kempton, 2024; Fraile & Hernández, 2024).

## Abortion in Negative Frames: Unintentional Media Bias

Mass media also can unwillingly convey a negative image of abortion to its audience even if they had an intention of advocating for the right to abortion when the media content does not match the reality of abortion. An analysis of four American and British television dramas from different television stations shows that even though these dramas positively portray abortion and highlight women's rights to seek abortion, they fail to portray abortion realistically (Freeman, 2022). Instead, the dramas portray the abortion procedure as surgical only and people seeking abortion as white, rich, and young. Freeman argues that television producers exclude information that viewers should know, like such alternatives to surgical interventions as medical abortion (i.e. taking oral medication), and the fact that all women can seek abortion, no matter where they live, their age, or the colour of their skin. Freeman (2022) further notes that such misinformation can 'exaggerate the risks of seeking abortion services' and can 'reinforce the assumption that abortion is violent and dangerous' to fuel abortion-related stigma (p. 600). What is more, when mass media does not cover the whole truth about abortion, it can be at risk of reinforcing the existing concerns associated with post-abortion complications and women's fears about seeking abortion services:

> More accurate representations of abortions (in terms of how an abortion is accessed, what will happen during the procedure, what will happen after, and who accesses abortions) may help to provide safer information to those who only access information about abortion through popular culture. (Freeman, 2022, p. 600)

Media coverage focussing on newsworthiness of issues regarding abortion can also foster biased information. When the voices opposing the legalisation of abortion are considered newsworthy, they are the most heard in the mass media and gain further prominence among audiences (Rohlinger, 2015; Sambaiga et al., 2019). In such countries as Tanzania and Uganda, which have restrictive laws on abortion and the majority of the population holds strong religious beliefs, the mass media focuses on anti-abortion movements' discourses because they are the most prominent (Larsson et al., 2015; Sambaiga et al., 2019). When the voices of activists supporting safe abortion and advocating for legal changes are few and of marginal interest to the public, they do not attract media attention and lose visibility in mass media. When mass media provides a public platform to voice opinions opposing women's rights to abortion, these rights are often ignored among the population (Davis Kempton, 2024).

## Abortion Coverage as Advocacy

While mass media can amplify dominant voices of power that demonise abortion, it can also advocate for abortion rights. The media can promote debates and give a voice to activists in order to influence public opinion and change conservative attitudes and restrictive laws (Feltham-King & Macleod, 2015). Mass media has the power to set the agenda and influence social norms around abortion, and media coverage has contributed to the amendment and repeal of restrictive laws and protection of women's rights to abortion (McDonnell & Murphy, 2019).

The increased coverage of incidents justifying the right of women to request abortion services brought about a change in the abortion law in the United States of America (Rohlinger, 2015). Although USA law allowed abortion in cases of sexual assault, incest, and foetal malformation during the 1940s and 1950s, Rohlinger narrates that this changed in the 1960s after increased coverage of the request for abortion by TV celebrity Sherri Finkbine, who realised that 'she had ingested a drug known to cause fetal deformity' (Rohlinger, 2015, p. 43). Her ordeal and travels to Sweden to obtain a safe abortion combined with the rubella measles epidemic received important TV coverage, and, as a result, abortion laws were amended in the country.

McDonnell and Murphy (2019) argue that mass media coverage of the 2012 death from sepsis after a prolonged miscarriage of Savita Halappanavar, who was refused an abortion because the law did not permit medical doctors to perform an abortion while the heart of the baby was still beating, brought about a similar change in Irish law. McDonnell and Murphy (2019) analysed how six Irish newspapers framed the issue of abortion to demonstrate that Savita Halappanavar's death provided an opportunity for newspapers to highlight the gap in the existing legislation which did not give medical doctors a clear framework. The law was accused of prioritising the rights of the unborn over the rights of the mother. The international media attention and debates reflected negatively on Ireland's image which gave way to a historical change in the Irish constitution, from 'the protection of the unborn' to ensuring that abortion was available on request up to 12 weeks (McDonnell & Murphy, 2019, p. 18).

## Abortion Coverage for Informed Decision-making

The mass media has significant power to provide factual information to assist individual women of reproductive age's decision-making about abortion services because mass media exposure allows them to acquire information on the existing laws guiding abortion in their countries and their rights to make decisions about their own bodies (Aalmneh et al., 2022; Ahinkorah et al., 2020; Dickson et al., 2018). For example, a 2018 study conducted in Ghana and Mozambique that identified socio-demographic factors influencing the termination of pregnancy among women in the two countries found that exposure to newspaper, radio, television, or social media impacted the likelihood that a woman would decide to terminate a pregnancy:

> The importance of media in providing information about how and where to terminate a pregnancy could account for the association between media exposure and the prevalence of pregnancy termination. Women who have access to social media may also be aware of the abortion laws in their country and are less likely to be stigmatised by society in their quest to have a pregnancy terminated. (Dickson et al., 2018, p. 8)

A 2020 study in Ghana further supports the relationship between mass media exposure and self-efficacy in abortion decision-making by revealing that adolescent girls and young women who consume mass media messages are more likely to develop independent decision-making about their own access to abortions than those who are not exposed to this information (Ahinkorah et al., 2020). Women's exposure to mass media provides them with a variety of ideas and knowledge about the importance of safe abortion, and the researchers recommend that to promote safe abortions, […] government should also ensure regular, periodic mass media campaigns to target adolescent girls and young women and provide education/knowledge on family planning and safe abortion practices. (Ahinkorah et al., 2020, p. 9)

Mass media's potential to build capacity for decision-making around abortion was also confirmed by a 2021 study of three popular media outlets in Kenya that found that when mass media provides adolescents with accurate information on sexual reproductive health and abortion, cultural mindsets can change and encourage adolescents to make informed, independent decisions about their reproductive health (Kafu et al., 2021).

## Conclusion

The review literature demonstrates that mass media coverage can be a double-edged sword when it comes to abortion. Coverage can satisfy either the pro-rights movement or the anti-rights movement. Mass media can serve as a model of the ideal public sphere, whereby the population has various opportunities to participate in public life by expressing their views on matters affecting them, but it is also a platform from which the dominant voices in this public sphere exercise the extant power dynamics and relationship, including men and governments who are against abortion rights. In other words, this can drown out other arguments for women's right to abortion and prevent accurate media coverage of abortion issues.

Mass media coverage of abortion, in general, reveals that abortion is a controversial subject worldwide even in countries where abortion is legalised. The consistently negative framing of the issue in the media can result in moral panic (McDonnell & Murphy, 2019; Nyathi & Ndhlovu, 2021). When media content amplifies negative attitudes towards abortion, this increases abortion stigma, discourages women from seeking safe abortions, and prevents activists from advocating for abortion (Nyathi & Ndhlovu, 2021, p. 1474). This can perpetuate the problem of women continuing with unwanted pregnancies or accessing unsafe abortion, and the latter is a significant factor in the high maternal mortality rates in Sub-Saharan Africa (Durojaye et al., 2021; Nyathi & Ndhlovu, 2021). When media content promotes independent decision-making and women's sexual and reproductive rights, it also has the power to influence not only an audience's attitudes and social norms around abortion but also abortion legislation.

Well-informed and responsible mass media coverage of abortion issues can result in a more informed public, reduced stigma, a more nuanced understanding of the complexities surrounding sexual and reproductive rights, and ultimately, better health outcomes and expanded options for women. While much of the available research focuses on the coverage of abortion in newspapers, television, and online media, there is little available literature on radio coverage of abortion. Given the influence of radio on its audience in Sub-Saharan Africa and its reach to all social groups (e.g. Chiumbu & Motsaathebe, 2021; Munoriyarwa, 2021), how radio covers and frames abortion needs more attention. This was the impetus behind a study conducted in 2024 into radio stations' coverage of the decriminalisation of abortion for minors in Rwanda.

# References

Aalmneh, T. S., Alem, A. Z., Tarekegn, G. E., Kassew, T., Liyew, B., & Terefe, B. (2022). Individual and community-level factors of abortion in East Africa: A multilevel analysis. *Archives of Public Health*, *80*(1), 184. https://doi.org/10.1186/s13690-022-00938-8

Ahinkorah, B. O., Seidu, A.-A., Mensah, G. Y., & Budu, E. (2020). Mass media exposure and self-efficacy in abortion decision-making among adolescent girls and young women in Ghana: Analysis of the 2017 Maternal Health Survey. *PLOS One*, *15*(10), e0239894. https://doi.org/10.1371/journal.pone.0239894

African Union. (2003). *Protocol to the African Charter on Human and People's Rights on the Rights of Women in Africa*. https://au.int/en/treaties/protocol-african-charter-human-and-peoples-rights-rights-women-africa

Chiumbu, S., & Motsaathebe, G. (Eds.) (2021). *Radio, public life and citizen deliberation in South Africa*. Routledge.

Cohen, S. (2002). *Folk devils and moral panics*. Routledge.

Davis Kempton, S. E. (2024). My body, my voice: Analyzing news sources in the *Roe v. Wade* reversal. *Newspaper Research Journal*, *45*(3), 299–310. https://doi.org/10.1177/07395329241248755

Dickson, K. S., Adde, K. S., & Ahinkorah, B. O. (2018). Socio-economic determinants of abortion among women in Mozambique and Ghana: Evidence from demographic and health survey. *Archives of Public Health*, *76*, 37. https://doi.org/10.1186/s13690-018-0286-0

Durojaye, E., Mirugi-Mukundi, G., & Ngwena, C. (2021). *Advancing sexual and reproductive health and rights in Africa: Constraints and opportunities*. Routledge.

Feldman, O., & Zmerli, S. (Eds.). (2019). Introduction: Liberal democracies and the study of political communicators. In *The psychology of political communicators: How politicians, culture, and the media construct and shape public discourse* (pp. 1–10). Routledge.

Feltham-King, T., & Macleod, C. (2015). Gender, abortion and substantive representation in the South African newsprint media. *Women's Studies International Forum*, *51*, 10–18. https://doi.org/10.1016/j.wsif.2015.04.001

Fraile, M., & Hernández, E. (2024). What is political and what is not? Illustrating how the salience of abortion in the media shapes public perceptions about its political nature. *Acta Politica*. https://doi.org/10.1057/s41269-024-00347-5

Freeman, C. (2022). Feeling better: Representing abortion in "feminist" television. *Culture, Health & Sexuality*, *24*(5), 597–611. https://doi.org/10.1080/13691058.2021.1874053

Goode, E., & Ben-Yehuda, N. (2009). *Moral panics: The social construction of deviance*. Wiley-Blackwell.

Habermas, J. (1989). *The structural transformation of the public sphere: An inquiry into a category of Bourgeois Society*. MIT Press.

Hadley, M. B. (2023). How do conversations on social media help to explain financial barriers to family planning services for Rwandan adolescent girls within the prevailing cultural and legal context? *Heliyon*, *9*(3), Article e14318. https://doi.org/10.1016/j.heliyon.2023.e14318

Jewkes, Y., & Linnemann, T. (2018). *Media and crime in the U.S.* Sage.

Kafu, C., Ligaga, D., & Wachira, J. (2021). Exploring media framing of abortion content on Kenyan television: A qualitative study protocol. *Reproductive Health, 18*, Article 12. https://doi.org/10.1186/s12978-021-01071-5

Lagos, C., & Antezana, L. (2018). Online framing on abortion and violence in South America: Dissonant sense making. In D. Harpe, J. Loke, & I. Bachmann (Eds.), *Feminist approaches to media theory and research* (pp. 131–148). Palgrave Macmillan. https://doi.org/10.1007/978-3-319-90838-0_9

Larsson, S., Eliasson, M., Klingberg Allvin, M., Faxelid, E., Atuyambe, L., & Fritzell, S. (2015). The discourses on induced abortion in Ugandan daily newspapers: A discourse analysis. *Reproductive Health, 12*, Article 58, 1–10. https://doi.org/10.1186/s12978-015-0049-0

McDonnell, O., & Murphy, P. (2019). Mediating abortion politics in Ireland: Media framing of the death of Savita Halappanavar. *Critical Discourse Studies, 16*(1), 1–20. https://doi.org/10.1080/17405904.2018.1521858

McQuail, D., & Deuze, M. (2020). *McQuail's media & mass communication theory.* Sage.

Munoriyarwa, A. (2021). A Habermasian critique of the democratic functions of open-line programme on Radio 702. In S. Chiumbu & G. Motsaathebe (Eds.), *Radio, public life and citizen deliberation in South Africa* (pp. 74–91). Routledge.

Munyati, B. M. (2018). African women's sexual and reproductive health and rights: The revised Maputo Plan of Action pushes for upscaled delivery. *Agenda, 32*(1), 36–45. https://doi.org/10.1080/10130950.2018.1438962

Nyathi, S. S., & Ndhlovu, M. P. (2021). Zimbabwean news media discourses on the intersection of abortion, religion, health and the law. *Media, Culture & Society, 43*(8), 1466–1479. https://doi.org/10.1177/01634437211029885

Poku, N. K. (2020). *Sexual and reproductive health and rights in Sub-Saharan Africa.* Palgrave Macmillan.

Purcell, C., Hilton, S., & Mcdaid, L. (2014). The stigmatisation of abortion: A qualitative analysis of print media in Great Britain in 2010. *Culture, Health & Sexuality, 16*(9), 1141–1155. https://doi.org/10.1080%2F13691058.2014.937463

Rohlinger, D. A. (2015). *Abortion politics, mass media and social movements in America.* Cambridge University Press.

Sambaiga, R., Haukanes, H., Moland, K. M., & Blystad, A. (2019). Health, life and rights: A discourse analysis of a hybrid abortion regime in Tanzania. *International Journal for Equity in Health, 18*(1), 135. https://doi.org/10.1186/s12939-019-1039-6

Starrs, A. M., Ezeh, A. C., Barker, G., Basu, A., Bertrand, J. T., Blum, R., Coll-Seck, A. M., Grover, A., Laski, L., Roa, M., Sathar, Z. A., Say, L., Serour, G. I., Singh, S., Stenberg, K., Temmerman, M., Biddlecom, A., Popinchalk, A., Summers, C., & Ashford, L. S. (2018). Accelerate progress—Sexual and reproductive health and rights for all: Report of the Guttmacher–*Lancet* Commission. *The Lancet, 391*(10140), 2642–2692. https://doi.org/10.1016/S0140-6736(18)30293-9

UNFPA. (2023). *Advancing rights, transforming lives: UNFPA strategic engagement with the United Nations human rights system to advance sexual and reproductive health and rights.* https://www.unfpa.org/publications/realisingrights

WHO. (2022). *Abortion care guideline.* https://www.who.int/publications/i/item/9789240039483

Chapter 8

# Mainstreaming Gender in Postgraduate Journalism and Communication Programmes in Ghana

*Aurelia Ayisi*

*Department of Communications Studies, University of Ghana, Ghana*

## Abstract

Gender representation in journalism and communication is crucial because it shapes how media reflects and constructs society. Extant literature on newsrooms and professional journalism indicate that women are under-represented in terms of numbers and the types of stories they cover. This 'problem' of representation within the profession of journalism itself has implications for the perpetuation of gender stereotypes and the framing of women and limits the public's understanding of women's issues. Journalism and communication educational institutions play a vital role in shaping the next generation of practitioners, who will take up roles in media organisations and be tasked with the issues of balanced gender reporting and representation. This document analysis examines the existence (or lack) of gendered perspectives, theories, ideologies, and gendered experiential learning opportunities within the postgraduate curricula in media and journalism in Ghana. Although the study establishes the availability of distinct gender courses, their integration is limited. The findings highlight the need to mainstream gender perspectives throughout postgraduate communication and journalism education to better equip future media

*Gender and Media Representation: Perspectives from Sub-Saharan Africa, 109–122*

doi:10.1108/978-1-83608-406-820251009

and communication practitioners to challenge stereotypes and present balanced coverage of women's issues within Ghanaian media.

*Keywords*: Gender mainstreaming; gender representation; journalism education; communication education; postgraduate education; Ghana

## Introduction

Academic discourse on gender and the media is not novel. The United Nations (UN) World Conference on Women held in Mexico City in 1975 identified the media as a site for action and a key component in shaping and challenging gender narratives. The UN delegates committed to looking more closely at the status quo of the roles and representations of women in their own countries. In Ghana, Kate Abbam's, a women's magazine publisher at the time, raised the issue of women's status in media organisations in 1975 (Gadzekpo, 2016). Abbam observed that only two of the 71 female employees at the state-owned Ghana Broadcasting Corporation held decision-making roles with most women occupying lower-level positions, making their presence in middle or upper management rare (Abbam, 1975). While significant progress has been made in improving women's status and representation in the media since the 1970s, these issues remain a topic of discussion both nationally and globally because of the inequalities that still exist.

The Global Media Monitoring Project (Macharia, 2021; Macharia et al., 2010), in over two reports, has consistently observed that women, as compared to men, have less opportunity to have their voice heard in the news, and their views are least heard in politics, government, the economy, and business. The 2020 report also indicates that stories in global media are more likely to reinforce than challenge gender stereotypes. More than half of the empowering stories on women were written by women reporters, even though women comprise only about a third of journalists (GMMP, 2020). These findings validate feminist strategies to improve the status of women within media organisations as well as news media discourses (Ross & Padovani, 2016).

Journalism and communication educational institutions are strategic stakeholders in the quest for gender representation because on their campuses, both male and female journalists acquire the requisite skills and training for their careers within the media industry. Yet, despite decades of efforts to bring gender parity to the profession, there remains a disproportionately large ratio of men to women in the journalism profession, and in undergraduate journalism and mass communication programme enrolment (and finally newsrooms), women still form the minority (Huang et al., 2006; York, 2017). The situation is no different in Ghana, where Yeboah-Banin et al. (2020), in a report on the Status of Women in the Ghanaian Media, showed that women exit the media industry early due to low wages and family commitments and that women are underrepresented in executive-level positions within media organisations. This study presumes that a multipronged approach is necessary for challenging and improving the status of women in the media – both in terms of the organisational levels they occupy and the ways they are represented in the media (Prince et al., 2020). The institutions of higher education that train communication practitioners and journalists are critical sites for the interrogation of the concerns about the status and representation of women. This chapter argues for curricular reform that mainstreams and prioritises gender theories, ideologies and gendered experiential learning opportunities as part of the graduate school programmes of journalism and communications. Scholars like Gadzekpo (2009), Ward and Grower (2020), and Heyder et al. (2021) have emphasised the need for current research to revisit and re-examine long-standing issues while also exploring the new opportunities and challenges that have emerged with the evolution of the media which has resulted in a more active and engaged society. To this end, this chapter focuses on the course descriptions for the journalism and communication studies programmes on the websites of two of the first institutions of higher education to be accredited to teach Journalism and Communication studies, namely the Department of Journalism at the University of Media, Arts and Communication and the Institute of Journalism (UniMAC-GIJ), and the Department of Communication Studies (DCS) at the University of Ghana.

## Aims and Significance

The study aimed to examine the extent to which the current MA programmes in these two premiere training institutions for journalists and communicators prepared their students for gender-balanced reporting. By examining the definite ways in which gender is infused into the journalism curricula, whether through the inclusion of dedicated courses on gender and journalism, the integration of gendered angles into other courses, or the use of gender-neutral language and examples throughout the course descriptions, the study sought to respond to the question, 'how do MA programmes in journalism and communication in Ghana prepare students to represent and report on gender issues fairly and accurately?' While this study does not offer an exhaustive examination of gender mainstreaming within all Ghanaian communication and journalism curricula, by focusing on UniMac-GIJ and the DCS, where postgraduate communication, journalism, and allied programmes are taught, the study contributes to scholarship on gender mainstreaming as a tool for balanced representation of women by acknowledging the role and contribution of a gender-responsive curriculum. The focus on graduate courses in communication and journalism reflects that graduate-level programmes in journalism and communication studies typically draw an enrolment of experienced professionals who have returned to classrooms for a graduate degree for diverse reasons and are thus more likely to go back to their communication or journalism careers upon completion of their degrees. The two institutions also have private universities that are affiliated with them for the purpose of accreditation to teach and award media and communication degrees; the DCS, however, runs only graduate-level programmes.

## Literature Review

The media plays an important part in shaping how the public views and understands the roles of women and men; its influence helps shape attitudes and perceptions of the general population (Diedong & Tuurosong, 2018), and when it comes to the subject of gender, the media has a long and troubling history of reinforcing stereotypes about masculinity and femininity. In the early 19th century, journalism was considered an unsuitable profession for women, who were expected to remain within domestic spaces (Tuchman, 1996). In the mid-19th century, white, middle-class women in the United States and the United Kingdom began working in newsrooms, focusing on writing 'women's stories' that catered to the expanding female readership (Chambers et al., 2004, p. 38). Women continue to be underrepresented as reporters and generally in the newsroom across the globe. The GMMP (2020) report suggests that women are only the subjects of roughly 25% of all news reporting globally, and when they are featured, their stories are often framed by persistent gender stereotypes. This underscores the critical need for journalism curricula to incorporate training on gender-sensitive reporting. Yeboah-Banin et al. (2020) note that women make up at least 40% of the people who work in the media. Their study found evidence of such persistent systemic inequalities that disadvantage women in media as their disproportional assignment of 'soft news' and social beats, unequal pay, discrimination in promotion opportunities, and the scarcity of women who occupy positions in the upper echelons of media organisations with decision-making positions. Sexual harassment was also common in Ghanaian newsrooms, with less than half of the organisations under study having policies to address the issues of gender-based violence in the workplace. These findings indicate that although there has been some improvement in the status of women in Ghanaian media, old challenges hinder women from realising their full potential in the media space. They further indicate that

> on the one hand, there is now a significant presence of young women in Ghanaian newsrooms who are more likely to work on beats traditionally considered the preserve of males. On the other hand, women's presence in top management and boardrooms remains abysmal. While some progress has been made to improve women's workplace conditions (e.g., maternity leave without risk of job loss), newsrooms are still quite inhospitable to women as they lack baby/child-friendly spaces to help them better manage their multiple roles. (Yeboah-Banin et al., 2020, p. 20)

In short, this Ghanaian study confirms Toff and Palmer's (2019) assertion that women's voices are less heard when it comes to discussing news topics, especially in areas like politics, government, the economy, and business. Thus, women's perspectives tend to be underrepresented in these important conversations. Likewise, the GMMP (2020) also shows that stories are more likely to reinforce than to challenge stereotypes in many regions of the world, except for Africa, where stories are equally likely to do so.

Other feminist scholars (North, 2010; Santos et al., 2018) have noted that more than half of the empowering stories on women were written by women reporters, even though women make up only a third of journalists. Blumell and

Mulupi (2024) argued that limited learning opportunities about gender issues and newsroom culture in university journalism courses help maintain the systemic gender inequality in the industry and the gendered stereotypes within the media. Appiah-Adjei (2021) elsewhere has argued that the growth of journalism education warrants an assessment to provide a clear picture of whether the courses taught have implications on how news is crafted and reported. Media and journalism schools can address the societal need for balanced gender representation in media by implementing gender-responsive syllabi.

## Gender Mainstreaming in MA Journalism Programmes

The concept of gender mainstreaming has been defined by various scholars and professionals, at the heart of gender mainstreaming is ensuring that any action like new laws, policies, or programmes considers how its impact will affect both women and men. It is thus a strategy designed to ensure that the perspectives and needs of both genders are included in the planning, execution, and evaluation of policies and initiatives. The goal of gender mainstreaming is to create equal benefits for everyone in society such that no one is left behind and inequalities are reduced or eliminated in all of society (Peterson & Jordansson, 2021; UN Women, 2022). Thus, the primary aim of gender mainstreaming is to promote gender equality. According to Unterhalter and North (2010), the concept evolved in the 1980s, driven by the efforts of women's groups during the UN Decade for Women (1976–1985). They highlight that gender mainstreaming emerged not only as a policy aimed at gender equality but also as a strategic approach to shaping policy development. As a result, gender mainstreaming can be seen both as a goal in itself and a means to achieve broader objectives. Although the policy was officially recognised at the Fourth World Conference on Women in Beijing in 1995, its practice had already been in place for over a decade (Geertsema-Sligh, 2014).

Gender mainstreaming has attracted both praise and condemnation. Chief among these criticisms is doubt about whether gender mainstreaming is effective in challenging and overturning patriarchal structures and replacing them with gender-balanced decision-making (Olsson & Sörensen, 2020). The UNESCO (2012) Report on Gender-Sensitive Indicators concludes that gender balance in education is crucial for media and journalism schools and universities and urges communication schools, training institutes, and NGOs to strive to address such critical areas of concern by focusing education and training on strategic objectives. From these policy and strategic standpoints, it is reasonable to argue that journalism programmes that prepare students to take up roles in an industry rife with gendered issues should mainstream gender in the programme of study because, as Morna and Shilongo (2004, p. 133) argue, 'improvement in media training [...] will lead to improvement in the biased and stereotypical gendered representations that exist within the media space'. Morna and Shilongo further argue that such improvements can include integrating gender awareness training into all types and aspects of media training. A study by Made (2010) in Southern Africa examined 25 institutions and discovered that only a handful had policies aimed at promoting gender equality. The focus on gender issues varied significantly depending on the individual instructors' knowledge and awareness. Gender-related topics were largely absent from course materials, student assessments, and faculty members' work.

Gender mainstreaming is an approach that requires all media and journalism educators to include gendered perspectives in journalism instruction. Geertsema-Sligh (2014) researched the impact of gender mainstreaming in journalism education and argued that well-rounded journalism education is essential for the next generation of journalists and a critical part of tackling gender bias and the many challenges women face in the media. Dralega et al. (2016, p. 12) found 'minimal, unclear and uncoordinated gender mainstreaming activities within most departmental policies, curricula, assessment and research' in Uganda, Rwanda, and Ethiopia, but this situation is not limited to Sub-Saharan Africa. For example, Geertsema-Sligh et al. (2020, p. 25) reporting on various national studies on mainstreaming gender in journalism curriculum indicate that only a quarter of Spanish universities that offer journalism studies included a subject with a gender perspective, and availability reflected the particular interests in gender issues of the faculty member teaching the course. In Australia there was 'no journalism programme offered a unit that specifically addressed the portrayal of women in the media, or the gendered production of news in gendered newsroom cultures'. A study from 2010 found that whether or not gender was covered in media and journalism programmes often depended on the personal interests of individual teachers. This meant that gender issues were often left out of the classroom (Made, 2010). These findings, along with other research, suggest a need to make gender a more central part of media education at every level. This is important if we want to see more women in media and journalism and ensure that their voices are heard. As Martin and Fisher-Ari (2021) observed, a curriculum that analyses gender imbalances in media can equip students with the critical skills needed to identify and challenge underrepresentation. This chapter specifically focuses the application of these gender mainstreaming strategies within communication and journalism education. Here, gender mainstreaming is understood as the strategic integration of gender perspectives into postgraduate communication and journalism programmes. I posit that this can be achieved through two methods, the incorporation of a gender lens across all existing courses or the inclusion of dedicated courses that explicitly address the dynamics of gender in media content production and distribution.

## Method

This study adopted a qualitative content analysis (QCA) approach to investigate whether the communication of gender and related issues is taught in journalism and communication postgraduate programmes at UniMAC-GIJ and the GCS. An examination of the published course descriptions of the MA degree programmes of these top postgraduate communication and journalism schools was conducted to identify the presence of gender communication in their curricula and the approaches to teaching these issues. A critical analytical method was used for the subjective interpretation of the contents of qualitative data in a systematic and context-dependent manner (Mayring, 2014), and QCA has become popular among researchers from different disciplines (Selvi, 2019). Hsieh and Shannon (2005) outlined three distinct approaches to QCA, each varying in its use of inductive reasoning. Conventional content analysis involves developing coding categories directly from the raw data through an inductive process. Directed content analysis begins with an existing theory or research findings that guides the initial coding process and summative content analysis that counts specific words or content features and then moves beyond counting to a deeper analysis of latent meanings and themes through close reading.

This study applied the summative QCA approach because the ultimate aim was to explore how words are used in a more open and inductive way. Krippendorff (2018) explains how content analysis techniques enable valid inferences from data to their context and are thus good techniques for contextual and text-based variables. These strengths of QCA informed its employment in this study to collect data from the graduate curriculum of the three selected journalism schools in Ghana and assess the extent to which gender is mainstreamed within their respective curricula.

## *An Overview of the Selected Universities*

Many gender and communication scholars alike have presented arguments for integration of gender perspectives into media and journalism education and practice to foster representative, critical, ethical, just, and balanced journalism. Dralega et al. (2016) established that while resource constraints are the attributed cause for the lack of gender mainstreaming, other prevailing factors include the absence of clear policy guidance and the 'know-how' to efficiently implement meaningful gender mainstreaming attempts as well as apathy among some staff towards the implementation of existing policies. The findings demonstrated an attitude of dismissiveness to the significance of gender mainstreaming in journalism curriculum that poses concerns about how journalism practice is perpetuating the hegemony of patriarchy. North (2009) argues that an investigation of the extent to which gender issues are transparent in university journalism courses is needed to address gendered newsrooms. Three questions therefore remain: 'if we do not teach them, how will they know? And if they do know, how will they practise?' The recent GMMP (2020) report presents perhaps the most compelling argument for the need for journalism education reform informed by how journalists are trained and prepared for their work.

UniMAC-GIJ, previously known as the Ghana Institute of Journalism (GIJ), was founded in 1959 during the era of Kwame Nkrumah to train journalists and foster a generation of professionals committed to Africa's liberation and development. In 1974, the National Redemption Council (NRC) officially recognised the institute through Legislative Instrument NRCD 275. Later, in 2006, Parliament passed the Ghana Institute of Journalism Act (Act 717), which elevated GIJ to a tertiary institution, empowering it to award degrees, diplomas, and certificates accredited by the National Accreditation Board. In 2020, under the University of Media, Arts and Communication Act (Act 1059), GIJ was merged with the National Film and Television Institute (founded in 1978) and the Ghana Institute of Languages (established in 1961) to form UniMAC, a unified public university. UniMAC-GIJ's School of Graduate Studies and Research manages postgraduate programmes across its faculties, offering four master's degrees in Public Relations, Development Communication, Journalism, and Media Management (UNIMAC-GIJ, 2023).

The DCS at the University of Ghana has a long-standing commitment to enhancing journalism and mass communication. Founded in 1972 as the School of Communications Studies, its mission was to improve media practice and deepen the public's understanding of communication. Initially, it offered a graduate diploma, serving both media professionals and the broader community. The school's name has changed over time, first in 1974 to the School of Journalism and Mass Communication and then in 1985 to the School of Communication Studies, reflecting a broader array of media-related courses. In 1998, the graduate diploma programme was upgraded to a master's programme, and currently, the institution offers both Master of Arts and Master of Philosophy and Doctor of Philosophy degrees. Its vision is to be a leading institution in training media professionals, academics, and researchers, advancing media practice through education and contributing valuable research that benefits the public and the media industry (University of Ghana, n.d.).

## Findings

The various strategies considered in the literature for gender mainstreaming in media and related environments situate this study within the broader context of improving gender representation in journalism: increasing the number of women in management positions in media organisations (Adjin-Tettey & Braimah, 2023; Guo & Fang, 2023), altering newsroom culture (Byerly et al. 2023; Shor et al., 2015), addressing media ownership issues (Blumell & Mulupi, 2024), and re-evaluating gatekeeping practices (York, 2017). While these approaches are valuable, this chapter argues for the mainstreaming of gender issues within media and journalism curricula as a foundational step towards achieving gender equity in media representation. Three key findings from the QCA of the graduate school handbooks of the MA in Communication offered by SCS and the MA-level courses in Communication and Journalism offered at UniMAC-GIJ as part of the MA programmes in Public Relations, Development Communication, Journalism, and Media Management support this argument. These findings on the nature of gender mainstreaming within the curriculum, the uncritical presentation of gender roles and stereotypes, and the limited intersectional perspectives are presented and discussed below.

### *Nature of Gender Mainstreaming Within the Curriculum*

#### *Courses Dedicated to Teaching Gender*

Thematic analysis of data from the QCA revealed a limited integration of gender into communication and journalism training in the postgraduate courses of the schools under study. One course, 'Gender and Communication', focuses on gendered issues within the media in the MA programme in Communications

Studies at the SCS and covers topics like gender communication, sensitive reporting, and the status of women in the Ghanaian media. What is more, this course is an elective. Although efforts at mainstreaming gender within the postgraduate programme were limited, the University of Ghana launched a gender policy in 2022 that aimed at mainstreaming gender in all university policies and procedures to create a gender-equitable environment (University of Ghana, 2024). Additionally, all first-year undergraduate students take a compulsory gender course offered by the Centre for Gender Studies and Advocacy. While this initiative does not directly target postgraduate communication and journalism students, it is an indication of mainstreaming efforts within the larger campus community.

At UniMAC-GIJ, of the four MA programmes offered by the School of Graduate Studies and Research (comprising regular, sandwich, and evening cohorts), there is also only one course, 'Gender, Representation and Development', that focuses on gender issues within media. It is also an elective. This means that journalism students can graduate from their programme of study at either institution without any training to orient them to gender perspectives in the media and communication landscape within which they will be working. At UniMAC-GIJ, there were also indications of attempts to mainstream gender in undergraduate courses: a fourth-year course (level 400) on 'Gender and Development' is mandatory for students specialising in Public Relations. Although these efforts are not directly targeted at postgraduate journalism and communication students, it is a strong indication of mainstreaming efforts within the university. Thus, at both these premier Ghanaian institutions, the postgraduate programmes in communication and journalism offer only a single, specialised, standalone gender course as an elective, and this [Peterson and Jordansson, 2021] note can potentially limit the impact and effectiveness of training gender-sensitive journalists and communication practitioners.

### Limited Integration of Gender Perspectives in the Curriculum

Gender was not integrated into the core journalism courses offered in either schools' MA in Communication or associated programmes. At UniMAC-GIJ, the gender perspective was not for journalism per se, but rather an incorporation of gender into development-communication approaches. This inherently limits the scope and approach because its specific goal is to

> provide students with the opportunity to think about gender and
> its representations with development, and to critically understand
> the changing gender representations in relation to development.
> (North, 2010)

In other words, gender is studied as a component of development communication rather than as a component of journalism and communication education in this course.

The Gender and Communication course offered by the DCS attempts to integrate gender into its broader communication mandate by focusing on 'the theoretical implications of the status and representation of gender in the media' (University of Ghana, n.d.). The course investigates the role of the media in assigning gendered roles through stereotyping, (the cultivation of) imagery, and the perpetuation of discrimination between the sexes and discusses the forms of anti-discriminatory reporting. This course is an elective, however, and because students decide whether to sign up limits its reach and accessibility and renders it superficial and peripheral in the MA programme.

### *Uncritical Presentation of Gender Roles and Stereotypes*

While the language used in the MA programmes at both institutions was gender-neutral and avoided perpetuating stereotypes, a critical analysis of course content reveals a lack of comprehensive integration of gender issues. This omission hinders the programmes' ability to challenge harmful gender narratives in the media (Yang, 2016). The MA in Communication Studies at the DCS offers some exceptions, where courses like 'Advanced Print Journalism' and 'Media, Culture and Society' incorporated gender within their content to a limited extent. Indeed, the Advanced Print Journalism course description includes among its aims to equip students with skills for 'covering major beats such as gender issues' (University of Ghana, n.d.). The 'Media, Culture and Society' course explores 'media representational practices' with a gender perspective (University of Ghana, n.d.). These examples suggest a limited and uncritical presentation of gender in the curriculum that contradicts Byerly et al.'s (2023) suggestion that a more systematic approach to gender mainstreaming in journalism curriculum is necessary for a deeper engagement with dismantling old and harmful narratives.

### *Limited Intersectional Perspectives*

Another clear gap was identified: lack of intersectionality in the two gender-oriented courses, namely 'Gender and Communication' (SCS) and 'Gender, Representation and Development'. Both courses largely focused on gender perspectives and issues in isolation from other social identities and without consideration of how gender intersects with, for example, status or religion, and shapes media coverage of women in communities.

## Discussion and Conclusion

The findings indicate considerable gaps and opportunities for improvement in mainstreaming gender within the graduate degree programmes in journalism and communication in Ghana. This confirms Heckman and Homan's (2020) and Geertsema-Sligh et al.'s (2020) assertions that gender courses are still missing in many African mass media schools and departments and that gender/women's studies departments must be created. This is crucial because Sub-Saharan African educational institutions need to equip future generations of media and communication practitioners to be more critical creators and consumers of media to promote an equitable and inclusive media environment.

A gendered, responsive curriculum plays an important role in providing the missing links in balanced representation and improving the status of women in the media. Critical media studies and communication training must take note of and endeavour to remedy these old concerns by defining and articulating gendered perspectives – either by integrating gendered perspectives into the core communication and journalism courses or offering dedicated, core courses on gender. Regardless of the approach, the most critical issue is to reflect seriously on gendered issues in the media and how postgraduate education, which is the nexus of journalism practice and theory, can position itself to redress some of these challenges. Leemann et al. (2010) have argued that to address gender concerns meaningfully in the educational sector, institutional constraints must be confronted and the curricula and research agendas in schools and departments must be revised to encourage better collaboration between academics and non-academics. UniMAC-GIJ is already making efforts. For example, on 27 October 2023, its faculty organised an all-lecturers workshop on *Creating a Gender Sensitive, Non-discriminatory and Inclusive Curriculum, Classroom and Work Environment* funded by the UNESCO Excellence in Journalism Education in Africa Project Grant (UniMAC-GIJ, 2023).

Kitta and Cardona-Moltó (2022) argue that mainstreaming gender in journalism education involves integrating gender perspectives, theories, and experiential learning opportunities throughout the entire curriculum. This approach, they argue, ensures continuous and deliberate exposure to gender issues and better prepare students to challenge and address gender biases in their professional careers. This study not only supports these scholarly positions but also recommends further studies on the process of mainstreaming and the specific topics that need to be mainstreamed within the Ghanaian context. Orienting students to deal with gendered issues and inequality is an important component of journalistic training that should not be overlooked. The currently superficial inclusion of gender in the MA journalism programmes flags that more work and effort need to be invested in designing gender and inequality courses that will form part of the foundational courses in postgraduate-level journalism programmes.

# References

Abbam, K. (1975). *Ghanaian women in mass media* [Unpublished paper]. Presented at a lecture to mark International Women's Year.

Adjin-Tettey, T. D., & Braimah, S. (2023). Assessing safety of journalism practice in Ghana: Key stakeholders' perspectives. *Cogent Social Sciences, 9*(1), Article 2225836. https://doi.org/10.1080/23311886.2023.2225836

Appiah-Adjei, G. (2021). Journalism education and ethnic journalism in Ghana: The case study of Ghana Institute of Journalism and University of Education, Winneba. In A. Gladkova & S. Jamil (Eds.), *Ethnic Journalism in the Global South* (pp. 23–47). Palgrave Macmillan.

Blumell, L. E., & Mulupi, D. (2024). How news organizations cultivate and maintain sexist newsrooms via gendered journalistic norms, sexual harassment, and the boys' club. *Women's Studies in Communication, 47*(3), 268–291. https://doi.org/10.1080/07491409.2024.2342842

Byerly, C. M., Sha, B.-L., Grant, R. L., Daniels, G. L., Pevac, M., & Nielsen, C. (2023). The versatility of intersectionality in journalism and mass communication research. *Journalism & Mass Communication Quarterly, 100*(2), 249–263.

Chambers, D., & Steiner, L., & Fleming, C. (2004). *Women and journalism*. Routledge. https://doi.org/10.1177/10776990231166941

Diedong, A. L., & Tuurosong, D. (2018). Establishing the rationale for media education for students in Ghana. *Journal of Communications, Media & Society*, *5*(1), 80–98. https://repository.gij.edu.gh/handle/123456789/77

Dralega, C, A., Jemaneh, A., Jjuuko, M., & Kantono, R. (2016). Gender mainstreaming in media and journalism education – An audit of media departments in Uganda, Rwanda and Ethiopia. *Journal of African Media Studies*, *8*(3), 251–266. https://doi.org/10.1386/jams.8.3.251_1

Gadzekpo, A. (2009). Missing links: African media studies and feminist concerns. *Journal of African Media Studies*, *1*(1), 69–80. https://doi.org/10.1386/jams.1.1.69_1

Gadzekpo, A. (2016). Media and gender socialization. In N. A. Naples, R. C. Hoogland, M. Wickramasinghe, & W. C. A. Wong (Eds.), *The Wiley Blackwell encyclopedia of gender and sexuality studies* (pp. 1–5). Wiley-Blackwell. https://doi.org/10.1002/9781118663219.wbegss213

Geertsema-Sligh, M. (2014). Gender mainstreaming in journalism education. In A. Vega Montiel (Ed.), *Media and gender: A scholarly agenda for global alliance for media and gender* (pp. 38–39). UNESCO. https://gamag.net/wp-content/uploads/2017/12/media_and_gender_scholarly_agenda_for_gamag.pdf

Geertsema-Sligh, M., Bachmann, I., & Moody-Ramirez, M. (2020). Educating journalism students on gender and inequality. *Journalism & Mass Communication Educator*, *75*(1), 69–74. https://doi.org/10.1177/1077695820901927

Guo, J., & Fang, K. (2023). Where are the missing girls? Gender inequality, job precarity, and journalism students' career choices in China. *Journalism*, *24*(10), 2099–2117. https://doi.org/10.1177/14648849221108768

Heckman, M., & Homan, M. (2020). The syllabus is a boys' club: The paucity of woman authors in journalism course materials. *Teaching Journalism & Mass Communication*, *10*(2), 15–21. https://community.aejmc.org/smallprogramsinterestgroup/publications/journals/previous-issues/volume-10-no-2

Heyder, A., van Hek, M., & Van Houtte, M. (2021). When gender stereotypes get male adolescents into trouble: A longitudinal study on gender conformity pressure as a predictor of school misconduct. *Sex roles: A Journal of Research*, *84*(1–2), 61–75. https://psycnet.apa.org/doi/10.1007/s11199-020-01147-9

Hsieh, H.-F., & Shannon, S. E. (2005). Three approaches to qualitative content analysis. *Qualitative Health Research*, *15*(9), 1277–1288. https://doi.org/10.1177/1049732305276687

Huang, E., Davison, K., Shreve, S., Davis, T., Bettendorf, E., & Nair, A. (2006). Bridging newsrooms and classrooms: Preparing the next generation of journalists for converged media. *Journalism & Communication Monographs*, *8*(3), 221–262. https://doi.org/10.1177/152263790600800302

Kitta, I., & Cardona-Moltó, M. C. (2022). Students' perceptions of gender mainstreaming implementation in university teaching in Greece. *Journal of Gender Studies*, *31*(4), 457–477. https://doi.org/10.1080/09589236.2021.2023006

Krippendorff, K. (2018). *Content analysis: An introduction to its methodology*. Sage Publications.

Leemann, R. J., Dubach, P., & Boes, S. (2010). The leaky pipeline in the Swiss university system: Identifying gender barriers in postgraduate education and networks using longitudinal data. *Swiss Journal of Sociology*, *36*(2), 299–323. https://doi.org/10.5167/uzh-41767

Made, P. A. (2010). *Gender in media education: An audit of gender in journalism and media education and training: Southern Africa*. Gender Links. https://genderlinks.org.za/gmdc/publications/gender-in-media-education-audit-2010-10-01

Macharia, S., O'Connor, D., & Ndangam, L. (2010). *Global media monitoring project 2010*. World Association for Christian Communication. https://whomakesthenews.org/

wp-content/uploads/who-makes-the-news/Imported/reports_2010/global/gmmp_global_report_en.pdf

Macharia, S. (2021). *6th Global Media Monitoring Project (GMMP) 2020*. World Association for Christian Communication. https://whomakesthenews.org/wp-content/uploads/2021/07/GMMP2020.ENG_.FINAL20210713.pdf

Martin, A. E., & Fisher-Ari, T. R. (2021). 'If we don't have diversity, there's no future to see': High-school students' perceptions of race and gender representation in STEM. *Science Education, 105*(6), 1076–1099. https://psycnet.apa.org/doi/10.1002/sce.21677

Mayring, P. (2014). *Qualitative content analysis: Theoretical foundation, basic procedures and software solution*. SSOAR. https://nbn-resolving.org/urn:nbn:de:0168-ssoar-395173

Morna, C. L., & Shilongo, P. (2004). Mainstreaming gender into media education: Forum section: Conference paper. *Ecquid Novi, 25*(1), 133–137.

North, L. (2009). Gendered experiences of industry change and the effects of neoliberalism. *Journalism Studies, 10*(4), 506–521. https://doi.org/10.1080/14616700902783911

North, L. (2010). The gender 'problem' in Australian journalism education. *Australian Journalism Review, 32*(2), 103–115. https://doi.org/10.3316/informit.898818248701411

Olsson, E. J., & Sörensen, J. S. (2020). What price equality? The academic cost of government supervised gender mainstreaming at Swedish universities. *Societies, 10*(4), 87. https://doi.org/10.3390/soc10040087

Peterson, H., & Jordansson, B. (2021). Gender mainstreaming in Swedish academia: Translating policy into practice. *Journal of Gender Studies, 31*(1), 87–100. https://doi.org/10.1080/09589236.2021.2004539

Prince, S. A., Roberts, K. C., Melvin, A., Butler, G. P., & Thompson, W. (2020). Gender and education differences in sedentary behaviour in Canada: An analysis of national cross-sectional surveys. *BMC Public Health, 20*, 1170. https://doi.org/10.1186/s12889-020-09234-y

Ross, K., & Padovani, C. (Eds.). (2016). *Gender equality and the media: A challenge for Europe* (1st ed.). Routledge. https://doi.org/10.4324/9781315709024

Santos, A., Cerqueira, C., & Cabecinhas, R. (2018). 'Challenging it softly': A feminist inquiry into gender in the news media context. *Feminist Media Studies, 22*(1), 66–82. https://doi.org/10.1080/14680777.2018.1465445

Selvi, A. F. (2019). Qualitative content analysis. In J. McKinley & H. Rose (Eds.), *The Routledge handbook of research methods in applied linguistics* (pp. 440–452). Routledge.

Shor, E., van de Rijt, A., Miltsov, A., Kulkarni, V., & Skiena, S. (2015). A paper ceiling: Explaining the persistent underrepresentation of women in printed news. *American Sociological Review, 80*(5), 960–984. https://doi.org/10.1177/0003122415596999

Toff, B., & Palmer, R. A. (2019). Explaining the gender gap in news avoidance: 'News-is-for-men' perceptions and the burdens of caretaking. *Journalism Studies, 20*(11), 1563–1579. https://doi.org/10.1080/1461670X.2018.1528882

Tuchman, G. (1996). Representation: Image, sign, difference. In H. Baehr & A. Gray (Eds.), *Turning it on: A reader in women and media* (pp. 150–174). Arnold.

University of Ghana. (n.d.). *MA in Communication Studies. Department of Communication Studies*. Retrieved April 3, 2025, from https://www.ug.edu.gh/commstudies/academics/graduate-programmes/ma-communication-studies

UN Women. (2022). *Handbook on gender mainstreaming for gender equality results*. https://unwomen.org/en/digital-library/publications/2022/02/handbook-on-gender-mainstreaming-for-gender-equality-results

UNESCO. (2012). *Gender-sensitive indicators for media: framework of indicators to gauge gender sensitivity in media operations and content*. UNESCO Report on Gender-Sensitive Indicators. https://unesdoc.unesco.org/ark:/48223/pf0000217831

UNIMAC-GIJ. (2023, August 29). *Workshop equips lecturers with skill-sets to be more gender-inclusive*. https://gij.edu.gh/faculty-of-integrated-and-communication-sciences/department-of-language-and-communication-skills/

University of Ghana. (2024). *VC inaugurates 13-member equal opportunities board*. https://www.ug.edu.gh/news/vc-inaugurates-13-member-equal-opportunities-board

Unterhalter, E., & North, A. (2010). *Assessing gender mainstreaming in the education sector: Depoliticised technique or a step towards women's rights and gender equality?* Taylor & Francis.

Yang, H. (2016). Transforming concepts into practices: Mainstreaming gender in higher education. *Asian Journal of Women's Studies*, *22*(4), 392–413. https://doi.org/10.1080/12259276.2016.1242940

Yeboah-Banin, A.A., Fofie, I. M., & Gadzekpo, A. S. (2020). *Status of women in the Ghanaian media: Providing evidence for gender equality and advocacy*. https://sics.ug.edu.gh/sites/sics.ug.edu.gh/files/Status%20of%20Women%20in%20Ghanaian%20Media%20Report%20opt1.pddf?

York, C. (2017, September 18). *Women dominate journalism schools, but newsrooms are still a different story*. Poynter. https://www.poynter.org/business-work/2017/women-dominate-journalism-schools-but-newsrooms-are-still-a-different-story/

Ward, L. M., & Grower, P. (2020). Media and the development of gender role stereotypes. *Annual Review of Developmental Psychology*, *2*, 177–199.

Section II

# Digital Media Spaces and Gender Empowerment

Chapter 9

# Digital Storytelling in Social Media: A Cultural Activity and a Media Style in Fighting Gender-based Violence in Tanzania

*Eva Solomon*

*University of Dar es Salaam, Tanzania*

## Abstract

This chapter describes digital storytelling (DST) in social media on gender-based violence (GBV) in Tanzania. It draws on narrative and feminist theories to answer two questions: What GBV themes are narrated in DST? What key roles does DST play in delineating GBV? Content analysis of the digital stories and netizens' comments on *Nitetee TV* on *YouTube* identified three emerging GBV themes, namely gender power struggle, GBV acts, and a family affair, which collectively demonstrate the power struggle and negotiations between not only men and women but also within institutions and authorities to create an interesting duality of women's empowerment and disempowerment. DST roles specific to GBV include warning, condemning GBV acts, amplifying marginalised voices, fleshing out GBV acts, giving netizens the autonomy to engage with the story, and providing a helping hand to GBV victims. Netizens' pursuit of information based on conventional legacy media's standards reaffirms DST as both a cultural activity and a media style. Overall, DST as a social action condemns GBV and empowers GBV survivors and marginalised female netizens.

*Keywords*: Digital storytelling; gender-based violence; social media; narrative theory; feminism; Tanzania

Gender and Media Representation: Perspectives from Sub-Saharan Africa, 125–139

doi:10.1108/978-1-83608-406-820251010

## Introduction

Storytelling comes naturally to humans (Fisher, 1984). Storytelling to make sense of the world and transmit information to future generations is one of the earliest forms of social communication (Markova & Sukhoviy, 2020; Shishko, 2022). The art of storytelling or 'oramedia', has always been central to human communication in traditional social and cultural contexts of Africa (Fayoyin, 2018; Mare & Tsarwe, 2012). Ugboajah (1985) proposed 'oramedia' to refer to media rooted in an indigenous culture that is created and consumed by its people who converse as a community. Oramedia shares many characteristics with social media in that it too facilitates the formation of a community of like-minded individuals through comments, voice notes, live chats, and wall posts in virtual communities (Fayoyin, 2018; Mare & Tsarwe, 2012).

DST on social media provides a reliable source of narrative sharing in the 21st century (Shishko, 2022). In Africa, DST in social media, arguably, entails migrating the human voice from offline to online spaces – from oramedia to social media (Mare & Tsarwe, 2012). In essence, DST connects one of the oldest social and cultural practices in human history – storytelling – with the latest and most used technology – the Internet, using such social media platforms as *YouTube*, *Facebook*, and *Instagram*. Indeed, technology is renewing the storytelling practice in Africa for, as Lewin (2011) argues, DST offers non-stereotypical images of individuals, gender roles, and relationships when there are so few true indigenous voices in mainstream media. Therefore, DST is essential for addressing a range of social issues, including GBV (Kannengießer, 2012).

Studies evaluating DST in social media as combating GBV in Tanzania are scant despite a sharp rise in social media usage in the country of more than 60 million people, of whom 37.6 per cent have Internet access and six million use social media (TCRA, 2022). The narrative and feminist theories employed in this chapter facilitate the exploration of how *Nitetee TV* on *YouTube* battles GBV in Tanzania through storytelling. The study specifically answers two key questions: What GBV themes are narrated in DST? What key roles does DST play in delineating GBV?

## Literature Review

### The Concept of DST

DST uses digital media to convey tales (Musfira et al., 2022). Dana Atchley first proposed and developed the DST idea in 1980 aiming at incorporating multimedia components into narrative presentations and gained widespread recognition when Atchley, Joe Lambert, and Nina Mulle established the Center for Digital Storytelling in California in 1990 (Rossiter & Garcia, 2010), currently a non-profit organisation for assisting people in using digital media to tell stories of their lives (Rasmussen, 2008). The phenomenal expansion of such digital tools as blogs and such platforms as *YouTube, Instagram, Facebook*, and *TikTok* has made DST profitable on a global scale. Smartphones, digital cameras, and general multimedia apps have made it easier for professionals and amateurs to create digital stories (Sandesh

& Srinivasa, 2017). DST has been employed for different motives by individuals of all ages, genders, and backgrounds in different nations (Şimşek, 2012) and has demonstrated its advantages in such fields as education, communication, journalism, marketing, campaigning, community development, and health (Musfira et al., 2022; Reed & Hill, 2010). Storytelling or narrative is a useful technique for communicating life experiences (Shishko, 2022). In Sweden and Brazil, digital tales on *Snapchat* and *Instagram* comprise individuals' activities, events, and locations (Amancio, 2017). In Africa, DST is used to tell a wide range of stories – political, economic, social, and cultural – that flow from offline to online and vice versa. For instance, DST fosters discussions on social media platforms among disadvantaged individuals sharing their own narratives and experiences (Mare & Tsarwe, 2012). Lewin (2011) argues that this trend could promote meaningful citizenship in post-colonial Africa for this globalised and digital age. Robin (2008) contends that personal experience-centred DST is most commonly used to capture significant life events and evokes emotional resonance for both the author and the audience. Personal accounts of GBV are poignant examples for such experiences (Mahmood & Shams, 2012).

### *DST: A Cultural Activity and a Media Style*

Conventional journalism seeks to reach its audience with facts, ideas, and opinions to inform, educate, persuade, warn, and connect society members, and storytelling entails sharing ideas and facts to fulfil similar roles (Mare & Tsarwe, 2012). Indeed, Tanzania's first media was the Kiswahili newspaper *Msimulizi*, which translates as 'The Storyteller', launched in 1888 by Anglican missionaries working under German colonial rule (Sturmer, 1998).

In the digital era, DST seeks to give common people a voice and democratise the creation of media content (Lundby, 2008). For instance, such combined multimedia elements as voiceover, photos, hypertext, audio, video, and text are used to create and tell a tale that can be heard on radio and television broadcasts or accessed on servers through the Internet (Balaman, 2018). What is more, DST has been broadly used on social media platforms for journalistic purposes (Mare & Tsarwe, 2012; Musfira et al., 2022). DST is therefore a cultural practice as well as a media style and a collaborative strategy that connects the age-old art of storytelling with contemporary media technologies (Shishko, 2022).

### *GBV and DST*

GBV affects women across the globe. There were 81,000 reported deaths in 2020, 58 per cent of which were at the hands of family members or intimate partners (Pycroft, 2022). The COVID-19 epidemic increased the rates of GBV because many women were trapped with their abusers during lockdowns (Dralega et al., 2022). The highest rates of domestic violence against women worldwide are reported in Sub-Saharan Africa (Ouedraogo & Stenzel, 2021).

DST has been used by female GBV survivors to create digital tales based on their GBV experiences in an effort to fight GBV (Rossiter & Garcia, 2010). Sawhney (2009) highlights African projects like 'Silence Speaks' that support the production of short films by female victims of abuse to share their stories. In

Pakistan, female GBV survivors also participate in DST initiatives to combat GBV (Mahmood & Shams, 2012). Developing a digital story is a healing process that enables marginalised individuals such as GBV survivors to develop resilience, find solace, and inspiration (McWilliam, 2009). Personal narratives have the power to uplift, inform, and unite different individuals to act as one against a common enemy (Shishko, 2022), and DST serves as a platform for change for the storyteller and the community at large (Lewin, 2011).

## Theoretical Framework

Erstad and Wertsch (2008) define narratives as cultural tools people use in telling their stories. Narrative, like DST, is a complex concept (Amancio, 2017). Tomaščíková (2009) flags how 'narrative' has been studied as a method, a theory, a social practice, as politics, and as a strategy, a diversity that underlines its complexity. Consequently, I examine narratives from a structuralist perspective as a form of communication to sidestep some of the complications related to the narrative concept not salient to the present investigation of DST and GBV in Tanzania (Amancio, 2017; Nguyen, 2011). This structuralist perspective considers communication to comprise four main parts: the story, the author, the discourse, and the audience. As Chatman (1978) explains, the author is the storyteller, the audience are listeners or viewers, the tale is the substance of a narrative (the 'what' describing the sequence of events), and the discourse is the form of narrative (the 'how' expressed through words, images, and videos).

Understanding narrative through structuralism emphasises the complexity of the act of telling stories just as DST focuses on online complexities and a variety of forms in use to tell stories (Amancio, 2017). Indeed, Nguyen (2011) contends that this complexity fits DST in establishing a connection between DST and narrative theory that is essential in understanding the practice of telling stories on social media platforms and streaming websites like *YouTube*. Nguyen (2011) uses the principal concepts of Fisher's (1984) narrative paradigm to provide a philosophical explanation of how DST is applied in social communication. Fisher employs narration as a theory of symbolic actions – words and/or deeds – that have meaning for those who live, create, and interpret them. This understanding aided in the investigation of *YouTube* GBV stories as a narrative in this study. Nguyen (2011) further demonstrates how Fisher's paradigm that describes how storytelling is ingrained in human nature, in the sense that human communication is surrounded by narratives encompassing such various intersectional factors as culture, history, social, politics, economy, religion, technology, education, and geographical location that can either encourage or discourage GBV.

Feminist theory (here used in its broadest definition) facilitates a better understanding of gender issues to solve oppressive gender relations (Sielbeck-Bowen et al., 2002). DST aligns with feminist theory in how it addresses the contemporary challenges women face, like gender stereotypes, biases, social injustice, and GBV. It also explores the interaction between oppression and power structures, thereby highlighting the need for open discussion in overcoming oppression (Kannengießer, 2012). To understand and dismantle gendered oppression, the intersectional factors imbedded in social, politics, economy, and culture must be considered, and feminist philosophy illustrates the experiences of women, especially those from marginalised and underrepresented groups (Sielbeck-Bowen et al., 2002). DST similarly offers a voice to such disadvantaged women as those suffering GBV (Mahmood & Shams, 2012; Reed & Hill, 2010; Sawhney, 2009; Shishko, 2022). From a feminist perspective, therefore, DST gives women the power and opportunity to share their own life stories, voice their concerns, and inspire social change against GBV (Crenshaw, 2021).

## Methodology

This study focuses on the *YouTube* channel, *Nitetee TV*. *Nitetee* is a Kiswahili word for 'fight for me', which well represents the channel's vehement opposition to GBV. Established in 2017, the channel has approximately 342,000 subscribers at the time of writing (August 2024) and an extensive collection of content aiming to combat GBV through storytelling. Two stories were purposively selected for analysis because they covered extreme GBV events and had the most viewers and comments. The first story or Story A (https://youtu.be/d0asQZ4v0-l?si=AYz4nhElwy-Ja7Qf), posted on 31 May 2022, had 99,751 views and 160 comments, and a follow-up story https://youtu.be/yFPgG-g59lU?si=m2RKbhqvygOeWd-P) posted 1 June 2022 had 85,936 views and 270 comments. In total, story A had 185,687 views and 430 comments as viewed on August 2023. The second story or Story B (https://youtu.be/ySxLuus1u8E?si=Z4y4wtyCzS9qA1bW), posted on 31 May 2023, had 71,677 views and 248 comments, as viewed on September 2023. Story A is about husband–wife murder-suicide. The husband accuses his wife of cheating, fatally shoots her seven times, and later kills himself by drowning in Lake Victoria. The deceased wife's sister narrates the story. Story B is narrated by a wife, who recounts how her husband severely injured her by slashing her with a machete for allegedly cheating on him.

Thematic analysis, as described by Braun and Clarke (2017), of the two stories and 678 netizens' comments served as the primary means of analysing the data. In other words, the data set comprised not only the Kiswahili stories in English but also literal translation of all the netizens' comments. Incorporating the comments as well as the stories themselves into the data set enabled an investigation of how netizens interact with the story. As Barthes and Heath (1977) argue, narrative communication is impossible without a narrator and an audience. Coding was conducted in two distinct stages: open coding and axial coding. Themes emerged from grouping codes, and each item was assigned to the appropriate theme. A thorough examination of themes determined the narrative contribution of each topic and was verified based on research questions.

## Findings and Discussion

The thematic analysis informed by narrative and feminist theories identified three themes: gender power struggle, GBV acts, and a family affair. These three themes connect with social, cultural, economic, technological, and legal structures and habits.

### Gender Power Struggle

The struggle for power between men and women is evident in what can also be described as 'women's disobedience' versus 'men's lack of tolerance' as presented below:

#### Women's Disobedience

Income source was the main cause of conflict, primarily the women's place of employment and working hours. In story A, a serious fight broke out between the husband and wife when she, a makeup artist, returned home late from work and had not prepared any food for the husband, who had been accusing her of cheating instead of working. This altercation resulted into the death of the wife, who was shot seven times by the irate husband, who then chose to drown himself in Lake Victoria. In story B, the husband also accused the wife of lingering for too long with her male customers, whom he suspected to be her lovers.

Gender dynamics have evolved, and women in traditional and conservative societies can leave the domestic spaces to support their families, achieve professional dreams, and pursue careers. This often leads to a perceived disobedience from wives, which as a netizen pointed out, can be a serious cause of GBV:

> @danieljoseph Usually, as a woman when you see your husband is angry, you must calm down. Your calmness might calm your husband in addition to preventing danger. Now your husband is angry, and you get angrier, you are in trouble. (Story B, September 2023)

McCleary-Sills et al. (2013) report that demographics play a considerable role in the toleration of GBV among women in Tanzania, where younger women (i.e. no older than their late 20s) are less tolerant of GBV than women over 30. They are less receptive to GBV and more likely to react, which men often interpret as defiance. Nevertheless, this younger generation of women seems to reject oppressive relations and fight back against patriarchy-engendered GBV in ways that are consistent with feminist theory (Sielbeck-Bowen et al., 2002). They also echo Lazar (2005) in opposing relations of power that systematically privilege men and disempower women to sustain a patriarchal social order. Older women, who are more likely to tolerate GBV, are more likely to be influenced by family properties, children, poor chances of remarriage, and the fear of negative social perception and stigma (McCleary-Sills et al., 2013).

Mobile phone usage, particularly smartphones, also emerged as common catalyst of GBV. Husbands accuse their spouses of using smartphones to commit adultery. The husbands also seize their wives' phones to prevent them from accessing support:

> He was complaining that she was not picking up his calls because she was cheating with other men. On that day she was to be shot dead, there were 47 missed calls on her phone, all from her husband. (narrator, Story A, August 2023)

> My husband and brother-in-law took my phone as a way of preventing me reaching out for help. (narrator, Story B, September 2023)

Not picking up calls as a form of disobedience attracted rebuke from netizens. As one observed:

> @elizaphankamando …You cannot hang up the phone even if you are busy working, respect your husband. (Story B, September 2023)

The role of smartphone technology in GBV has become a major issue in Tanzania. Passwords and recordings are used to protect communications from suspicious spouses and punish those who want to quit clandestine relationships. Extortion has emerged as a viable source of income for bad actors, and the application of advanced artificial intelligence technologies to produce deepfakes intensifies these fears and dangers. Extortion is a form of GBV that affects celebrities, politicians, wealthy business owners, and ordinary people, and women are its major victims.

*Men's Lack of Tolerance*

Men were also condemned for lacking tolerance, a major cause of marital rifts and GBV. As one netizen narrated:

> @ruthysarakikya If you see your wife is not impressing you take her to her father's home. It is better to stay out of her life than to beat her. And you [women] if you see danger run away, stop being stubborn. (Story B, September 2023)

But is this lack of tolerance or a struggle for power? GBV reflects power inequalities and inequities between women and men as the former are more commonly the victims of GBV, and men can leverage their socially sanctioned power over women (Lokot, 2023). Grabska (2014) refers to men who abuse macho power to oppress women and put them under their firm control as 'guardians of patriarchy' (Grabska, 2014). Kandiyoti (1998), however, warns that women do not always behave in accordance with gender ideologies portend. Because men's (ab)use of power usually involves physical violence (which has immediate and often significant effects), women's similar (ab)use of power (usually assumed to be peaceful) is often overlooked and unreported (Lokot, 2023). As one netizen lamented:

> @kapesatv Marriages have challenges and children are the victims. Women are the main cause. (Story A, August 2023)

In other words, the economic power that women in Story A and Story B gained through employment need not necessarily have been exercises in benevolent ways (Allen, 1998). Being a woman does not preclude the abuse of power (e.g. extortion), immoral behaviour (e.g. adultery), or the use of violence against others, including husbands, daughters-in-law, and children (Lokot, 2023). To avoid such scenarios, netizens urged men to fulfil their gender roles as family providers:

> @ monicambuya If you do not want your wife to do business, make her stay at home [embrace domesticity], provide everything for her. Do not be jealousy if you have low income, a woman must go out to look for a job. (Story B, September 2023)

From this netizen's viewpoint, the gender power of men is arguably negotiable and attainable through power struggles that are either pinned on women's disobedience or men's lack of tolerance. McCleary-Sills et al. (2013), however, highlight what they refer to as a 'culture of silence' in traditional African societies where violence against men is deeply ingrained but rarely discussed due to stigma and masculinity-based norms. In other words, men are also vulnerable to abuse from women with stronger wills, egos, and prowess and less likely to report it or ask for help.

### *Acts of GBV*

In story A, the narrator explains how her sister was battered to unconsciousness and hospitalised before the murder-suicide:

> That man said one of them [him or his wife] would die. He took his gun, dragged my sister, severely beat her, and pushed her onto the floor. She fainted. We took her to the hospital, where it took her four hours to regain consciousness and they administered six bottles of drip on her. (August 2023)

On the tragic day of her murder, neighbours explained how they had heard bangs but never considered they might be gun-shots because that was very unusual in their neighbourhood. Indeed, some had never heard a gunshot before and could not fathom the danger lurking in the neighbourhood:

> I heard a loud bang noise several times. My kids were shouting, gun! gun! I never took them seriously, thinking it was just explosives. Not knowing my neighbour was being murdered. (August 2023)

A video shot at the deceased's home shows blood covering the sitting room floor (August 2023). The husband's body was picked on Lake Victoria's shores; he had a gun-shot wound in the head, presumably self-inflicted before he drowned himself.

In story B, the victim/narrator still has fresh machete wounds on her head, is covered with blood, and has yet to be attended to by a doctor when she is telling the story. She recounts with tears streaming down her face how she escaped death at the hand of her husband:

> He took a machete and started sharpening it. He then aimed it at me. I started running, but he managed to land it on my head twice. The third time he aimed it at my neck, but somehow my son saved me and I managed to escape. (Story B, September 2023)

As she narrates her ordeal, the camera focuses on a pillow and bed sheets stained with her blood. The narration coupled with poignant visuals encourages netizens to sympathise with her, condemn the perpetrators of GBV, and calling for instituting serious measures (explained later in 'DST roles' section). As many narrative theorists argue, the narration and visual aspects of DST play a crucial role in raising public awareness of the dangers of GBV (Chatman, 1978; Fisher, 1984; McWilliam, 2009; Tomaščíková, 2009). Narrating GBV is not only a source of empowerment for survivors but also a social action as public condemnation of violence against women.

## A Family Affair

The women victims in Story A and Story B had received advice from their parents and relatives not to leave their marriages for their children's sake. This is consistent with the McCleary-Sills et al.'s (2013) finding that the family is the first step in seeking help for GBV, but that families can consider the reconciliation of marriages more important than addressing women's critical concerns. As a result, these wives suffered tragic consequences. The wife in story A ended up dead, her body riddled with her husband's bullets.

In story B, the wife went to the police after not getting any help from within the family. But the police – as though reading from a stereotypical patriarchal notebook – also advised her to stay for the sake of the children: 'The police told me to stay in the marriage for my children not to be street kids' (September 2023). A similar view is also emphasised by netizens:

> @AnestaJosephat Do not leave your children behind because men do not go to the labour ward. The mother is the one who knows the pain of bearing a child, not the father. (September 2023)

> @zainabubalama Do not leave the children behind; they will be sexually abused. Who will protect your children? (September 2023)

Many women do tough it out and bear immeasurable agony to tolerate GBV, and some netizens condemned this decision as a criticism of the 'sophistication' or 'elegance' of these women:

@serengetiduma The father is saying tolerate. Indeed, African families! Now you have lost your daughter. (Story A, August 2023)

@angelinamwakilufi What killed this girl is her father's word 'TOLERATE'. (Story A, August 2023)

This tendency encourages often unrepentant men to commit GBV and discourages women from seeking law enforcement to get justice for past wrongs:

@user-lo Men do this because strict legal measures are not taken against them to teach them a lesson. (Story A, August 2023)

McCleary-Sills et al. (2013), however, argue that pursuing justice through the court system signifies a sharp deviation from the culturally entrenched emphasis on 'family affairs' reconciliations in many Sub-Saharan African cultures like Tanzania. McClearly-Sills adds that few women in these societies have any familiarity with the legal system and may not feel comfortable to take that complicated and intimidating route operated by professional gatekeepers, namely bureaucrats and lawyers.

Overall, Story A, Story B, and their comments from the netizens of the *You-Tube* community demonstrate an interesting duality of empowerment and disempowerment. While DST empowers women to condemn GBV, cultural norms and societal perceptions perpetuate it. The stories of exceptional women who can overcome such hindrances, like the narrator of Story B, reveal what ultimately results from this duality is women's struggle for survival as they endure GBV. Indeed, DST provides an alternative bridge between oppressed women and authorities that bypasses many of the structures of the oppressor that sustain patriarchal system. Thus, for family affairs (as findings in this study disclose), men shun digital space.

## DST Roles

Although this study reveals roles performed by DST that are also performed by traditional media, like educating, informing, and raising awareness (evidence of DST being a media style), there are roles specific to DST in alignment with the specific goals of combatting GBV. These include warning, condemning GBV acts, amplifying marginalised voices, fleshing out GBV acts, giving viewers autonomy to engage with the story, and providing a helping hand to GBV victims.

### Warning

A neighbour in story A cautions: 'It should serve as a lesson to the youth on how to manage and control anger' (August 2023). Netizens echoed this didactic message in the comments:

@mrs I hope this will be a lesson. Domestic violence should be prohibited, and parents should not force marriages onto their children. (Story A, August 2023)

These comments reaffirm the relevance of DST not only as a teaching strategy (Kannengießer, 2012), but also as a way of bringing together people of varied backgrounds and experiences to raise a collective, common voice against GBV (Reed & Hill, 2010; Shishko, 2022).

*Condemning Acts of GBV*

Video of a bloody sitting room floor in story A is powerful, evocative evidence that draws attention to and raise awareness about the dangers of GBV. Story B also includes video of fresh machete wounds, and the camera's focus on a blood-strewn pillow and bed sheets signify the macabre and dangerous GBV acts. As Sandesh and Srinivasa (2017) have argued, the multimedia presentation of content heightens the dangers of GBV in addition to exposing the grisly criminal acts. This footage triggered a high tempo of condemnation from the netizens:

@kabwelasutiviraka Nothing justifies murder even in broken relationships. Poverty is the cause for women to remain in abusive relationships, beaten, wounded and eventually murdered. Bride price in marriages is like buying a woman who ends up serving as a pleasure tool for a man, doing domestic chores and bearing children. Where is the value of Tanzanian women? (Story A, August 2023)

This netizen associates GBV with poverty, and poverty is aggravated for women with limited access to property and capital in a male-dominated socio-economic environment such that women tolerate GBV to sustain their lives. This comment is also consistent with Lokot (2023) in that it claims that dowry and bride price can encourage GBV in marriages because the financial nature of this relationship substantiates her treatment as property.

*Amplifying Marginalised Voices*

DST can and does report GBV issues that could otherwise not receive attention in mainstream media. The comments area offers a great deal of democracy and space for netizens' thoughts, and traditional media cannot give the same consideration (Solomon, 2023). What is more, media-shy women can choose to openly express their ideas freely without having to reveal their identities by using pseudonyms. From a feminist perspective, DST tends to empower marginalised women by giving them authority and capacity to amplify the dangers of GBV and influence social change against GBV (Crenshaw, 2021; Kannengießer, 2012).

### Fleshing Out Acts of GBV

DST serves as a tool for victims to expose GBV acts usually treated as mundane or concealed under the veil of silence that encourages the matter to remain in family circles. In both Story A and Story B, families persisted in telling the victims to endure the suffering as sacrificial lambs, but this more digital-savvy generation of women not only rely on DST to tell their stories but also are more likely to seek outside help (McCleary-Sills et al., 2013). Fleshing out these GBV acts via DST promotes awareness, transformation, and social change in patriarchal societies (Kannengießer, 2012; Lazar, 2005; Musfira et al., 2022; Shishko, 2022).

### Giving the Viewers Autonomy to Engage with the Story

Netizens can bring meaning to a *YouTube* channel video through interactive comments, which (as revealed in the findings of this study) encourages the storyteller to make a follow-up and hence makes the story even more comprehensive and meaningful. As Barthes and Heath (1977) maintain, there is no narrative without an audience, and streaming sources like *YouTube* strongly promote direct feedback from viewers. Consequently, Story A had a follow-up story posted 1 June 2022 (as explained in the methodology section) regarding the family of the deceased husband as requested by netizens:

> @bakarimwalimu We should also hear from Saidi's side [the husband's family]. You should not make us believe that only Saidi has mistaken. (Story A, August 2023)

> @budebamussa I am neutral until I hear about the other side [the husband] on what caused the conflict. (Story A, August 2023)

This space for contradiction from viewers adheres to the principles of legacy media of providing a 'balanced' story. Netizens also raised ethical issues since a minor participated in story A. These are typical tendencies of traditional media and further evidence of DST conforming to the media style (Balaman, 2018).

> @70SIXER7 ... in other countries forcing a child to talk is a big lawsuit and a jail sentence. (Story A, August 2023)

The ethical standards of legacy media require that the child's facial identity and name be safeguarded and not the focus of inquiries that would remind him of the atrocities that had just occurred. Musfira et al. (2022) have also flagged this ethical concern regarding DST.

Story B's narrator also faced a dilemma over which issue to prioritise: the media or her own health?

@mwanakijiji Women will be finished, you are hurt instead of going to the police to get PF3 for hospital treatment, you go to the media. It is their [women's] mistake that is why they do not go to the police they instead go to the media to defend themselves. (September 2023)

This netizen sees the police as the appropriate channel for justice, whereas this woman had once reported GBV to the police but was discouraged. She opted to take her story to DST as a tool to fight GBV. Overall, this view point raises critical questions regarding appropriate DST practice. For instance, why precisely do netizens wish DST practice to include standards of older media? How much does DST practice need to diverge from or mimic traditional media practice to be more successful?

*DST as a Helping Hand to GBV Victims*

DST connects GBV victims to relevant authorities that can provide the much-needed help. In story A, for instance, the Minister for Community Development, Gender, Women and Special Groups, Dr Dorothy Gwajima, issued a statement via phone: 'It is time men should assess themselves. We cannot have such extreme anger issues and continue parading as men. The law will be enforced'. Such statements from authorities might eventually result in action against GBV leading to social change.

## Conclusion

The GBV themes unite narrators and netizens through *Nitetee TV* on *YouTube* to capture the timeless quality of storytelling as a cultural expression. Such DST roles as enlightening, teaching, and raising awareness reflect those of conventional media. The character of DST is revealed by netizens' pursuit of information that adheres to journalistic standards like 'balancing' and ethical considerations, thereby reaffirming DST as a media style. The study also reveals that audio-visual DST is more effective in addressing GBV. It serves as a warning, a denouncement of acts of GBV, a forum for amplifying marginalised voices, and offers solutions to victims. This unique approach elicits emotional responses from netizens that encourages them to interact with the content and act.

## References

Allen, A. (1998). Rethinking power. *Hypatia, 13*(1), 21–40. https://doi.org/10.1111/j.1527-2001.1998.tb01350.x

Amancio, M. (2017). *"Put it in your story": Digital storytelling in Instagram and Snapchat stories*. Uppsala Universitet.

Balaman, S. (2018). Digital storytelling: A multimodal narrative writing genre. *Journal of Language and Linguistic Studies, 14*(3), 202–212.

Barthes, R., & Heath, S. (1977). *Image, music, text: Essays selected and translated by Stephen Heath*. Fontana Press.

Braun, V., & Clarke, V. (2017). Applied qualitative research in psychology. *Applied Qualitative Research in Psychology, 0887*(2006), 77–101. https://doi.org/10.1057/978-1-137-35913-1

Chatman, S. B. (1978). *Story and discourse: Narrative structure in fiction and film*. Cornell University Press.

Crenshaw, K. (2021). Demarginalizing the intersection of race and sex: A black feminist critique of antidiscrimination doctrine, feminist theory and antiracist politics. *Droit et Société, 108*, 465.

Dralega, C. A., Jjuuko, M., & Solomon, E. (2022). Caught between a rock and a hard place: Impact of COVID-19 on feminist media in Uganda, Rwanda and Tanzania. In C. A. Dralega & A. Napakol (Eds.), *COVID-19 and the media in Sub-Saharan Africa: Media viability, framing and health communication* (pp. 19–33). Emerald Publishing. https://doi.org/10.1108/978-1-80382-271-620221002

Erstad, O., & Wertsch, J. (2008). Tales of mediation: Narrative and digital media as cultural tools. In K. Lundby (Ed.), *Digital storytelling, mediatized stories: Self-representation in new media* (pp. 21–40). Peter Lang.

Fayoyin, A. (2018). African oramedia in a digital age: Explorations in remediation. In K. A. Omenugha, A. Fayoyin, & C. M. Ngugi (Eds.), *New media and African society: Essays, reviews and research* (pp. 22–39). Nairobi Academic Press.

Fisher, W. R. (1984). Narration as a human communication paradigm: The case of public moral argument. *Communication Monographs, 51*(1), 1–22. https://doi.org/10.1080/03637758409390180

Grabska, K. (2014). *Gender, home & identity: Nuer repatriation to Southern Sudan*. James Currey.

Kandiyoti, D. (1998). Gender, power and contestation: "Bargaining with patriarchy" revisited. In C. Jackson & R. Pearson (Eds.), *Feminist visions of development* (pp. 135–151). Routledge.

Kannengießer, S. (2012). *Digital storytelling as a feminist practice*. Association for Progressive Communications. http://www.genderit.org/es/node/3657

Lazar, M. M. (2005). Politicizing gender in discourse: Feminist critical discourse analysis as political perspective and praxis. In M. M. Lazar (Ed.), *Feminist critical discourse analysis: Gender, power and ideology in discourse* (pp. 1–28). Palgrave Macmillan. https://doi.org/10.1002/9781118584248.ch9

Lewin, T. (2011). Digital storytelling. *Participatory Learning and Action, 63*, 54–62. http://pubs.iied.org/14606IIED.html

Lokot, M. (2023). Gendered power struggles beyond the male-female dichotomy: Syrian mothers-in-law exercising power within patriarchal structures. *Anthropology of the Middle East, 18*(1), 35–55. https://doi.org/10.3167/ame.2023.180104

Lundby, K. (2008). *Digital storytelling, mediatized stories: Self-representation in new media*. Peter Lang.

Mahmood, Q. K., & Shams, S. (2012, July). Digital storytelling and self healing of women survivors of violence: Evidence from Pakistan. In G. Bradley, D. Whitehouse, & A. Lin (Eds.), *IADIS international conference ICT, society and human beings* (pp. 59–66). International Association for Development of the Information Society.

Mare, A., & Tsarwe, S. (2012). Social journalism as storytelling in Africa: Participatory journalism. *Rhodes Journalism Review, 20*(32), 44–45. https://doi.org/10.10520/EJC134101

Markova, V., & Sukhoviy, O. (2020). Storytelling as a communication tool in journalism: Main stages of development. *Journal of History Culture and Art Research, 9*(2), 355. https://doi.org/10.7596/taksad.v9i2.2516

McCleary-Sills, J., Namy, S., Nyoni, J., Rweyamamu, D., Salvatory, A., & Steven, E. (2013). *Help-seeking pathways and barriers for survivors of gender-based violence in Tanzania: Results from a study in Dar es Salaam, Mbeya and Iringa regions*. International Center for Research on Women (ICRW).

McWilliam, K. (2009). The global diffusion of a community media practice: Digital storytelling online. In J. Hartley & K. McWilliam (Eds.), *Story circle: Digital storytelling around the world* (pp. 37–75). Wiley-Blackwell Publishing Ltd.

Musfira, A. F., Ibrahim, N., & Harun, H. (2022). A thematic review on digital story-telling (DST) in social media. *Qualitative Report, 27*(8), 1590–1620. https://doi.org/10.46743/2160-3715/2022.5383

Nguyen, A. (2011). *Negotiations and challenges in creating a digital story: The experience of graduate students*. University of Houston.

Ouedraogo, R., & Stenzel, D. (2021). *The heavy economic toll of gender-based violence: Evidence from Sub-Saharan Africa*. International Monetary Fund. https://www.imf.org/en/Publications/WP/Issues/2021/11/19/The-Heavy-Economic-Toll-of-Gender-based-Violence-Evidence-from-Sub-Saharan-Africa-509667

Pycroft, H. (2022). *Violence against women, statistics around the world*. Action Aid. https://www.actionaid.org.uk/blog/2022/11/01/violence-against-women-statistics-around-world

Rasmussen, E. D. (2008). Center for digital storytelling. https://elmcip.net/node/2820

Reed, A., & Hill, A. (2010). "Don't keep it to yourself!": Digital storytelling with South African youth. *Seminar.Net, 6*(2), 268–279. https://doi.org/10.7577/seminar.2447

Robin, B. R. (2008). Digital storytelling: A powerful technology tool for the 21st century classroom. *Theory into Practice, 47*(3), 220–228. https://doi.org/10.1080/00405840802153916

Rossiter, M., & Garcia, P. (2010). Digital storytelling: A new player on the narrative field. *New Directions for Adult and Continuing Education, 126*, 37–48. https://doi.org/10.1002/ace.370

Sandesh, B. J., & Srinivasa, G. (2017). Text-mining based localisation of player-specific events from a game-log of cricket. *International Journal of Computer Application in Technology, 55*(3), 213–221.

Sawhney, N. (2009). Voices beyond walls: The role of digital storytelling for empowering marginalized youth in refugee camps. In *Proceedings of the 8th international conference on interaction design and children (IDC '09)* (pp. 302–305). Association for Computer Machinery. https://doi.org/10.1145/1551788.1551866

Shishko, B. (2022). Storytelling in the digital era: Perspectives on age and gender. *Trames, 26*(4), 397–411. https://doi.org/10.3176/tr.2022.4.03

Sielbeck-Bowen, K. A., Brisolara, S., Seigart, D., Tischler, C., & Whitmore, E. (2002). Exploring feminist evaluation: The ground from which we rise. *New Directions for Evaluation, 2002*(96), 3–8. https://doi.org/10.1002/ev.62

Şimşek, B. (2012). Enhancing women's participation in Turkey through digital storytelling. *Cultural Science Journal, 5*(2), 28–46. https://doi.org/10.5334/csci.45

Solomon, E. (2023). Female gender stereotyping and President Samia Suluhu Hassan's political communication on Twitter: A blessing for female political leaders? *Information, Communication & Society, 26*(13), 1–17. https://doi.org/10.1080/1369118X.2023.2239889

Sturmer, M. (1998). *The media history of Tanzania*. Ndanda Mission Press.

TCRA. (2022). *Tanzania top social networks and social media*. https://www.tcra.go.tz/uploads/text-editor/files/Communications%20Statistics%20December%202021%20(1)_1645554800.pdf

Tomaščíková, S. (2009). Narrative theories and narrative discourse. *Bulletin of the Transilvania University of Braşov, 2*(51), 281–290.

Ugboajah, F. O. (1985). Oramedia in Africa. In F. O. Ugboajah (Ed.), *Mass communication, culture and society* (pp. 165–176). Hans Zell Publishers.

# Chapter 10

# Gender Mainstreaming in AI-enhanced Journalism Practice, Education, and Research in African Contexts

*Carol Azungi Dralega*

NLA University College, Norway

## Abstract

This chapter explores the integration of gender mainstreaming in artificial intelligence (AI)-enhanced journalism, journalism education, and research within African contexts, emphasising both the opportunities and challenges presented by emerging technologies. AI tools, while transformative, risk perpetuating existing gender biases if not implemented with a gender-sensitive approach. In African media, where patriarchal structures persist, the use of AI can further marginalise women's voices and perspectives in newsrooms, education, and research. This chapter not only identifies key gender-related issues in AI-enhanced media environments, such as biased content algorithms, underrepresentation in AI education, and insufficient gender-sensitive research but also offers a practical solution through gender mainstreaming toolkits. These toolkits serve as essential guides for media professionals, educators, and researchers, helping them to critically reflect upon and engage with the intersection of AI, and media, and to implement strategies that promote gender equity within local contexts. By addressing these challenges, the chapter provides a framework for ensuring that AI technologies contribute to a more inclusive and decolonised media landscape, advancing gender equality and diverse representation in African journalism.

*Keywords*: Gender mainstreaming; artificial intelligence (AI-enhanced newsrooms); journalism education; decolonisation; intersectionality; toolkits

Gender and Media Representation: Perspectives from Sub-Saharan Africa, 141–160

doi:10.1108/978-1-83608-406-820251011

## Introduction

The integration of gender mainstreaming into journalism practice, education, and research within African contexts is critical for promoting gender equality and creating diverse, equitable media landscapes (Dralega, 2016; GMMP, 2020). Gender mainstreaming refers to the systematic assessment of gender implications in all areas of policy and practice (United Nations, 2002). Despite efforts to mainstream gender in global media, challenges persist, worsening gender imbalances in content production, representation, and decision-making (Gadzekpo, 2011; Gallagher et al., 2023; Kassova, 2020). These challenges are further complicated by the intersection of gender with other social categories such as race, class, ethnicity, sexuality, location, education, age and income (Buolamwini & Gebru, 2018; Crenshaw, 1991) and lately science and technology (Grzanka and Bhatia 2023) as well as the broader need for decolonising media practices to reflect African realities and indigenous perspectives (Kamlongera & Katenga-Kaunda, 2023a; Ndlovu-Gatsheni, 2015; Dralega, 2023a; Dralega, 2023b). In this chapter, we explore the issues, challenges, and potential solutions surrounding AI-enhanced journalism practice,[1] journalism and media education,[2] and research.[3] For a better understanding of this, there is a need to briefly revisit the current 'traditional' or longstanding challenges in gender mainstreaming in newsrooms, journalism education, and research within African contexts:

African newsrooms, with a few exceptions, remain male-dominated spaces where women are underrepresented, particularly in decision-making roles. Despite constituting a growing part of the workforce, women are often excluded from key editorial and leadership positions (Byerly, 2011; Ejigu Kassa & Sarikakis, 2020; Gallagher et al., 2023; Kaija, 2013; Kassova, 2020). This is compounded by the 'leaking pipeline' in journalism with the progressive reduction in the number of women as they move from journalism education into newsrooms and eventually leadership positions, highlighting systemic barriers that hinder their career advancement (Byerly, 2013; Kaija, 2013). Within newsrooms, women are also less likely to cover 'hard news' beats like politics, economics, and governance, where they are marginalised both as professionals and sources (Maractho, 2017). According to the Global Media Monitoring Project (GMMP, 2020), women constitute only 24% of news sources in Africa, reinforcing the invisibility of women's voices in public discourse. This underrepresentation not only limits the diversity of viewpoints but also perpetuates stereotypes that cast women in narrow roles, often as victims or passive figures, rather than active agents of change.

---

[1] In this study, AI-enhanced journalism refers to the application/practice of artificial intelligence technologies to optimize journalistic processes, automate tasks, and generate data-driven insights, with a critical focus on the integration of gender mainstreaming to challenge and transform existing biases within media practices.

[2] The examination of education emphasizes how journalism and media educational programmes incorporate gender sensitivity into AI-related courses, fostering a critical understanding of both AI and gender dynamics.

[3] The research focus underscores the imperative of gender sensitivity in academic inquiry, exploring the intersections of AI, gender, and journalism to advance equitable and inclusive scholarship that challenges traditional biases and promotes gender equity.

Journalism education in Africa is still largely rooted in curricula that overlook the need for gender-sensitive training (Geertsema-Sligh, 2014; Made, 2010; Morna, 2002). Traditional journalism schools often adopt Western frameworks (Ezumah, 2019; Wasserman & de Beer, 2009) that do not fully address the complexities of gender inequalities in African societies (Kamlongera & Katenga-Kaunda, 2023b). Courses seldom integrate gender studies or intersectionality, leaving future journalists ill-equipped to report on issues of gender with nuance (Kamlongera & Katenga-Kaunda, 2023a, 2023b; Musa & Domatob, 2011). The absence of such training contributes to the perpetuation of patriarchal narratives in media content. Additionally, the sparsity of research on gender mainstreaming in African journalism education reflects a significant gap in efforts to promote equity in media institutions (Dralega et al., 2016).

The research landscape around gender and media in Africa faces its own set of challenges. While the GMMP (2020), Kamlongera and Katenga-Kaunda (2023a), and Steeves and Awino, I. (2015) and other initiatives have begun to document gender disparities, there remains a significant gap in intersectional research that explores how gender interacts with race, class, and other social dimensions in media representation and practice. This gap is particularly critical given the growing demand for decolonised research frameworks that challenge the dominance of Eurocentric models and offer more contextually relevant understandings of gender in African journalism (Dralega, 2023b; Kamlongera & Katenga-Kaunda, 2023b; Ndlovu-Gatsheni, 2015 Rodny-Gumede, 2022). Moreover, women in academia face similar barriers to those in the newsroom, including underrepresentation in leadership positions and marginalisation in key decision-making processes (Mwaura & Balliah, 2024).

### AI, Gender, and Journalism: Emerging Issues

As AI increasingly becomes a driving force in the media, its implications for gender equality in journalism cannot be ignored. AI technologies are transforming African journalism by automating content production, enhancing reporting accuracy, and improving audience engagement (Dralega, 2023b; Munoriyarwa et al., 2021; Mutsvairo & Bebawi, 2023). Despite this African Journalism faces several context-related challenges including but not limited to knowledge gap; resource constraints; inadequate business strategies for AI; lack of collaboration between media and other stakeholders; scarce, costly and dirty data concerns over algorithmic harm and job insecurity fears; cultural resistance in the newsroom; language shortage; poor policy and legal frameworks (Dralega, 2023c; Mutsvairo, 2019; Ogola, 2023).

In developing mitigating measures to these general challenges, it is important to note that without inclusive especially, gender-sensitive frameworks, AI systems risk reinforcing gender biases embedded in the historical datasets on which they are trained (Kassova, 2020; Mutsvairo, 2019; UN Women 2024; West et al., 2019). To illustrate this continuity within AI-enhanced newsrooms in African newsrooms, Kassova's (2020) study informs:

> The decision-makers within most of the newsrooms were male as were the journalists. This was also the case for the emergent new roles such as audience engagement editors, UX designers,

> data visualisers, and data scientists. Institutionalized practices of gender exclusion were therefore being baked into new journalistic practices and newsroom structures. (Kassova 2020, p. 11)

In fact, the challenge of gender mainstreaming related to AI underscores existing challenges females face with access and use of information and communication technologies (ICTs) generally (AU, 2015; Jjuuko & Njuguna, 2019; Kassova, 2020). The AU report based on a study in eight countries of Angola, Botswana, Naminia, Malawi, Mozambique, South Africa, Zambia, and Zimbabwe documents that women face significant barriers to accessing ICTs due to factors such as insufficient infrastructure, high costs, limited availability, language challenges, low literacy rates, and restrictive social norms. These obstacles hinder the transformative potential of ICTs in advancing women's empowerment. Additionally, the lack of strong gender-focussed provisions in media laws and policies exacerbates these challenges, further impeding progress (AU, 2015).

AI systems are implicated in reproducing the same inequalities they were designed to overcome by underrepresenting women and marginalising them in key subject areas like politics and leadership (Kassova, 2020; O'Connor & Liu, 2024). These systems also risk perpetuating harmful stereotypes and making women invisible in news coverage, reinforcing patriarchal narratives already prevalent in African media spaces. Intersectional dimensions must therefore be considered, as AI may amplify not only gender biases but also ethnic, class, geographic, and digital disparities previously highlighted (Buolamwini & Gebru, 2018).

The need for decolonising AI technologies in journalism is crucial. AI systems and data are largely developed in the Global North and often do not account for African realities, thereby reinforcing Eurocentric models of media production and representation (Ai & Masood, 2021; Dralega, 2023b; Ndlovu-Gatsheni, 2015). In this chapter, measures that promote gender mainstreaming in AI-driven media environments deemed vital to ensure that these technologies do not exacerbate existing disparities but instead contribute to more inclusive, decolonised media practices.

### *AI-related Gender Challenges in Newsrooms, Education, and Research*

AI technologies are increasingly deployed in African newsrooms for content automation, reporting, and audience analytics (Dralega, 2023b; Kothari & Cruikshank, 2022; Munoriyarwa, 2024). However, these systems are frequently trained on datasets that reflect historical gender biases, including the underrepresentation of women in critical areas like politics and economics (Manasi et al., 2022; Munoriyarwa et al., 2021; Mutsvairo, 2019; Mutsvairo & Bebawi, 2022). Additionally, the adoption of AI without a gender-sensitive framework risks entrenching the very stereotypes it was intended to overcome. Measures that can guide media organisations in addressing gender biases within AI systems are therefore essential to fill the gaps and promote equity in newsrooms.

AI adoption in journalism education is on the rise in Africa, offering new opportunities for teaching digital literacy and innovation.[4] However, without integrating

---

[4]Various courses taught in universities such as: University of Rwanda, University of Stellenbosch, University of Cape Town, University of Dar es Salam and so on.

gender-sensitive and intersectional approaches, AI-enabled journalism education risks perpetuating the same gender disparities seen in traditional media practices (Dralega et al., 2016; Geertsema-Sligh, 2014; Made, 2010). Current curricula often lack a focus on gender and AI, leaving students unaware of how these technologies can either exacerbate or mitigate gender inequalities – a discursive and ethical challenge Jaakkola (2023) underscores in addition to teaching conceptual, didactic, AI ethics, and competences to budding journalist students. Developing frameworks or guidelines for gender-sensitive AI training in journalism schools is therefore necessary to prepare future journalists for equitable reporting and content production.

The intersection of AI, gender, and journalism research in Sub-Saharan Africa is still an emerging field. While AI has the potential to revolutionise media research, it also brings new challenges, particularly when it comes to gender equity. The current research landscape is sparse on critical empirical focus on how AI systems may perpetuate historical gender biases in media content and representation (Kassova, 2020; Kothari & Cruikshank, 2022; Munoriyarwa et al., 2021; Mutsvairo & Bebawi, 2023). This gap is compounded by the lack of intersectional analysis in existing research, which often overlooks how AI may affect women differently based on other identity markers such as race, class, ethnicity, geography, universal access, and information poverty in local context. Decolonising AI research in journalism is also crucial to ensure that African realities and diverse gender perspectives are fully integrated into the future of media research.

In a nutshell, the integration of gender mainstreaming in African journalism practice, education, and research remains essential for fostering inclusive media landscapes. Traditional challenges, such as the underrepresentation of women in newsrooms, gender-blind journalism education, and the lack of intersectional research, continue to hinder progress. However, as AI becomes more prevalent in African media, these challenges are compounded by new concerns over how AI technologies may reinforce or disrupt existing gender biases. Addressing these issues requires not only gender-sensitive frameworks but also a decolonial approach that centres African realities and challenges the dominant, eurocentric models of AI development and media representation. Below is an endeavour to address the current gaps in the form of toolkits for journalism practice, education, and research. These can be strengthened and adjusted to suit local contexts.

## Methodology for Developing Gender Mainstreaming Toolkits in AI-enhanced Spaces

The study draws from a mixed-methods approach, incorporating theoretical research, case example, and policy analysis to ensure that the toolkits for gender mainstreaming in AI-enhanced journalism practice, education, and research are robust, grounded in both theory and practice, and adaptable to various contexts, particularly in Africa.

### Theory

Theoretical foundations are drawn from several key areas, including gender and technology studies, which highlight the potential for AI algorithms to perpetuate existing gender biases (Noble, 2018; Wajcman, 2004). Additionally, feminist communication theories provide critical insights into the representation and participation of women in media and newsrooms, guiding the creation of more equitable AI-enhanced spaces (Byerly, 2011; Gallagher, 2014). Intersectionality theory, as articulated by Crenshaw (1991), Grzanka and Bhatia, (2023) was integral to ensuring that the framework addressed overlapping identities such as race, class, and ability. This approach is vital in avoiding the reinforcement of multiple forms of oppression through AI-driven processes in both newsrooms and educational settings.

### Good Practices

In addition to theoretical research, this methodology includes a review of strong existing case with good practices, which identified actionable steps for gender mainstreaming, particularly in the fields of journalism and education, such as UNESCO (2020) and the European Institute for Gender Equality (2024[5]). Also, key insights from journalism practice (BBC 50:50[6]) informed the development of specific guidelines to support gender equity in AI-enhanced environments.

### Policy and Framework Analysis

A significant component of this methodology is policy and framework analysis, which involved reviewing existing gender mainstreaming policies such as European Institute for Gender Equality (2024) and AI ethical frameworks (Floridi et al., 2018). This review ensured that the toolkits align with global standards for gender-sensitive AI practices. A comparative analysis of the UNESCO guidelines for gender equality in media (FOJO, 2021[7]; Grizzle, 2012) and the OECD principles on AI (OECD, 2019) further adapted these global frameworks to meet the specific needs of AI-driven platforms in African newsrooms and educational settings. The combination of theoretical insights, best practices, and policy frameworks forms the basis of a comprehensive and contextualised toolkits for gender mainstreaming in AI-enhanced journalism and education.

### The BBC's 50:50 Project as a Model for Gender Balance

An exemplary model for gender balance in AI-enhanced journalism practice is the BBC's 50:50 Project, a data-driven initiative aimed at achieving gender parity in media content established in 2017. Initially launched as a manual gender diversity framework, the project has grown to include 750 BBC teams, 145 partner organisations in 30 countries (BBC, 2022) and expanded beyond just gender diversity to include ethnicity and disability. In collaboration with Stanford University, the project integrated AI to track gender representation in real time, using data-driven systems that provide dashboards to editorial teams. These dashboards flag imbalances and enable producers to correct underrepresentation of women before content is published or aired. By 2021, the initiative had significantly increased the visibility of women across BBC programming, with over 70%

---

[5]The Gender Equality Plan and toolkit for academia and research here: https://eige.europa.eu/gender-mainstreaming/toolkits/gear.
[6]www.bbc.co.uk/5050
[7]https://sojethiopia.org/wp-content/uploads/Gender-in-Ethiopian-Media-Landscape-March-2021.pdf

of participating teams achieving gender parity (BBC, 2021[8]). The project also works in collaboration with other partners including academia, such as journalism schools at the University of Newcastle, Liverpool John Moores University, Nottingham Trent University, and the University of the West of Scotland.[9] This project exemplifies how, AI can be leveraged (through practice, education, and research collaboration) to enhance gender balance in media.

## Toolkits for Gender Mainstreaming in AI-enhanced Journalism, Education, and Research

To address the challenges of gender inequality in AI-enhanced spaces, gender mainstreaming toolkits offer practical solutions for ensuring that AI technologies promote gender equity in journalism. These toolkits are designed to equip media professionals, educators, and researchers with resources to understand and address the gendered nature of AI technologies (Fig. 10.1). For journalism practice, the toolkits help media professionals critically assess how AI systems may reproduce gender biases and provide strategies for mitigating these issues (Gallagher, 2014). In journalism education, gender-sensitive AI curricula prepare future media professionals to use AI technologies in ways that challenge rather than reinforce, patriarchal structures.

Moreover, these toolkits promote decolonised approaches to AI in African media by incorporating Indigenous knowledge systems and prioritising the representation of African women's voices. By doing so, they offer a pathway to more inclusive and equitable media practices across the continent. These crosscutting toolkits should be viewed as part of a broader approach to gender equity, complementing other strategies for sustainable social change within the media and education sectors.

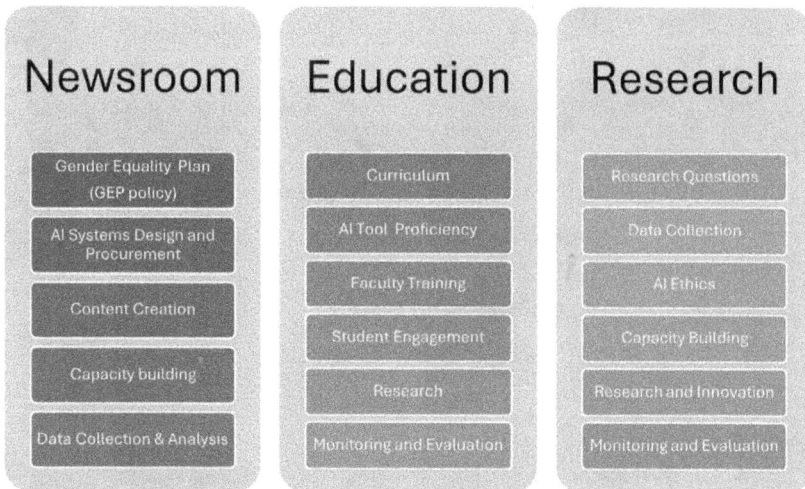

| Newsroom | Education | Research |
|---|---|---|
| Gender Equality Plan (GEP policy) | Curriculum | Research Questions |
| AI Systems Design and Procurement | AI Tool Proficiency | Data Collection |
| Content Creation | Faculty Training | AI Ethics |
| Capacity building | Student Engagement | Capacity Building |
| Data Collection & Analysis | Research | Research and Innovation |
| | Monitoring and Evaluation | Monitoring and Evaluation |

Fig. 10.1.   Overview of Areas Covered in the Three Toolkits.

---

[8]BBC 5050 Impact Report 2021: https://www.bbc.com/5050/documents/50-50-impact-report-2021.pdf.
[9]https://www.bbc.co.uk/5050/stories/academia

## *Toolkit I: Gender Mainstreaming in AI-enhanced Newsrooms*

As African newsrooms increasingly adopt AI technologies for *content* creation, curation, and distribution, integrating gender mainstreaming in these digital transformations becomes essential. Toolkit one (Table 10.1) offers guidance for media houses to ensure that AI deployment upholds gender equity, avoids bias, and enhances gender-sensitive reporting.

Gender mainstreaming in AI-enhanced newsrooms is essential to fostering equity and representation in the rapidly evolving media landscape. African media houses must approach AI not just as a technological innovation but as a tool for reinforcing gender-sensitive journalism. This toolkit integrates gender sensitivity into the AI-driven future of African newsrooms, addressing both technical and ethical dimensions. By incorporating these steps, media houses can become leaders in the fight for gender equity in journalism, leveraging AI to bridge existing gaps.

Table 10.1.   Toolkit I: Overview for Newsrooms.

| Task | Activity | Key Action |
|---|---|---|
| Policy and Strategy Development *Objective: Set up a gender-responsive AI strategy within media organisations* | *Gender mainstreaming policy:* Develop an overarching policy that includes AI usage guidelines emphasising gender equality in editorial decisions and newsroom operations | Formulate gender-responsive editorial guidelines, ensuring AI systems in place are designed or selected to enhance rather than diminish gender balance. For instance, ensure inclusive language standards; bias detection and mitigation; balanced representation in content; data and algorithm transparency; content moderation and reporting tools, etc. |
| | *AI and gender advisory committee:* Create a standing committee within the newsroom to oversee the integration of AI technologies with an explicit gender focus | Ensure gender balance in decision-making panels related to AI system procurement and deployment |
| AI System Design and Procurement *Objective: Obtain AI tools that actively prevent gender bias* | *Bias auditing tools:* Implement AI bias auditing tools that assess the datasets and algorithms for gender discrimination | Collaborate with AI developers to ensure training data is diverse and includes gender-sensitive labels. AI technologies that source data from social media, for instance, should be checked for gender stereotyping or misinformation |
| | *Inclusive AI training:* Ensure the algorithms used in news generation reflect African gender realities, considering local languages, dialects, and gender nuances | Incorporate gender-neutral or gender-diverse names, images, and stories in AI-generated content |
| Gender-sensitive Content Creation with AI | *Promoting diverse sources:* Train AI systems to diversify the sources and voices featured in news coverage, especially highlighting female experts, activists, and leaders | Ensure that AI tools employed for source selection and interviews include a high percentage of women experts |

*(Continued)*

Table 10.1.   (Continued)

| Task | Activity | Key Action |
|---|---|---|
| *Objective: Create AI-enhanced content that reflects gender inclusivity and balance.* | *AI-generated content review protocol*: Set up a review process where AI-generated content is evaluated for gender sensitivity before publication | Utilise natural language processing (NLP) tools to flag potential gender biases in written content, ensuring gender-neutral language and representation. |
| Capacity Building for Newsroom Staff *Objective: Build gender awareness and AI literacy across newsroom staff* | *AI and gender training*: Conduct regular workshops to upskill newsroom staff on both AI use and gender-sensitive reporting. This should include training on how to critically engage with AI-generated content through a gender lens | Train staff on how AI works, its limitations in terms of gender bias, and how to complement AI with human editorial oversight for balanced reporting |
| | *Gender audit of AI tools*: Introduce regular gender audits of AI tools in use to evaluate their impact on gender representation in content | Periodically assess whether AI-generated content, bylines, or data trends skew disproportionately towards male-centric perspectives or topics |
| Data Collection and Analysis *Objective: Collect gender-disaggregated data on the performance and outcomes of AI tools* | *Tracking gender representation*: Use AI-powered analytics to track the gender representation in news coverage, identifying disparities and trends | Develop dashboards that visualise gender representation metrics, ensuring newsroom staff can monitor progress over time |
| | *Regular reporting*: Establish quarterly reporting on gender balance in AI-generated content, including key performance indicators (KPIs) such as the proportion of female experts interviewed, the percentage of women in leadership, and gender portrayal in news | Media houses should publish these reports publicly as part of their commitment to gender equity |

## Toolkit II: Gender Mainstreaming in AI-enhanced Journalism Education

As journalism education in Africa adapts to the growing use of AI in the media industry, integrating gender mainstreaming into journalism curricula and assessment is essential. This toolkit (Table 10.2) proposes strategies and actions to incorporate gender sensitivity into AI-driven journalism training. It ensures that future journalists are not only adept at using AI technologies but also equipped to recognise and mitigate gender biases, thereby promoting inclusive journalism practices.

Integrating gender mainstreaming in AI-enhanced journalism education is critical to preparing future journalists who are equipped to navigate the ethical and social complexities of AI. Jaakkola (2023) highlights the discursive (in addition to conceptual, didactic, and competence) challenges of AI in journalism training pointing to the need to address societal issues such as (gender) inequality. By incorporating gender-sensitive approaches into curriculum design, tool proficiency training, faculty development, and student engagement, journalism schools can ensure that AI technologies enhance rather than hinder gender equity in African newsrooms. This toolkit can empower journalism educators to ensure that gender mainstreaming is integrated into the evolving landscape of AI in journalism, preparing students to lead with both technological expertise and ethical responsibility.

Table 10.2.    Toolkit II: Overview for Education.

| Task | Activity | Key Action |
|---|---|---|
| Gender-responsive Curriculum Development Objective: *Embed gender-sensitive AI practices into the core of journalism education* | *Gender and AI modules:* Introduce dedicated modules on AI and gender within journalism programmes to discuss gender bias in AI, algorithmic discrimination, and the importance of gender inclusivity in media technologies | Develop courses that focus on how AI systems can both perpetuate and dismantle gender stereotypes, particularly in African media contexts |
| | *Decolonisation and intersectional approach:* Curriculum should address intersectionality, highlighting how AI impacts different gender identities across race, class, and geography, etc. | Include case studies from African contexts, analysing how AI systems have affected different genders across various socioeconomic backgrounds |
| AI Tool Proficiency with a Gender Lens Objective: *Train journalism students on AI tools while highlighting potential gender biases* | *AI training with gender focus:* Provide practical workshops on AI-powered tools such as automated news writing, data journalism, and content curation, coupled with discussions on gender bias detection | Teach students how to critically assess datasets for gender biases and how to use AI ethically in journalism practice |
| | *Practical assignments on gender-sensitive AI use:* Incorporate AI-related assignments that challenge students to produce gender-balanced content, identifying biases in AI-generated outputs and suggesting improvements | Students should be required to audit AI-generated news for gender representation, use gender-neutral language, and ensure diverse sourcing in their reports |
| Faculty Training and Awareness Objective: *Equip educators with the skills to teach gender-sensitive AI use in journalism* | *Faculty development workshops:* Regularly train lecturers on the intersection of AI and gender issues, ensuring that they can effectively guide students on how to avoid algorithmic bias | Conduct workshops on the latest AI technologies used in journalism, with an emphasis on gender equity in content creation and analysis. |
| | *Gender-inclusive teaching materials:* Develop and update teaching resources to include gender-balanced case studies, examples of AI in journalism, and literature on gender mainstreaming | Ensure that all course materials reflect gender diversity, using examples of women and non-binary individuals who have contributed to AI in journalism. |

| | | |
|---|---|---|
| Student Engagement and Gender Sensitisation *Objective: Foster a gender-sensitive learning environment for students in AI-enhanced journalism courses* | *Gender and AI awareness campaigns:* Organise awareness campaigns within journalism schools to encourage discussions on gender and AI, creating platforms for students to engage with these issues critically | Create events such as panel discussions, guest lectures, or hackathons focussed on addressing gender biases in AI tools used for journalism |
| | *Mentorship programmes with a gender focus:* Establish mentorship programmes connecting students with professionals who specialise in gender and AI in journalism, encouraging gender-conscious career development | Match students with mentors who can guide them on how to navigate AI technology while advocating for gender equity in their journalism careers |
| Research and Innovation in Gender and AI *Objective: Promote research on AI, gender, and journalism, fostering innovation in gender-sensitive AI applications* | *Research on gender bias in AI journalism tools:* Encourage students and faculty to engage in research that explores how AI can perpetuate or mitigate gender bias in journalism | Develop research projects that assess the impact of AI on gender representation in African newsrooms, suggesting ways to counteract these biases |
| | *Gender-sensitive AI innovation labs:* Establish innovation labs within journalism schools where students can develop AI tools that promote gender inclusivity in news production | Fund student-led projects that explore how AI can be used to amplify women's voices and highlight gender diversity in news repo journalism schools should track how male, female, and non-binary students engage with AI tools, ensuring that no group is marginalised in AI-related coursework or career opportunities |
| Monitoring and Evaluation *Objective: Track and assess the effectiveness of gender mainstreaming efforts in AI-focussed journalism education* | *Gender Disaggregated Data in Education Outcomes:* Collect and analyse gender-disaggregated data on student performance, participation, and career progression to identify gaps and opportunities for gender mainstreaming | Journalism schools should track how male, female, and non-binary students engage with AI tools, ensuring that no group is marginalised in AI-related coursework or career opportunities |
| | *Regular curriculum audits:* Conduct regular audits of journalism programmes to ensure that gender sensitivity and AI integration are being effectively addressed | Use external reviewers to evaluate the extent to which the curriculum and pedagogy reflect gender mainstreaming in AI-related topics |

### *Toolkit III: Gender Mainstreaming in AI-enhanced Journalism Research*

As AI continues to revolutionise journalism, integrating gender into research on AI in journalism is vital to addressing systemic biases and ensuring equitable representation. This toolkit (Table 10.3) proposes strategies for researchers (both experienced and students) to integrate gender-sensitive methodologies and ethical considerations into their AI-related journalism research, particularly in African contexts. It promotes an approach that fosters gender equality, avoids reinforcing stereotypes, and critically examines AI's impact on media ecosystems.

This toolkit provides a comprehensive framework for integrating gender mainstreaming into AI and journalism research, particularly within African contexts. By focussing on gender-sensitive research design, ethical considerations, data inclusivity, and innovative methodologies, researchers can ensure that AI enhances gender equity in journalism rather than perpetuating existing biases. Through capacity building and collaborative networks, research institutions can lead the way in promoting gender-sensitive AI research that drives equitable change in African media. By following this toolkit, researchers in journalism and AI can ensure that their work not only advances the field of AI but also contributes to reducing gender bias and promoting equity within African journalism. The recommendations provided can help foster a more inclusive and fair media environment, ensuring that AI's potential benefits are realised for all genders.

Table 10.3. Toolkit III: Overview for Research.

| Task | Activity | Key Action |
|---|---|---|
| Gender-sensitive Research Design<br>*Objective: Embed gender equity into the research design process for AI and journalism studies* | *Gender-inclusive research questions:* Formulate research questions that explicitly address how AI impacts gender representation in journalism, focussing on the African context | Develop research projects that investigate how AI-generated content, algorithms, and automated news systems affect the representation of different genders in newsrooms and media outputs. What consequences emerge for society |
| | *Intersectional approach:* Apply an intersectional lens to research, examining how AI affects different genders in relation to race, class, ethnicity, and geographic location within Africa | Ensure that research on AI and journalism reflects the diverse experiences of African women, and other marginalised groups, avoiding one-dimensional gender analysis |
| Data Collection and Analysis<br>*Objective: Ensure that data collection and analysis processes are gender-sensitive and inclusive* | *Gender-disaggregated data:* Collect and analyse gender-disaggregated data in AI journalism research to understand the differential impact of AI on men, women, and non-binary individuals | Develop data collection strategies that track the representation of different genders in AI-generated news stories, focussing on sources, subjects, and experts |
| | *Inclusive datasets:* Ensure the datasets used for AI and journalism research are diverse and free from inherent gender biases. This involves curating data that accurately represent women, non-binary individuals, and gender-diverse communities | Collaborate with AI developers to ensure that training datasets for AI systems reflect gender diversity and avoid reliance on Western-centric or male-dominated data sources |
| Ethical Considerations in AI and Gender Research<br>*Objective: Address ethical challenges in AI research with a focus on gender mainstreaming* | *Ethical AI framework:* Develop ethical frameworks for AI journalism research that prioritise gender equity and inclusivity. Ensure that AI technologies used in newsrooms do not perpetuate gender stereotypes or discriminatory practices | Incorporate ethical review processes that evaluate AI tools and methodologies for their impact on gender representation and avoid harm to marginalised communities |

*(Continued)*

Table 10.3.    (*Continued*)

| Task | Activity | Key Action |
|------|----------|------------|
| | *Transparency and accountability*: Ensure transparency in how AI systems are designed, trained, and applied in journalism, and hold systems accountable for gendered outcomes | Researchers should document how AI tools were used in media research, the sources of data, and their implications for gender equity, ensuring that these are published in research findings |
| Capacity Building for Gender-Sensitive AI Research<br>*Objective: Build research capacity for gender mainstreaming in AI and journalism* | *Training for researchers*: Provide targeted training for journalism researchers on gender-sensitive methodologies and the ethical use of AI in media studies. This should include workshops on recognising gender bias in AI technologies | Develop training programmes that equip researchers with the tools to critically engage with AI systems, focussing on gender representation and inclusion in AI-based media research |
| | *Collaborative research networks*: Encourage collaboration among researchers, particularly across African universities and gender advocacy organisations, to advance AI research that centres gender equity. | Establish regional and international networks (and funding) that foster collaborative projects, sharing best practices in gender-sensitive AI research |
| Promoting Gender-sensitive Innovation in AI<br>*Objective: Encourage innovative research that develops AI tools and methodologies promoting gender equity in journalism* | *AI innovation with a gender lens*: Promote the development of AI tools and platforms that enhance gender inclusivity in newsrooms, ensuring that women and non-binary individuals are well-represented in both the content and the creation process | Fund research projects that explore the development of AI models aimed at balancing gender representation in media stories, sources, and news subjects |
| | *AI and gender policy advocacy*: Conduct research that informs policy on the ethical and gender-sensitive use of AI in African media, advocating for regulatory frameworks that prevent bias in AI systems | Partner with governments and media regulatory bodies to provide research-backed recommendations on AI and gender policies that protect against discrimination and promote inclusivity |

| Monitoring and Evaluating Gender Outcomes in AI Research *Objective: Regularly monitor and evaluate the gender outcomes of AI-focussed journalism research* | *Gender equity metrics*: Develop and apply gender equity metrics to assess the outcomes of AI and journalism research, ensuring that research findings contribute to gender balance in media practices | Use metrics that evaluate the impact of AI research on gender equity, such as the proportion of female or non-binary sources in AI-generated content or the diversity of voices highlighted in news coverage |
|---|---|---|
| | *Periodic reviews of research impact*: Conduct periodic reviews of AI-related research projects to evaluate their long-term impact on gender representation in journalism and the media industry | Establish a review mechanism where research projects are assessed for their contribution to reducing gender bias and enhancing inclusive journalism practices |

## Concluding Remarks

The integration of AI in journalism practice, education, and research presents both opportunities and challenges for gender equality in African contexts. Without gender mainstreaming and decolonised approaches, AI systems risk perpetuating the same patriarchal and Western norms that have long dominated African media landscapes. The toolkits for gender mainstreaming offer a practical solution to these challenges, ensuring that AI technologies contribute to a more equitable, inclusive, and decolonised media environment. Despite this, we are reminded of African realities such as resource constraints, bureaucratic hurdles, patriarchal cultural beliefs, and unequal access to technology that may complicate adoption and the mainstreaming of gender in AI newsrooms, education, and research. For instance, many educators and researchers lack familiarity with AI, creating a capacity gap that must be addressed before implementing gender-responsive AI curricula. Also, investing in infrastructure, AI tools, and training is critical to overcoming some of these barriers. Addressing these structural, cultural, and financial barriers at different levels is essential for AI to support gender-sensitive transformations across the continent.

## References

Ai, M., & Masood, M. (2021). De-westernization in journalism research: A content and network analysis of the BRICS journals. *Scientometrics, 126*(12), 9477–9498.

AU. (2015). *Media portrayal of women and media gender gap in Africa.* Gender Links.

Buolamwini, J., & Gebru, T. (2018). Gender shades: Intersectional accuracy disparities in commercial gender classification. *Proceedings of Machine Learning Research, 81,* 1–15.

Byerly, C. M. (2011). *Global report on the status of women in the news media.* International Women's Media Foundation.

Byerly, C. M. (2013). *The Palgrave international handbook of women and journalism.* Palgrave Macmillan.

Crenshaw, K. (1991). Mapping the margins: Intersectionality, identity politics, and violence against women of color. *Stanford Law Review, 43*(6), 1241–1299.

Crenshaw, K. (2021). *Intersectionality matters: American policy forum* (Podcast). https://podcasts.apple.com/us/podcast/intersectionality-matters/id1441348908

Dralega, C. A. (2016). Media, capacity building and gender parity: Why we should not look away. *Journal of African Media Studies, 8*(3), 247–427.

Dralega, C. A. (Ed.). (2023a). *Digitisation, AI and algorithms in African journalism and media contexts: Practice, policy and critical literacies.* Emerald Publishing Limited.

Dralega, C. A. (2023b). AI and the algorithmic-turn in journalism practice in Eastern Africa: Perceptions, practice and challenges. In C. A. Dralega (Ed.), *Digitisation, AI and algorithms in African journalism and media contexts* (pp. 33–52). Emerald Publishing Limited.

Dralega, C. A. (2023c). An agenda for developing critical literacies for journalism education in an era of datafication. In C. A. Dralega (Ed.), *Digitisation, AI and algorithms in African journalism and media contexts* (pp. 155–160). Emerald Publishing Limited.

Dralega, C. A., Jemaneh, A., Jjuko, M., & Kantono, R. (2016). Gender mainstreaming in media and journalism education – An audit of media departments in Uganda, Rwanda and Ethiopia. *Journal of African Media Studies, 8*(3), 251–266.

Dralega, C. A., Jjuuko, M., & Solomon, E. (2022). Caught between a rock and a hard place: Impact of COVID-19 on feminist media in Uganda, Rwanda and Tanzania. In C. A. Dralega and A. Napakol (Eds.), *COVID-19 and the media in Sub-Saharan*

*Africa: Media viability, framing and health communication* (pp. 19–33). Emerald Publishing Limited.

Ejigu Kassa, B., & Sarikakis, K. (2020). Mainstreaming gender into media: The African Union backstage priority. In J. Servaes (Ed.), *Handbook of communication for development and social change* (pp. 1257–1275). Springer Singapore.

Ezumah, B. (2019). De-westernizing African journalism curriculum through glocalization and hybridization. *Journalism & Mass Communication Educator, 74*(4), 452–467.

Floridi, L., Cowls, J., Beltrametti, M., Chatila, R., Chazerand, P., Dignum, V., Luetge, C., Madelin, R., Pagallo, U., Rossi, F., Schafer, B., Valcke, P., & Vayena, E. (2018). AI4People – An ethical framework for a good AI society: Opportunities, risks, principles, and recommendations. *Minds and Machines, 28*, 689–707.

Gadzekpo, A. (2011). Battling old ghosts in gender and African media research. *African Communication Research, 4*(3), 389–410.

Gallagher, M. (2014). *Gender and media: Progress and challenges in policy and practice.* UNESCO.

Gallagher, M., Luxton, L., & Padovani, C. (2023). Women, gender, feminism: Status, scholarship, and advocacy. In J. Becker & R. Mansell (Eds.), *Reflections on the international association for media and communication research* (pp. 93–122). Palgrave Macmillan. https://doi.org/10.1007/978-3-031-16383-8_7

Geertsema-Sligh, M. (2014). Gender mainstreaming in journalism education. In A. V. Montiel (Ed.), *Media and gender: A scholarly agenda for global alliance for media and gender* (pp. 38–39). UNESCO.

Global Media Monitoring Project (GMMP). (2020). *Who makes the news?* [Global Media Monitoring Project 2020 Report]. WACC.

Grizzle, A. (Ed.). (2012). *Gender-sensitive indicators for media: Framework of indicators to gauge gender sensitivity in media operations and content.* United Nations Educational, Scientific and Cultural Organization.

Grzanka, P. R., Brian, J. D., & Bhatia, R. (2023). Intersectionality and science and technology studies. *Science, Technology, & Human Values,* 01622439231201707. https://www.researchgate.net/publication/373140596_Intersectionality_and_Science_and_Technology_Studies

Jaakkola, M. (2023). *Reporting on artificial intelligence: A handbook for journalism educators.* UNESCO.

Jjuuko, M., & Njuguna, J. (2019). *The discourse of digital inclusion of women in Rwanda's media.* Amsterdam University Press.

Kaija, B. (2013). Uganda: Women near parity but still leaving newsrooms. In C. M. Byerly (Ed.), *The Palgrave international handbook of women and journalism* (pp. 315–329). Palgrave Macmillan UK.

Kamlongera, M. I., & Katenga-Kaunda, A. K. (2023a). 'What is gender to you?': An Africana Womanist take on perceptions of gender reality on women's agency among a rural Malawian Community. *Gender and Education, 35*(3), 299–314.

Kamlongera, M. I., & Katenga-Kaunda, M. W. (2023b). Researchers' reflections on ethics of care as decolonial research practice: Understanding Indigenous knowledge communication systems to navigate moments of ethical tension in rural Malawi. *Research Ethics, 19*(3), 312–324.

Kassova, L. (2020). *The missing perspectives of women in news.* Bill and Melinda Gates Foundation.

Kothari, A., & Cruikshank, S. A. (2022). Artificial intelligence and journalism: An agenda for journalism research in Africa. *African Journalism Studies, 43*(1), 17–33.

Made, P. (2010). *Using gender to transform media education and journalism training curriculum at tertiary level.* GenderLinks. https://genderlinks.org.za/wp-content/uploads/imported/articles/attachments/12171_patmade_using-gender-to-transform-media-education.pdf

Manasi, A., Panchanadeswaran, S., Sours, E., & Lee, S. J. (2022). Mirroring the bias: Gender and artificial intelligence. *Gender, Technology and Development, 26*(3), 295–305.

Maractho, E. C. (2017). *Mass media, women and public life in Uganda: Interrogating representation, interaction and engagement* [Unpublished doctoral dissertation]. University of Kwazulu-Natal.

Morna, C. L. (2002, November 12–15). *Promoting gender equality in and through the media. A Southern African case study* [Report presentation]. United Nations Division for the Advancement of Women (DAW) Expert Group Meeting on "Participation and Access of Women to the Media, and the Impact of Media on, and Its Use as an Instrument for the Advancement and Empowerment of Women," Beirut, Lebanon.

Munoriyarwa, A. (2024). Unravelling socio-technological barriers to AI integration: A qualitative study of Southern African newsrooms. *Emerging Media, 2*(3), 474–498. https://doi.org/10.1177/27523543241288814

Munoriyarwa, A., Chiumbu, S., & Motsaathebe, G. (2021). Artificial intelligence practices in everyday news production: The case of South Africa's mainstream newsrooms. *Journalism Practice, 17*(7), 1374–1392. https://doi.org/10.1080/17512786.2021.1984976

Musa, B., & Domatob, J. K. (2011). Gender mainstreaming in African media curricula: Bridging the gap in journalism education. *Journalism and Mass Communication Educator, 66*(2), 181–196.

Mutsvairo, B. (2019). Challenges facing development of data journalism in non-western societies. *Digital Journalism, 7*(9), 1289–1294.

Mutsvairo, B., & Bebawi, S. (2022). Journalism and the Global South: Shaping journalistic practices and identity post "Arab Spring" special issue: Remembering the Arab Spring: Pursuing possibilities and impediments in journalistic professional practice across the Global South. *Digital Journalism, 10*(7), 1141–1155.

Mwaura, J., & Balliah, D. (2024). Championing inclusivity: Underrepresentation of women in African academic leadership and scholarly journal management. *Evidence Based Library and Information Practice, 19*(3), 42–59.

Ndlovu-Gatsheni, S. J. (2015). Decoloniality as the future of Africa. *History Compass, 13*(10), 485–496.

Noble, S. U. (2018). *Algorithms of oppression: How search engines reinforce racism.* NYU Press. https://www.degruyter.com/document/doi/10.18574/nyu/9781479833641.001.0001/html

O'Connor, S., & Liu, H. (2024). Gender bias perpetuation and mitigation in AI technologies: Challenges and opportunities. *AI & SOCIETY, 39*(4), 2045–2057.

OECD. (2019). *OECD principles on artificial intelligence.* OECD. https://www.oecd.org/en/topics/ai-principles.html

Ogola, G. (2023). *AI, journalism and public interest media in Africa: Scoping study to map the current state of artificial intelligence use in public interest media in Africa.* IMSforfreemedia. www.mediasupport.org.

Rodny-Gumede, Y. (2022). The triple oppressions: Race, class and gender in south African journalism. In *Women journalists in South Africa: Democracy in the age of social media* (pp. 15–29). Cham: Springer International Publishing.

Steeves, H. L., & Awino, I. (2015). Gender divides and African journalism practice. *African Journalism Studies, 36*(1), 84–92.

UN Women. (2024). *The gender digital divide and AI: Opportunities for inclusion.* https://www.unwomen.org/en/news-stories/explainer/2024/05/artificial-intelligence-and-gender-equality

UNESCO. (2020). *Artificial intelligence and gender equality: Key findings from Africa.* https://unesdoc.unesco.org/ark:/48223/pf0000374174

United Nations. (2002). *Gender mainstreaming: An overview.* UN Women.

Wajcman, J. (2004). *TechnoFeminism.* Polity Press.

Wasserman, H., & de Beer, A. S. (2009). Towards de-westernizing journalism studies. In K. Wahl-Jorgensen & T. Hanitzsch (Eds.), *The handbook of journalism studies* (pp. 448–458). Routledge.

West, S. M., Whittaker, M., & Crawford, K. (2019). *Discriminating systems: Gender, race, and power in AI.* AI Now Institute.

Chapter 11

# Digital Safety: Perspectives from Women Journalists in Uganda

*Fred Kakooza[a] and Samuel Kazibwe[b]*

[a]*Makerere University, Uganda*
[b]*Uganda Christian University, Uganda*

## Abstract

The Internet has been recognised as a tool or space for universal access to information that fosters diversity and plurality of voices. Yet in this space, journalists have been a regular target of online attacks, intimidation, and bullying that threaten the diversity of voices and information. Women journalists face a double burden of risk based on their gender, such that the safety and security of women journalists require a paradigm shift from focussing on physical harm alone to considering digital and online security as well. This chapter explores Ugandan women journalists' safety and security experiences in online environments and how women journalists negotiate their online media environments to deliver journalistic work. Discussed through the media affordance and objectification theoretical perspectives, the findings indicate that women journalists use digital spaces as an enabler to their profession but are challenged with threats, violations, and harassment online. We emphasise continuous training of women journalists on digital safety and security, including rallying media organisations to ensure online safety for women journalists.

*Keywords*: Women journalists; social media; digital spaces; digital safety; digital security; online harassment; press freedom

Gender and Media Representation: Perspectives from Sub-Saharan Africa, 161–174
doi:10.1108/978-1-83608-406-820251012

## Introduction

The Internet is an enabler for universal access to information as evidenced by the plurality of voices online. Journalists use online digital spaces to check what organisations are doing, keep in touch with their audiences, search for breaking news, and gather additional information through such sites as Facebook or X (formerly Twitter), and this has positively impacted their professional work (NewsLab, 2019). Journalists, however, have also become regular targets of online attacks, including bullying and intimidation, which puts plurality and diversity of voices at risk (HRNJ-Uganda, 2013). This requires a re-conceptualisation of journalists' security from mere physical protection from harm to reflect how 21st-century threats to journalists' safety and security involve digital risks, especially to those who operate within the online environment. Threats often appear in the comments sections of articles authored by women journalists, but such threats may also include graphic imagery in their inboxes or pop-ups on their social media profiles that allude to rape or physical violence.

The last decade has seen an increased drive by international organisations and civil society to focus on raising awareness about the safety and security issues that confront women working in the media across the world. Some steps have been taken to ensure online safety for women journalists at the international level. For example, the International Federation of Journalists (IFJ, 2018) launched an awareness campaign on social media, the Byte Back Campaign, using the hashtag #DefendMyVoiceOnline to encourage women not to abandon this virtual space when faced with abuse. A safety handbook for women journalists has been developed by the International Association of Women in Radio and Television (IAWRT, 2017) with support from UNESCO as a concrete and practical guidebook on safety and security with recommendations for women journalists working in war and conflict.

Despite such interventions, a recent case of gendered online harassment targeting Maria Ressa, a journalist in the Philippines, resulted in 90 trolling hate messages per hour, and several legal cases have been brought against her online publication, *The Rappler*. Ressa was recently acquitted of tax evasion (Associated Press, 2023). This high-profile example shows that measures to improve online security and safety are still too limited and contain no guarantees that harassers will be punished (IWMF, 2016). This chapter explores the safety and security experiences of Ugandan women journalists in online environments through three key questions:

1.   What is the nature of harassment that women journalists encounter online?
2.   How do women journalists navigate for their safety online?
3.   What are recommendations for female journalists' security and safety online?

## Media and Internet Freedom in Uganda

Uganda has a vibrant media environment whose operations are guaranteed by the constitution. Article 29(1) of the 1995 Ugandan constitution proclaims that everyone shall have the right to 'freedom of speech and expression which shall include freedom of the press and other media'. This provision is in tandem with the codification of access to information as a basic human right under Article 19 of the Universal Declaration of Human Rights, which includes freedom of opinion, expression, and information. In Uganda, the right to access information is explicit in Article 41 of the 1995 Constitution:

> Every citizen has a right of access to information in the possession of the state or any other organ of the state except where the release of the information is likely to interfere with the security of the state or the right to the privacy of any other person.

Uganda currently boasts of over 250 radio stations and over 40 television stations (Government Citizen Interaction Centre (GCIC), 2022), and the majority of these organisations publish and broadcast a variety of print and online media. The utilisation of the Internet for media in Uganda aligns with the recognition of the Internet as critical to the promotion of the right to access to information by the United Nations (CIPESA, 2017). Indeed, statistics indicate that there are about 11.7 million Internet users in Uganda (Kemp, 2023), and the number is growing steadily, thanks in large part to the adoption of mobile phones. A total of 30.55 million cellular mobile connections are active in Uganda (Kemp, 2023). Furthermore, as part of the 'MYUG' free Wi-Fi project that is being rolled out at the time of writing, Uganda currently has 300 active sites that provide free Internet access in the Kampala central business district and parts of Entebbe in central Uganda (Uganda National Information Communication Technology-NITA, 2023). If the full roll-out is successful, then the increased online penetration will also reach rural populations who will benefit from the affordances of digital spaces. The number of online publications in Uganda is already growing, and the mainstream media has an online presence to connect and grow their audience. This means that digital spaces are new and important work environments for women journalists.

Despite these encouraging developments, the latest 2024 World Press Freedom Index ranked Uganda at 128 out of 180 countries assessed. The report reveals further that Ugandan journalists, who are critical of government continue to face intimidation and violence from security services on daily basis (RSF, 2024). This raises safety and security concerns for women journalists in Uganda because they are not spared from arbitrary arrests or beatings (RSF, 2019). Moreover, Uganda has instituted a social media law that discourages online activity, stifles free expression, and creates new restrictions (Wanyama, 2022). Such a hostile environment is rife with protection risks that may be faced by women journalists online. The country has witnessed media and social media shutdowns, ongoing arrests, threats, and harassment of journalists and bloggers, all of which paints a worrying scenario (Eckey, 2017). The intimidation of journalists often works, and self-censorship breeds an information gap and lack of accountability to the public (Kaija, 2018). What is more, Ugandan journalists continue to face fear of arrest, harassment, low remuneration, a lack of policies to secure female journalists, and long working hours (Okoth, 2018).

## Coping with or Negotiating Online Harassment

Female journalists in Uganda have adopted several strategies to deal with online harassment. Walulya and Selnes (2023) established that some women journalists in Uganda have abandoned beats that are more susceptible to online harassment. Other strategies used to deal with online harassment include withdrawing from spaces where mob harassment and negative messages are prevalent and blocking perpetrators from their contacts (Semakula, 2019). In persistent cases, the victims (female journalists) report to their superiors and government authorities. As Semakula (2019) reports:

> Respondents harassed by perpetrators on social media platforms such as WhatsApp and Facebook (cyber harassment) said they either refuse to reply, block their accounts, and if the practice persists, report to a higher authority, including media managers and Police. (p. 60)

Another technique women journalists employ to negotiate online harassment is self-censorship to prevent attacks against them and their media outlets. They do this by double-checking their messages before sharing them to edit out statements or words with the potential to annoy sections of online mobs (Nakiwala, 2020; Walulya & Selnes, 2023). Alier (2021) observed that censorship may sometimes include avoiding sensitive stories or choosing soft angles or a story published but with all the important facts omitted for the safety of the journalist. This censorship is detrimental to journalism and society at large, since it deprives citizens of critical information necessary for the functioning of a democracy (Walulya & Selnes, 2023). Women journalists also hide their identities online as a defence mechanism. Instead of using their actual names and pictures, some use pseudonyms and dummy pictures to confuse their potential attackers – both online and offline (Alier, 2021).

## Theoretical Framework

How digital spaces facilitate the work of women journalists in Uganda is an important aspect of how these women navigate their safety and security in online environments and can be appreciated by applying the theoretical lens of technological affordance. Affordance is a key concept that enables the understanding and analysis of social media technology and the relations between the technology and its users (Bucher & Helmond, 2018). We view social media platforms as open spaces for the expression of opinions without gatekeeping that give everyone an equal opportunity to engage, interact, and share their views. Consequently, women journalists, as goal-oriented actors, perceive social media in terms of how it can be used, including how it can help them meet their journalistic goals (Pozzi et al., 2014; Schrock, 2015; Volkoff & Strong, 2017). A single technology can result in multiple action possibilities because individuals have agency over their user practices and habits (Schrock, 2015). In these online spaces, women journalists engage with the public, and this interaction is affected by how they are perceived by their audiences in those spaces.

The study also employed objectification theory to understand the interaction of women journalists in online spaces. The theory highlights elements of 'degrad[ation] and coercion' (Cuklanz, 2016, p. 9) that women face in digital media environments that hinder their participation. It gives a framework through which we can understand the genesis of the threats and violations that women encounter in digital spaces while practising journalism. Women journalists worldwide are challenged with gender power struggles within traditional and online media environments because they are culturally looked at as women first and foremost. Objectification theory postulates that the lived experiences of particular groups of people can generate knowledge, perspectives, and ways of thinking about a given situation (Winn & Cornelius, 2020). It allows scholars and researchers to appreciate the impact of sexual objectification on the lives of women 'as well as how they manage, cope with, and resist these experiences' (Szymanski et al., 2011, p. 7). As Calogero (2012) noted, women journalists are objectified sexually online through sexual comments, exposure to sexualised images, sexual harassment, and sexual violence, among other behaviours. The theory of objectification therefore provides a framework for examining how women journalists in Uganda experience the digital media environment.

## Methodology

A qualitative research approach comprising both focus group discussions (FGDs) and in-depth interviews was adopted for data collection to enable an intensive and detailed examination of a case (Bryman, 2012). Five FGDs (numbered 1 through 5, each between 7 participants) were conducted with 35 women drawn from a database at the Uganda Media Women Association of 400 women journalists using a simple random sampling technique. This sample size is consistent with Israel's (1992) recommendation of 10–30 participants for small-scale studies. The approach encouraged highly participatory and interactive engagements on issues related to the safety and security of women journalists. Each of the five FGDs dealt with a sub-theme under the broader topic of 'safety and security of women journalists in online and offline environments', and the data presented in this chapter was collected during FGD 4, which specifically discussed the sub-theme of 'handling of personal safety and security in online environments', FGDs were appropriate because we sought to explore attitudes, opinions, and perceptions through flexible and open discussions between the selected respondents (Kumar, 2011).

In-depth interviews were conducted with two women journalists, referred to pseudonymously here as 'Respondent 1' and 'Respondent 2', who had recently experienced online safety threats and security violations. These two case stories of women journalists were important for the gathering of personal reflections on the research question that was included in the FGDs data collection. Respondent 1 was a reporter with a leading private broadcast media house who faced online harassment from a high-ranking general in the Uganda Peoples' Defence Forces and his followers that transitioned into physical threats. This respondent had to quit her job. Respondent 2 had faced many online attacks (which had also further degenerated into physical threats) for stories uploaded online. The discussion in this chapter is based solely on the findings derived from the two in-depth interviews and the FGD that specifically examined the safety and security experiences of Ugandan women journalists in online environments.

## Findings

The majority of the women journalists sampled were younger than 35 – in other words, they fall under the youth category who utilise online platforms in their daily life. The youth in Uganda (18–30 years) make up 22.7 per cent out of 45.9 million people (UBOS, 2024). Overall, 78 per cent of Uganda's population are under 35, and these figures are expected to double in the next 25 years (Lirri, 2021). Increased Internet access has given these young people more latitude to actively participate in online spaces (Deutsche Welle, 2018). The participants reported an average professional experience of five years as journalists. This makes them novice journalists and vulnerable to digital threats as they interact in online environments. The study participants had all worked with media houses that have online platforms and reported several challenges they faced while interacting in these spaces as 'women journalists'.

### *Nature of Harassment Encountered Online*

Respondents reported that they use digital platforms to execute their journalistic duties and identified their many benefits to support faster communication and dissemination of information while in the field, more efficient engagement with sources and follow up on stories, and a larger readership, as well as getting story tips. Oftentimes, women journalists are harassed because of the stories they post online:

> Besides journalism, I sometimes express my opinions online, and, of course, there are people who don't like what we post. I had just posted a video of the Uganda Peoples' Defence Forces fracas in Kayunga over land. The people were exchanging and confronting the armed UPDF personnel. I then received harsh comments on my Twitter (X) platform from people accusing me of putting the national army in a bad light. (Respondent 2)

This statement shows how critical online safety is in the digital era, when most journalists rely on the Internet to perform their tasks efficiently. Respondents confirmed various forms of online harassment either through personal experiences or having heard about them from colleagues and sources. For example, a respondent reported online cases of objectification where netizens can make the subject personal, beyond the story. 'This is very common where people attack you not in line with what you do, but they focus on your personality' (Respondent 2). Respondent 1 confirms online attacks against her family for simply reporting a political story: 'If you write a "critical" story about the National Resistance Movement or about the National Unity Platform, they will attack you'.

The findings also established that women journalists face gender-related safety risks and threats in digital spaces, including cyberstalking, trolling, obscene remarks, unwanted sexual advances and sexually evocative pictures, and sexually explicit jokes. These acts go beyond online spaces to the physical environment where women journalists also face physical threats and abuse. These threats are enabled by cyberstalkers who collect personal information and updates available online that can be used to blackmail and harm women journalists. One respondent described how a person who has

> stalked you, knows where you stay through Facebook, and can track you to assault you physically. [...] There is a story I did in 2023, and somebody posted my picture on Twitter and said, 'don't think you are very far; I can get you wherever you are'. I felt that this was no light threat, and I was shaken. (Respondent 2)

Online platforms have also been used for blackmail and to damage the reputation of women journalists through, for example, releasing of unpleasant information about them. Another respondent shared a bad experience of receiving personal information about their family and their whereabouts from attackers:

> I received photos of my father's house in the village and of my father. They were letting me know that they know where my family is, they know who my parents are, they know who my siblings are, and where they stay. They have their contacts, and they can reach out to them and harm them. (Respondent 1)

Sexual harassment both online and offline was reported to be a major issue affecting women journalists as they go about their work. Women journalists also noted that while doing their work in digital spaces, they get persistent advances from male sources and colleagues who assume that the women will welcome the sexual or romantic interest at some point:

> Annoyingly, the perpetrators think it is okay. They think that these are two consenting adults and therefore [it's] a matter of negotiating. It also has repercussions when you reject them, particularly if you are searching for a job as a journalist. (Respondent 2)

One FGD participant shared when she had once found herself in this situation:

> I was on air one time presenting, and then, all of a sudden, I just saw the computer lighting [up] only to look, and it was a sex video. I realized that someone had done it intentionally because, after some minutes, my supervisor walked in [...] and started telling me funny words. It disturbed me psychologically because he wanted to kiss me.

Women journalists are concerned about hackers who obtain their personal information by manipulating digital security to access their online accounts. 'I do not know how many times my accounts have received notifications of people trying to hack into my social media accounts' (Respondent 2). Another respondent shared that: 'When my account got hacked into, I was called by my cousin that they were seeing bad (nude) pictures [...] I checked and deleted them' (Respondent 1). An FGD participant reported that some people use fake or bot accounts to troll women journalists: 'They use bots to troll you, to degrade you, and to show the public that you are disqualified and that you don't fit to be a journalist'. Participants in FGDs were also concerned about the contradictory comments they receive when they make posts on given subjects and how these are often the first manoeuvre in what degenerates into abusive attacks: 'They will always comment to the contrary [...] they will provoke you in their comments'. Another interview respondent noted that there were so many forms and tones of harassment and how they are all based on the audience's expectations: 'because you work on TV and they hear you on radio, they expect you to belong to a certain (high-class) category, and when they realize that you are not in that category, they will go all out on you' (Respondent 1).

### How Women Journalists Navigate Safety Online

Respondents were not sure about in-house policies that specifically tackled online safety and security and opined that individual journalists must guard their safety. A respondent shared that it was easy for women journalists to be harassed and abused because the perpetrators are sure that it is their nature not to react: 'When you react back, it also becomes an issue; they will start questioning your qualifications, your ethics, your employer, and how you ended up in that media house – when you disrespect the viewers' (Respondent 1).

There are different levels of censorship (both by the regulator and the employer) on online standards – that indicate a journalist should not express their opinions. From this point of view, participants observed that safety and protection start with the individual and advised female journalists to 'be alert with ears on the ground, be careful with personal information on social media like Facebook and to be smart in taking decisions while in the field' (FGD participant). One respondent shared her encounter with security personnel when she was summoned over a comment she made on the social media platform X:

> I was scared, I was amidst powerful men, who would do anything to me, I could not fight them, they are in position of power and would not be held accountable. Even my media house would not protect me because I was on suspension for two weeks. After all, they had been pressured ... so, if anything had happened to me in that dungeon, they were not certainly going to look for me. (Respondent 2)

Women journalists feel that journalism is not safe for their gender, and this has resulted in many abandoning the profession such that there are few women covering hard news or political beats, and the public are denied a diversity of voices and opinions. Many female journalists report on health, where they deal with press conferences and ministerial press releases and reports, without venturing into investigative pieces:

> The situation limits you and because you are human you have emotions, you have a family telling you what do you lose if you don't do this, safety first, what do you lose if you let it be? So, you ask yourself; is it worth it? (Respondent 2)

Another respondent admits that she found herself doing stories that she never enjoyed:

> I became more of a press conference person; I became a person who was scared of reporting objectively and that did not fit my expectations of being a journalist. I looked up to guys [journalists] who would even go to war zones to document stories, and who would put leaders on the spot. (Respondent 1)

The findings indicate that women journalists feel that they are not safe when practising journalism. They now tread carefully to the extent of abandoning the profession to be safe from online harassment. The safety of women journalists in online spaces needs to be given due attention and consideration if they are to survive and thrive in such harsh environments.

### Recommendations for Women Journalists' Security and Safety Online

Respondents observed that newsrooms needed to do much more to protect and ensure the safety of women journalists online because they are more vulnerable to safety and security violations and threats than men. Women journalists feel that they need to be believed when they come out to expose the violations and unpleasant situation they experience while executing their work rather than being questioned. Women journalists expressed knowledge of the laws that protect journalists against digital safety risks and violations while going about their work. For example, they were able to list some of the offenses defined in the Computer Misuse Act of 2011, including offensive communication and cyberstalking. Nevertheless, women journalists need to be well informed about digital safety tools:

> It starts with the gadget that you use. Different gadgets have different safety protocols. It depends on the different insecurities and threats you face, but we have to be up to speed with these tools. (Respondent 2)

Limited knowledge of digital protection laws and the responsibility of Internet service providers in ensuring the protection of personal data was identified as another challenge to women journalists' safety and security online. This calls for training of women journalists. As one respondent testified, such training would have helped protect her online accounts from hackers: 'I would have lost both my Facebook and X accounts if I didn't know other safety protocols that require another layer of authentication besides two-factor authentication' (Respondent 2).

Other women journalists learn to cope with abusive attacks as a form of resilience in executing their work:

> From the Twitter body shaming, I was told that I could not fit into the categories of women to be dated and that I could not be a goddess like his wife. I maintained that I am just a goddess in a small package and that is how I ended up being called a small goddess. I had to embrace it for me to cope with the harassment and abuse, and it worked. (Respondent 1)

The preceding data reveals the nature of online harassment faced by female journalists, the coping mechanisms they employ, and their proposed recommendations for the improvement of online safety for women journalists.

## Discussion

Online harassment has taken various forms, including trolling, cyberstalking, obscene remarks, unwanted sexual advances, sexually evocative pictures, and sexually explicit jokes. Sometimes women journalists face physical attacks because of their online activities. These experiences further illustrate the mechanisms adopted by women journalists in Uganda to navigate online challenges. The respondents also proposed a number of steps that ought to be taken to alleviate the already precarious situation. This section discusses these key findings in light of the presented literature and theoretical perspectives.

The majority of women journalists who participated in the study were young and still early in their journalism careers. Digital media platforms facilitate the accomplishment of their journalistic roles and the development of their experiences and competencies. This finding that online platforms offer women journalists faster communication and dissemination of information is consistent with affordance theory's approach to understanding and analysing social media technology and its relations with users (Bucher & Helmond, 2018). Despite the media affordances that digital platforms offer, they are also a source of oppression and discrimination against women (Gallagher, 2003). The present study's findings indicate that there is a great deal of objectification of women journalists in online spaces, where they are attacked for their gender and not their journalistic work or abilities. This pattern of behaviour is the focus of the objectification theory, which highlights the structures of power that systematically portray women as objects rather than active subjects in the production of media content (Gallagher, 2003). The findings have also revealed that women journalists have braved varying forms of online threats, including physical violations.

Attacks on women journalists while in online environments are a powerful factor that influences women journalists to keep off digital spaces to avoid the dangers that might arise from posting journalistic material. The struggles that women face in the media environment have hindered their potential to advance in the profession (Cuklanz, 2016). Our findings demonstrate that women journalists tend to concentrate on such safer beats as health, fashion, tourism, and press conferences, which often limits their journalistic potential. For instance, in 2017, NTV reporter Gertrude Uwitware was attacked by security officers for using Facebook to express her support for a local campaign that was aimed at compelling the government to provide free menstruation supplies (i.e. sanitary towels) to all school-going girls. Uwitware was kidnapped at gunpoint, forced into a car, and driven to an unknown location, where she was tortured and threatened (RSF, 2017). She was also ordered to delete all her Twitter and Facebook posts deemed too critical of the first family. She consequently quit active journalism. Respondents agreed that such violations have created a situation of self-caution and self-censorship among women journalists and media houses that negatively impacts their role not only of disseminating news and information but also of watching over government actions. This finding aligns with Walulya and Selnes's (2023) finding that women journalists have abandoned reporting certain beats that are more susceptible to online harassment. This is a real contemporary problem that needs urgent attention since studies (Nakiwala, 2020; Walulya & Selnes, 2023) have shown a striking absence of female voices in news items that concern women in specific ways.

The women journalists who participated in this study are often threatened by the repeated use of electronic communication to harass them. Hackers take advantage of their information online to damage their reputation and journalistic integrity. They are concerned about stalkers who get into their physical space aided by online information to blackmail and threaten their lives, sometimes by releasing private information. Those who do not withstand such challenges usually leave the profession, and this results in fewer women's voices and the under-representation of their issues in the media. This is self-censorship, a technique that women journalists have embraced to prevent online attacks against them (Nakiwala, 2020; Walulya & Selnes, 2023). The findings further revealed that women journalists were not adequately protected by their media organisations and are usually on their own as they fight off threats and violations in digital spaces. As they cope with self-censorship, women journalists expressed discomfort about how media houses censor their use of digital spaces such that their appreciation of the affordances offered by digital spaces for the execution of journalistic work is curtailed.

The study established that there was a general lack of knowledge on digital security and protection, including matters of safety risks, violations, and protection. Women journalists need to be trained in digital safety and security because such training will be beneficial in building their confidence and resilience around digital spaces as a way of coping and advancing their journalistic calling. Indeed, the presence of women in the media is an opportunity for gendered discourse that may create a sense of self-determinism to naturally embrace challenges within online spaces (Ryan & Deci, 2002). In other words, targeted training will give women journalists an opportunity to actualise their sense of self and human potential to overcome such work challenges, including the pervasive sexual harassment that extends from digital spaces to physical environments.

## Conclusion

This chapter discussed how women journalists in Uganda have faced threats and violations in digital spaces as they strive to have their voices heard or represented in the media. While online spaces have been projected as free and open, where users are supposed to interact at an equal level, this study of women journalists' interactions reveals that gender biases are exported from physical environments to online spaces and vice versa. The study has established that women journalists encounter digital security threats and violations in online spaces that hinder their work. They experience gender-related violations, abuses, and safety risks that oftentimes transcend to offline environments yet, when reported, their descriptions are rarely believed. We argue that as digital spaces become more crucial for media work, attention needs to shift to make them safe for women journalists to freely work. Women voices should be promoted in digital spaces, and media organisations must support women journalists through online safety policies and training such that they can thrive. Different stakeholders should ensure that online safety is strengthened to facilitate transparent and accountable mechanisms for the protection of media diversity.

## References

Alier, G. J. (2021). *Coping strategies and mechanisms of private journalists operating in hazardous environment: A case of South Sudan* [Unpublished Master's dissertation, Uganda Christian University].

Associated Press. (2023). *Nobel-winning Philippine journalist Maria Ressa is acquitted in tax evasion case*. NPR. Retrieved June 03, 2024, from https://www.npr.org/2023/09/12/1198878729/nobel-winning-philippine-journalist-maria-ressa-is-acquitted-in-tax-evasion-case

Bryman, A. (2012). *Social research methods* (4th ed.). Oxford University Press.

Bucher, T., & Helmond, A. (2018). The affordances of social media platforms. In J. Burgess, A. Marwick, & T. Poell (Eds.), *The SAGE handbook of social media* (pp. 233–253). SAGE Publications.

Calogero, R. M. (2012). Objectification theory, self-objectification, and body image. In F. C. Thomas (Ed.), *Encyclopaedia of body image and human appearance* (pp. 574–580). Academic Press.

CIPESA. (2017). *The state of access to information in Uganda* [Position paper]. Retrieved May 15, 2024, from https://cipesa.org/wp-content/files/briefs/report/Position-Paper-The-State-of-Access-to-Information-in-Uganda.pdf

Cuklanz, L. (2016). Feminist theory in communication. In K. B. Jensen, E. W. Rothenbuhler, J. D. Pooley, & R. T. Craig (Eds.), *The international encyclopedia of communication theory and philosophy* (pp. 1–11). John Wiley & Sons. https://doi.org/10.1002/9781118766804.wbiect157

Deutsche Welle. (2018). *Internet opening up a new future for Ugandan youth* [interview]. Retrieved June 03, 2024, from https://akademie.dw.com/en/dw-akademies-miriam-ohlsen-internet-opening-up-a-new-future-for-ugandan-youth/a-43653785; https://p.dw.com/p/2xALJ

Eckey, S. (2017, June 2). Freedom of expression a must for sustainable development. *The Daily Monitor*. Retrieved May 04, 2024, from https://www.monitor.co.ug/OpEd/Commentary/Freedom-of-expression-a-must-for-sustainable-development/689364-3952318-wbqp1kz/index.html; https://allafrica.com/stories/201706020015.html

Gallagher, M. (2003). Feminist media perspectives. In A. N. Valdivia (Ed.), *A companion to media studies* (pp. 1–19). Blackwell Publishing.

Government Citizen Interaction Centre (GCIC). (2022). *Approved radio stations in Uganda*. Retrieved May 28, 2024, from https://www.gcic.go.ug/radios/https://www.gcic.go.ug/radios/

HRNJ-Uganda. (2013, May 2). *Report assesses safety of journalists in Uganda*. IFEX. https://www.ifex.org/uganda/2013/05/02/hrnj_u_press_statement/

IAWRT. (2017). *What if...? Safety handbook for women journalists*. Retrieved May 15, 2024, from https://www.iawrt.org/sites/default/files/field/pdf/2017/11/IAWRT%20Safety%20Manual; https://iawrt.org/wp-content/uploads/2017/11/IAWRT-Safety-Manual.Download.10112017.pdf

International Federation of Journalists (IFJ). (2018). *Byte back campaign: Fighting online harassment*. South Asia Media Hub. Retrieved May 04, 2024, from https://samsn.ifj.org/ifj-byteback-campaign/

Israel, G. D. (1992). *Determining sample size*. University of Florida IFAS Extension. Retrieved May 04, 2024, from https://www.tarleton.edu/academicassessment/documents/Samplesize.pdf

IWMF. (2016, February 12). *Challenges to the safety and protection of journalists*. Global Investigative Journalism Network. Retrieved May 18, 2024, from https://gijn.org/2016/02/12/challenges-to-the-safety-and-protection-of-journalists/

Kaija, B. (2018, October 28). *We must all protect a free press*. The New Group. https://x.com/newvisionwire/status/1054392200988123136/photo/1; Retrieved May 04, 2024, from https://www.facebook.com/thenewvision/posts/we-all-must-protect-a-free-press-police-interrogated-me-professionally-and-cordi/10156934629039078/

Kemp, S. (2023, February 14). *Digital 2023: Uganda*. DataReportal. Retrieved June 03, 2022, from https://datareportal.com/reports/digital-2023-uganda

Kumar, A. (2011). *Research and writing skills*. Lulu Press.

Lirri, E. (2021, February 2). Uganda has world's youngest population. *Daily Monitor*. Retrieved June 20, 2024, from https://www.monitor.co.ug/uganda/special-reports/uganda-has-world-s-youngest-population-1497730

Nakiwala, A. S. (2020). Risk perception and negotiation of safety among Ugandan female journalists covering political demonstrations. In A. G. Larsen, I. Fadnes, & R. Krøvel (Eds.), *Journalist safety and self-censorship* (pp. 130–147). Routledge.

NewsLab. (2019). *Why journalists use social media*. Retrieved May 18, 2024, from https://newslab.org/journalists-use-social-media/#:~:text=More%20than%20half%20of%20the,for%20gathering%20information%20and%20reporting.&text=About%2073%20percent%20of%20the,there%20is%20any%20breaking%20news

Okoth, C. (2018, April 19). UNESCO rolls out mechanisms for protection of journalist. *The New Vision*. Retrieved June 03, 2024, from https://www.newvision.co.ug/new_vision/news/1475965/unesco-rolls-mechanism-\protection-journalists

Pozzi, G., Pigni, F., & Vitari, C. (2014, August 7–9). *Affordance theory in the IS discipline: A review and synthesis of the literature* [Proceedings paper]. AMCIS 2014 proceedings, Savannah, USA. https://aisel.aisnet.org/amcis2014/SocioTechnicalIssues/General Presentations/2https://aisel.aisnet.org/AMCIS2014

RSF. (2017, April 10). *TV reporter kidnapped and beaten over post about First Lady*. Retrieved May 18, 2024, from https://rsf.org/en/tv-reporter-kidnapped-and-beaten-over-post-about-first-ladyrsf.org/en/news/tv-reporter-kidnapped-and-beaten-over-post-about-first-lady

RSF. (2019). *Twenty-Seven women journalists held in appalling conditions*. https://linkprotect.cudasvc.com/url?a=https%3a%2f%2frsf.org%2fen%2ftwenty-seven-women-journalists-held-appalling-conditions&c=E,1,m95jqYnyLydAC8I7TY6OnCVVL9t HmDlt59udSjaPCzRCVEcf4btVHq1vNtrEvRDGXq8DrJGMkJV_QVSm3lO2n9 u4LsTn2ZB9eXncy4H_4UGIvJo94LN42bJ-VNw,&typo=1

RSF. (2024). *World press freedom index*. https://rsf.org/en/region/africa

Ryan, R. M., & Deci, E. L. (2022). Self-determination theory. In F. Maggino (Ed.), *Encyclopedia of quality of life and well-being research* (pp. 1–7). Springer. https://linkprotect.cudasvc.com/url?a=https%3a%2f%2fdoi.org%2f10.1007%2f978-3-319-69909-7_2630-2&c=E,1,Mq7NjfiSwZquRU9XxFf0jo1tPEyXQ5kuQ6TR6u-IAIlIbxbY2JywQJ4LIHtqPHolu_ZiQPRMAIMvxplPotQyUKZFc1iVXiuFJGp WPI562BA,,&typo=1

Schrock, A. R. (2015). Communicative affordances of mobile media: Portability, availability, locatability, and multimediality. *International Journal of Communication, 9,* 1229–121246. https://ijoc.org/index.php/ijoc/article/view/3288

Semakula, J. (2019). *Sexual harassment of female journalists in Ugandan media* [Unpublished Master's thesis]. Uganda Christian University.

Szymanski, D. M., Moffitt, L. B., & Carr, E. R. (2011). Sexual objectification of women: Advances to theory and research 1ψ7. *The Counselling Psychologist, 39*(1), 6–38. https://doi.org/10.1177/0011000010378402

Uganda Bureau of Statistics (UBOS). (2024). *The National Population and Housing Census 2024 – Preliminary report*, Kampala, Uganda. https://www.ubos.org/wp-content/uploads/publications/National-Population-and-Housing-Census-2024-Preliminary-Report.pdf

Uganda National Information Communication Technology-NITA. (2023). *Key milestones* [Infographic]. NITA Uganda. Retrieved May 18, 2024, from https://www.nita.go.ug/

Volkoff, O., & Strong, D. (2017). Affordance theory and how to use it in IS research. In R. D. Galliers & M.-K. Stein (Eds.), *The Routledge companion to management information systems* (1st ed., pp. 1–14). Routledge. https://doi.org/10.4324/97813156193 61https

Walulya, G., & Selnes, F. N. (2023). "I thought you are beautiful": Uganda women journalists tales of mob violence on social media. *Digital Journalism, 11*(10), 1962–1981. https://doi.org/10.1080/21670811.2023.2170899

Wanyama, E. (2022). *Uganda passes regressive law on "misuse of social media" and hate speech*. CIPESA. Retrieved May 18, 2024, from https://cipesa.org/2022/09/uganda-passes-regressive-law-on-misuse-of-social-media-and-hate-speech/

Winn, L., & Cornelius, R. (2020). Self-objectification and cognitive performance: A systematic review of literature. *Frontiers in Psychology, 11,* 20. Retrieved May 31, 2024, from http://www.frontiersin.org/articles/10.3389/fpsyg.2020.00020/full

Chapter 12

# YouTube Videos as Agents of Social Inclusion and Therapy Among Gender-based Violence Survivors

*Anne Anjao Eboi*

*Daystar University, Kenya*

## Abstract

The reviewed literature demonstrates how new media platforms are increasingly offering survivors of gender-based violence (GBV) a forum for the promotion of social justice. Data indicate that one in three Kenyan women has experienced GBV, and this study explores how YouTube videos can be agents of social inclusion and therapy for survivors of GBV. Six key informant interviews and a focus group discussion were conducted and guided by media ecology and networked public theories within the qualitative research paradigm. A narrative analysis reveals how YouTube videos act as sources of information, therapy, and comfort to those survivors who watch both GBV- and non-GBV-related content. Additionally, YouTube videos offer education and training for GBV awareness and allow survivors to share experiences, find support, and learn coping strategies. Despite these positives, YouTube videos also generate comments that support gender stereotypes and other negative attitudes that may deny victims social justice. While men are also victims of GBV, they are often excluded from male-related GBV videos. The study argues that YouTube should strengthen its innovation policies to promote social justice for GBV survivors and other stakeholders should invest in YouTube by creating content specific to GBV and social justice for all genders.

*Keywords*: YouTube videos; gender-based violence; social inclusion; therapy; survivors

Gender and Media Representation: Perspectives from Sub-Saharan Africa, 175–189
doi:10.1108/978-1-83608-406-820251013

# Introduction

Research has well established that YouTube is associated with certain benefits for survivors of GBV. On the one hand, YouTube affords some intimacy to vulnerable users through digital storytelling and sharing of experiences among audiences (Jenkins et al., 2009). When the marginalised share their painful experiences, it helps them to reclaim and restore their identities, thereby preventing further suffering (Shishko, 2022). Miller and Demirbilek (2023) have argued that YouTube provides opportunities for awareness raising, advocacy, and support through sharing information, personal stories, and resources related to GBV. On the other hand, commenters demonstrate how YouTube videos can contribute to GBV-related cases in deleterious ways. Compared to male YouTubers, female YouTubers receive more negative video comments, including sexism, racism, and sexually aggressive hate speech (Döring & Mohseni, 2020). Since women are most objectified, attacked, and harassed on social media platforms, there is a need for effective policy in digital spaces (Capella-Castro, 2021).

GBV has been defined as a social justice issue, a global concern, and a gross violation of victims' fundamental human rights, including the right to life, safety, liberty and security, and the right to equal protection under the law as well as the right to sound physical and mental health (United Nations High Commissioner for Refugees (UNHCR), n.d.; World Vision, 2022). GBV results in such psychological and emotional disturbances as isolation, depression, suicide attempts, and, in severe instances, death (UNHCR, n.d.; World Vision, 2022). The United Nations' (UN) Sustainable Development Goals underscore the issues related to GBV in Goal 5 (Gender Equality), which foregrounds the elimination of all forms of violence against girls and women.

## Problem Statement

GBV is a sensitive issue such that, in some contexts, survivors are reluctant to discuss or report. This reluctance remains despite several attempts and initiatives to provide relief and social justice, including medical treatment, provision of safe spaces, legal aid, psychosocial support, physical security, mentorship programmes, community-based peer support, and livelihood support (UNHCR, n.d.; World Vision, 2022). These social services are often delivered by rescue centres, hotlines, hospital support, and other organisations. The media has also offered support. The Nation Media Group (NMG), the leading media house in East and Central Africa (Nation Media Group, n.d.), for example, established a gender desk in its editorial section in 2019. Thereafter, NMG started observing *16 Days of Activism Against Gender-Based Violence*, an annual global campaign initiated by the inaugural Women's Global Leadership Institute in 1991 that raises awareness about violence against women and girls as a human rights issue (Kassova & Addy, 2022).

While YouTube videos provide important information on issues of social justice in relation to GBV, there is a dearth of literature on their potential to address these issues in the Kenyan context that this chapter endeavours to address. This study draws on qualitative research approaches to explore the lived experiences and perceptions of YouTube viewers on GBV and how YouTube videos can serve as sources of knowledge and therapy for the survivors and promote social inclusion. The study's specific objectives are threefold:

- to identify which specific videos are frequently watched by GBV survivors and why;
- to gather data about the lived experiences of the study participants, namely journalists (who work in mainstream media or as freelancers), while watching or hosting these videos; and
- to establish YouTube's potential as a source of information and spaces for therapy and social inclusion for survivors.

## Literature Review

### *YouTube and GBV*

The few extant studies on YouTube's role in the promotion of social justice in Kenya have generally focussed on addressing GBV in broader terms. Vahedi et al. (2024), for example, investigated how GBV service providers navigated the process of digitalising GBV prevention and response during the COVID-19 crisis. Ndaka (2023) portrays YouTube as a networked community that links decentralised and fragmented voices in Kenya, but the study does not focus on GBV. Baker (2018) details how young women globally, including Kenya, are 'taking back' technology to demand their rights and challenge violence. Although these empirical studies are not directly focussed on the relationships between GBV and YouTube, they well-demonstrate the need for more research on social inclusion in digital environments. Indeed, most of the reviewed literature does include a discussion of the advantages or disadvantages of YouTube as a platform.

The case of Cecily Bolden, who was murdered by her boyfriend for not disclosing her HIV status prior to having sex (Anderson, 2014), provides a poignant example of YouTube discussions on GBV matters. It was particularly disturbing in this case that the comments overwhelmingly blamed Cecily and called to set the perpetrator free (Anderson, 2014). But there is also strong evidence that YouTube hosts information on GBV that may be useful for survivors and offer social inclusion and therapy. For instance, World Vision (2022) has a 10-minute video on a GBV initiative they implemented in Nairobi and Narok counties. A *Citizen TV* 'Monday Report' edition provided a platform for critical conversations on GBV on 15 May 2023 that is uploaded to their YouTube channel. *YouthAction-Net* (2015) posted a six-minute advocacy video on how to avoid GBV.

### *Definition of Terms*

The United Nations High Commissioner for Refugees (UNHCR, n.d.) documents how people are exposed to insecurity and vulnerable to threats against their lives and to sexual abuse, rape, forced prostitution, and trafficking when they are forced to flee their homes. The Gender Violence Recovery Centre (2022), a charitable trust of the Nairobi Women's Hospital, reports that one in three Kenyan women has experienced an episode of sexual violence before the age of 18, one of the highest rates of GBV in the world, and that 5% of boys and 3% of Kenyan men are GBV survivors. One in four women in Kenya has experienced violence from an intimate partner (Kenya News Agency, 2023). Femicide (killings may be unintentional) is also on the rise in Kenya, where more than 500 women have been reported killed since 2016 (Africa Data Hub, 2024). Social justice initiatives and programmes are concerned with what hinders fairness and equality for people (Lowery, 2023).

The UNHCR (n.d.) defines gender inequality as, first and foremost, the denial of the equal enjoyment of rights, responsibilities, and opportunities for all people. This definition is linked to the understanding of social inclusion as the process of improving the ability, opportunity, and dignity of those disadvantaged by their identity (World Bank, n.d.). Gender is one such identity that confronts barriers that prevent full participation in political, economic, and social life (World Bank, n.d.). This chapter argues that institutions should institute such GBV-related measures, programmes, and services as legal redress and therapy to facilitate social justice in relation to GBV in Kenya.

Psychotherapy and Counselling Federation of Australia (PACFA, n.d.) defines therapy as a process where a trained professional (counsellor or psychotherapist) meets with a client to help resolve problematic beliefs, behaviours, feelings, and related physical symptoms. The treatment involves interpersonal relationships to help clients develop self-understanding so that they can make changes in their lives. Vahedi et al. (2024) suggest that prevention and response activities and services can be digitised to the advantage of GBV survivors. This chapter investigates whether this digitisation can be applied to YouTube videos as a source of therapy.

## Theoretical Framework

This chapter's analytical framework is informed by two theories, namely networked publics and media ecology. The theory of networked publics emphasises that digital technologies enable the formation of networked communities that exist and interact primarily in online spaces by sharing experiences, opinions, and views (boyd, 2008). Boyd contends that social media platforms amplify voices, build communities, and create awareness and activism. Papacharissi (2014) explores what mediated feelings of connectedness do for politics and networked publics in the digital age and concludes that even though technologies network us, it is our stories that connect us.

Media ecology theory suggests that the form of media and communication channels influence the way people perceive reality and interact with their surroundings (McLuhan, 1964). Postman (1970) offered the founding definition of media ecology where he metaphorically saw media as environments and environments as media and was explicitly concerned about their forms, effects, and evolution. Milberry (2012) indicates that the symbol systems and technologies people use to think, communicate, and represent their experiences play an integral role in how we create and understand reality. As conceptualised in this study, these two theoretical perspectives support the understanding that online spaces both mirror and reshape societal dynamics and that they can be leveraged to address GBV effectively. In other words, while YouTube provides opportunities for awareness, activism, and support, it can also reinforce negative behaviours and stereotypes.

## Method

This study draws on the social constructivism paradigm, where the goal of research mainly relies on the participants' views of the situation to better understand the world in which they live and work (Creswell, 2007). The qualitative research methodological approach employed six in-depth interviews with key informants (KIs) and a focus group discussion (FGD) comprised of eight members from whom data were gathered. In-depth interviews with participants helped to elicit rich descriptions of their experiences, emotions, interpretations, and reflections on GBV and YouTube. The FGD participants responded to the same questions, all of which sought to explore issues of social justice and social inclusion. The data collection process followed Creswell's (2007) recommendation that the researcher should gather data in a natural setting while being sensitive to the people and places under study. Consent was obtained from each participant for both in-depth interviews and FGDs prior to field research, and all the FGD participants reported that they had healed and are now public advocates against GBV. I took detailed field notes during interviews and FGDs and documented non-verbal cues and reactions.

The study participants were identified through purposive and snowball sampling. Inclusion criteria were: a GBV victim who watches YouTube videos or a journalist (including YouTubers) who may or may not be a GBV survivor but who reports on GBV on YouTube. Invitations to participate were sent through the Association of Media Women in Kenya, Media Sisters Kenya, and Women in Media WhatsApp groups. Five interview informants were GBV survivors, and one was a non-survivor. All watched YouTube videos. The sample included two journalists (one survivor, one non-survivor), who also provided perspectives as professionals. In-depth interviews used together with FGDs helped to triangulate the results.

Consistent with the standards of qualitative research, data were simultaneously collected and analysed. Narrative analysis was used to interrogate the responses created by the informants into an understanding of their experiences with GBV and YouTube videos. I thoroughly checked the transcribed data to ensure it was free from error and for qualitative reliability (consistency).

## Research Findings

This study aimed to identify the specific videos frequently watched by GBV survivors and why, to understand the lived experiences of the study participants, and to establish YouTube's potential as a source of information and spaces for the social inclusion of survivors of GBV. The discussion of findings is organised according to these objectives. Quotations drawn from the interviewees are cited as KI-1 through KI-6, and the FGD participants as FGDP-1 through FGDP-8.

### Most Frequent Videos Watched and Why

All the informants interviewed were frequent users of YouTube and logged in daily. The six informants identified the following nine channels as their most frequently watched on YouTube: Abel Mutua, Engage Talk, Muthoni's Mission, Lynn Ngugi, Usikimye Kenya, Shared Moments with Justus, Comedian YY, Tuko/Tuco-Kenya, and Legally Clueless. They also reported watching other, less prominent channels on such topics as African stories, news, health and mental wellness, historical moments, sermons, meditation, religion, music, investigation, and family matters, as well as documentaries like Africa Titanic and the Defenders' Coalition channel.

The reasons that participants provided for their engagement with YouTube videos included information and self-education, meditation and therapy, training, mental wellness, getting news, and entertainment: 'YouTube has a lot to offer and is a good way to pass time, do research to gain knowledge, engage in critical thinking and relax' (KI-5). They explained that these genres help them to connect and have a sense of belonging with their ability to contribute to discussions in the comments section. Indeed, some informants had, over the years, increasingly formed online networks with the people whom they had met online in the comments section of their watched YouTube channels.

### Informants' Lived Experiences

FGDP-7 brought up a 21 September 2023 episode 'I stayed in an abusive marriage for years, could not find the strength to walk out but I finally did' from Lynn Ngugi Network's (LNN) *LNS Rebuilding Series* that she had watched several times while noting down nuggets that assisted her in healing and rebuilding her life. Several FGD participants flagged how the comments section of this video showed how issues of therapy and social inclusion played out on YouTube and read out some specific comments from LNN to demonstrate:

> I've watched this episode and I've seen myself in it all through, from dating the wrong person, to your mum having an itch about the partner, the emotional abuse, healing and finally giving myself a second chance to love .... (Selected by FGDP-3)

> I experienced the same and gathered courage to walk out after 23 years. That was the best decision I ever made. (Selected by FGDP-5)

> I'm watching this crying, I can relate to her story I went through this for 9 years and I thank God I came out of it. (Selected by FGDP-7)

The rebuilding series has had a huge impact on my life as a woman and a mother. Thank you, Lynn ... People are healing and rebuilding their lives from hurt, pain, deceit, revenge ... etc. (Selected by FGDP-2)

LNN, this is me, this is my life story ooh I thank God for He rescued me and my 3 beautiful daughters. I can say am healed and still healing. One day I will share the story of my life. Sharing helps many many others (selected by FGDP-4). Lynn Ngugi (2023, September 21). *I stayed in an abusive marriage for years, could not find the strength to walk out but I finally did* (Video). YouTube: https://www.youtube.com/watch?v=xbleHFXYIBs&t=375s

The informants also singled out Usikimye Kenya, a channel specifically dedicated to GBV, whereas LNN is more broadly focussed on 'stories that have the ability to impact the communities around us' (Lynn Ngugi, n.d.). Unfortunately, Usikimye Kenya's presence on YouTube is not as pronounced as LNN. For instance, the channel's segment on survivor stories only has 21 videos on its playlist (Usikimye Kenya, n.d.) despite being in existence since 2019 (Kagonye, 2021).

KI-6 shared her subjective experiences and interpretations concerning YouTube and GBV. She reported not having yet come across a YouTube video specifically committed to helping GBV survivors. Unable to take in the abuse, she turned to YouTube for solace and humour. Initially, she searched for videos that directly spoke about GBV and how to handle it, but she found very little. Instead, she found solace in such channels as *The Flight Channel*, which produces content about historical flight accidents: 'Do you know I became so engrossed in the Flight Channel that I started to forget about the abuse?' Another KI revealed that she too found YouTube a useful distraction from GBV trauma: 'I was withdrawn and traumatized. I started going for therapy at a local clinic, but soon abandoned it when I found Legally Clueless on YouTube. It became my therapy' (K1-1). This informant reported being more affected by people's reactions to GBV than the act of GBV that she experienced itself:

Even a police lady told me to change the story to look like this guy wanted to rob from me but not to assault me. This lack of understanding broke my heart. Then I remembered watching something similar on YouTube. (KI-1)

KI-2 shared that she was sexually abused by her uncle at the age of 11 and carried that trauma for a long time. She had attended therapy to no avail until she watched a video called 'A Dangerous Silence: Domestic Violence Documentary'. I found it depressing but watched it to the end and realised there was too much evil in the world, especially against women, and there was nothing much I could do about my life than to pick myself up. (KI-2)

KI-3 is a survivor of sexual violence who is now working with GBV survivors living in safe homes. She narrated her ordeal as a teenager and her experience with domestic violence as a young adult:

> When I started this work, I would pity myself a lot. I would relate with what the survivors had gone through. It started with me working from a passionate point of view, then emotional. Right now, I wouldn't say radical, but my perception has changed in terms of advocating for GBV and advocating for opportunities and equality for survivors. (KI-3)

This same informant reported that the few survivors at the rescue centre watch YouTube videos, mostly comedy, and that they watch for comic relief because some of them are too young; *Churchill Television's Churchill Show* episodes are favourites among the girls.

KI-5, a journalist, had not experienced GBV, but had been reporting on these issues for such a long time that she described feeling like she had experienced it. She observed that reporting GBV was a daunting task because of empathy. She further opined that while more women than men reported GBV, men too suffer violence and stigma owing to societal stereotypes:

> When the men do report that their wives have engaged in physical conflict with them, they face stigma. I remember any time we reported that a man had been beaten by his wife, the audience was a bit skeptical since society has normalized GBV. (KI-5)

This informant also showed how YouTube had become an indispensable tool for informed, well-researched coverage of GBV stories:

> The issue of men as victims sent me to YouTube to find out the situation globally. I came across an American video, 'What happens when men are domestic violence victims?' Like in Africa, the men face stigma and will not reveal that they are abused, and the society expects them to be tough! These are the real issues of social inclusivity. (KI-5)

As a defender of human rights, KI-4's experience with GBV was primarily professional, but she had experienced a non-physical type of violence. She explained that she had been targeted on Facebook, where explicit mudslinging, vile talk, and vitriol was used against her. She further explained:

> I have also been profiled by people I believe were state agents. Recently, I led a couple of grassroots feminists in a protest where we had gone to court in a case involving a politician accused of neglecting his daughter, but we were called all sorts of names from

body shaming, being labeled as lesbians, etc. Equality? No, we have miles to cover. (KI-4)

The data from the FGD are similar to that provided by the KI interviews, but the informants from the FGD emphasised that they drew heavy inspiration from LNN even though the channel did not exclusively deal with GBV:

> I was going through a very rough patch in my marriage and wouldn't leave until I watched that episode on LNN about a Biology/Chemistry teacher who went through hell. And I asked myself, 'Why is she tolerating all this?' I then burst out laughing because in reality, I was speaking to myself! The following day, I was out. That was therapy 101. (FGDP-6)

Another FGD participant reported a similar relationship to GBV-related content:

> It's the way Justus [YouTube journalist] allows the narrator to tell their story uninterrupted. Most of Justus' shows are not about GBV, but watching them continuously contributed to my healing. The show about a lady who had been gang-raped by 24 men did it for me. I asked myself what could be worse than what that woman had gone through, so I left. (FGDP-1)

These testimonials of the informants' lived experiences with GBV and how other experiences shared on YouTube helped them to cope with their own situations demonstrate how social media platforms can be good therapeutic tools for GBV victims.

### *YouTube's Potential for Social Justice*

The data from both in-depth interviews and FGDs indicate that YouTube videos offer a platform where survivors can receive information, therapy, and social inclusion. The informants, however, saw this as a negligible contribution and suggested that more could be done to enrich this space for GBV survivors. Informant KI-5, for example, had yet to watch a channel on YouTube that is solely devoted to GBV or that especially offered comfort to survivors: 'I haven't specifically come across one that gives comfort, feedback or information on what actions survivors could take. But LNN occasionally attempts to offer linkages and personal comfort'.

The FGD informants described how YouTube fills the space once occupied by traditional social support systems. Survivors find safety in social media spaces, where they can open up, listen to others, and share their experiences. Some also obtain material and financial help, as is evident on LNN, Tuko/Tuco-Kenya, and Usikimye Kenya. Participants in both interviews and the focus groups also flagged the importance of digital media in raising awareness about GBV and exposing the prevalence of GBV and its consequences:

> Previously, there was no social media, so it appeared calm on the domestic front, save for the occasional drunk and village batterer. But social media platforms are now amplifying voices we would never have heard of. (FGDP-8)

> I think it helps in terms of showing reality. Government some-times denies that such issues happen, but when you put a face, it's a reality that those things are happening. (KI-4)

The informants observed further that YouTube videos offer anonymity, which they view as a good starting point on issues of equality because they foster safe spaces without people judging the victim on a personal level. The continual nature of content on YouTube channels like LNN was reported as a factor in its transformative potential to support and empower GBV survivors: 'If I put what happened to me, that content is ageless. I mean, a survivor can access it 10 years from now and find hope' (KI-2).

Ten of fourteen informants expressed that YouTube does offer them solace, comfort, and therapy. KI-3, for example, estimated that she receives 80% of her solace and therapy from social media spaces, as compared to socialisation with friends and family, even though there were times when certain shows brought back memories she would rather forget. A focus group participant corroborated this opinion that YouTube was not a safe place for GBV survivors since it only amplifies the negative situation and promotes exclusivity. She added that there is no social inclusivity when the target of ridicule and emotional stress is the woman and criticised LNN for this very behaviour as seen in her perspective below:

> I have a reservation about Lynn Ngugi's site because sometimes I see her as a person who reopens the wounds but doesn't offer the victims a platform for healing. Maybe issues of social inclusivity and gender equality need to be taught to these hosts. (FGDP-3)

When asked whether she had experienced content that traumatised her on YouTube, KI-1 explained that although she had not, she was aware there was 'not-so-good' content on social media. KI-3 had not witnessed negativity against her on YouTube, but she had encountered it on another social media platform: 'I would be referred to as "Jezebel," "Deceitful Eve," "the other gender," etc. on Facebook. But I have learned to block people and move on with life' (KI-3).

For KI-5 and a few other FGD members, sharing stories online can cause harm: 'I feel that these sites could be detrimental by exposing survivors to more harm if the perpetrators are still within reach and if there are no protective meas-ures' (KI-5). KI-5 also worried about the impact of unintended media exposure on the children of affected families, even when their identities had been hidden.

She added that even without facial recognition, people had a way of identifying them. Further, the comments section could traumatise survivors who are sometimes bullied and blamed for the violence.

FGDP-2 felt that language could be a barrier to YouTube's potential to help GBV survivors. She explained how she had once logged onto YouTube to follow a certain channel and discovered that it was in Kikuyu and without translation. This spoke directly to how YouTube channels can be agents of social exclusion. Another informant felt that YouTube could make its platform more survivor-centred by introducing policies that discourage shaming, trolling, or traumatising the survivors and was not doing enough to prevent undesirable behaviour against GBV survivors (KI-4). KI-5 supported policy formulation to limit the production of shows covering sensitive subjects on YouTube to those trained to handle issues around therapy and social inclusion. While YouTube does have policy in these regards (YouTube, n.d.), it could be extended to GBV:

> There should be policies to guide the procedure of creating a GBV video. The Media Council can work on policies, guided by professional and ethical principles concerning advocacy. In fact, this is the right forum to sensitize journalists on therapy and social inclusivity. (KI-5)

All the informants agreed that YouTube can promote therapy and inclusivity among GBV survivors, and that since there are agencies and organisations with the capacity and skills to offer therapy, socio-psychological support, and legal advice, YouTube should devise ways to better publicise such organisations and their services to netizens.

## Discussion

The informants of this research have provided rich data to validate YouTube as an agent for therapy and social justice for, among others, survivors of GBV. All 14 informants reported that they heavily consume YouTube for news and information, education and entertainment, meditation and critical thinking, therapy and mental wellness, research and training, and connection and belonging. These findings are consistent with media ecology theory (Milberry, 2012), in that they demonstrate how YouTube videos influence how people perceive reality and interact with their surroundings. That some informants deliberately log in to leave a comment, have their voices projected, and form networks illustrates Boyd's (2008) theory of networked publics in that this pattern of behaviour is an example of people glued together digitally by GBV as a common issue. The theory of networked publics also well accounts for concerns raised by informants about the safety of those who share their stories online and Anderson's (2014) warning about the potential harm in victims sharing their stories in virtual spaces.

The reviewed literature is consistent with the reasons informants gave for logging onto YouTube, including digital storytelling (Shishko, 2022); participatory culture (Jenkins et al., 2009); information, awareness, and educational content

(Miller & Demirbilek, 2023); sharing experiences and seeking support and validation (Shishko, 2022); connecting with others and coping with trauma (Miller & Demirbilek, 2023); granting the marginalised a voice as well as healing and therapy (Shishko, 2022). LNN was the most frequently accessed and popular YouTube channel among study participants because survivors find it relevant and important. In addition to its three series, namely the *Lynn Ngugi Show*, *LNS Rebuilding*, and *Global Inspire*, the channel's host, Lynn Ngugi, who handles a variety of themes, often covers content revolving around GBV.

None of the informants could recall watching an LNN show that covered or referenced a man who was a victim of GBV, but men are also vulnerable to GBV. Their voices have been silenced by cultural expectations such that they suffer social exclusion. In other words, the media ecology may not favour men speaking out against GBV (Papacharissi, 2014). Similarly, some women GBV survivors experience negativity and feel left out of the social justice equation. What they have experienced is similar to what happened in the Cecily Bolden case (Anderson, 2014). Anderson posits that YouTube can create a platform for stereotypes and magnify dangers for survivors.

The data show that YouTube is a powerful platform where viewers can derive therapy and inclusivity. The discussion in the focus groups flagged how the comments section on LNN has created networked publics that freely share experiences, although their identities are public. Survivors seek information, healing, therapy, belonging, and more from these channels and their hosts. One informant considered watching videos containing worse accounts than their own therapeutic, but this finding challenges PACFA's (n.d) definition of therapy as a professional intervention by trained personnel to assist with healing.

Findings also reveal that channels focussed on GBV, such as Usikimye Kenya, do not have a strong presence on YouTube as they should, yet informants thought that such interventions can do well on the YouTube platform. As described by media ecology theory, forms of media and communication channels influence the way people perceive reality and interact with their surroundings, so it is this study's position that not-for-profit organisations like Usikimye Kenya can be supported to consistently produce professional programmes on YouTube for survivors' benefit.

Another key finding was that survivors consume non-GBV videos as distractions from trauma, and that this strategy has worked. This raises questions about the role of social media in creating programmes on gender, therapy, and social inclusion. The more deliberate the media is about filling YouTube with relevant GBV content, the less unintentional perpetuation of unrealistic, stereotypical, and marginalising perceptions there will be. Indeed, another concern raised by participants was that most survivors are not aware of online support systems. Nevertheless, many survivors of GBV have found out that YouTube channels provide a safe space while recovering, where they can voice their opinions as well as challenge undeserving opinions. This finding supports the conclusions of Shishko (2022) that victims reclaim their narrative and create a sense of community on YouTube; it is consistent with networked publics theory and its framework for the study of social media platforms as public spaces to share stories, raise awareness, mobilise support, and thereby challenge traditional power dynamics.

YouTube has great potential for advocacy and raising awareness (World Bank Report, 2019). YouTube channels can produce and distribute training programmes, workshops, and seminars on safety, policy, therapy, and social inclusivity. Yet some studies indicate that social media only amplifies the negative situation (Döring & Mohseni, 2020). The informants also raised concerns about YouTube's policies that allow harmful GBV content, echoing Capella-Castro's (2021) call to action to make these platforms more inclusive, therapeutic, and survivor-centred.

## Conclusion

This chapter explored the lived experiences and subjective perceptions of YouTube viewers regarding GBV and how YouTube videos serve as sources of information and agents of therapy and social inclusion. The findings indicate that there are few YouTube channels dedicated to GBV-related issues globally, yet survivors experience comfort, peace, therapy, and a sense of belonging whenever they watch GBV-related shows on such YouTube channels as Usikimye Kenya, Tuko/Tuco-Kenya, and the Lynn Ngugi Network. YouTube also offers a platform for news, education, training, sharing experiences, raising awareness, providing support, and coping strategies. A YouTube channel viewer can spend time on the platform doing research, learning, engaging in critical thinking, meditating, and relaxing. While YouTube can help transform and empower survivors, some shows may act as triggers and there are videos likely to further harm survivors and their families. The study has also established the lack of adequate policies to protect GBV survivors on YouTube.

Social justice issues concerning gender on YouTube are real. The comments sections on GBV-related videos point towards social injustice against women in that commenters often blame victims for the violence. What is more, men who experience GBV face social exclusion mainly due to gendered social and cultural norms and are not represented on the YouTube channels with which the participants were familiar. The findings challenge definitions of therapy as a service that can only be provided by trained professionals because survivors do obtain many of the benefits of therapy from engaging with YouTube channels, their content, and their communities. Insisting that only medical practitioners offer therapy when the same can be offered on YouTube may work against social justice. There is a need for deliberate conversation about harnessing the power of YouTube, a privately owned and operated platform (by Alphabet) that generates revenue from advertising (Ceci, 2024) to tell GBV stories for the benefit of survivors rather than shareholders.

The study proposes that governments, civil society, the media, and other relevant bodies create YouTube channels that produce content to address GBV-related issues. For instance, the Ministry of Health in Kenya can create shows aimed at offering therapy from professional perspectives in addition to supporting shows like Usikimye Kenya and LNN that have shown promise. To further promote social justice, the study recommends the creation of a YouTube channel producing content that specifically addresses GBV issues that affect men. YouTube can also be petitioned to refocus its policy and better ensure the safety of GBV survivors. Although a few channels, like LNN and Tuko/Tuco-Kenya, deploy translation tools to reach larger and more diverse audiences, inclusive language should be a priority for YouTube channels on GBV. Finally, YouTube content developers (including journalists and other communicators) should receive training on sensitivity and social inclusivity to improve online reporting on GBV issues.

This study acknowledges its limitations: the sample was small, and some informants may have been reluctant to share deeper insights about their experiences. The interviews conducted reached saturation levels, however, and further studies into these issues are recommended. Quantitative anonymous surveys for comparative purposes, comparative studies between nations and societies, and a deeper content analysis of a single channel to explore the coverage of GBV are three potentially fruitful avenues to explore.

# References

Anderson, J. N. (2014). *Killing her socially: YouTube narratives of the Cicely Bolden case* [Conference presentation]. Medicine 2.0'14 Summit & World Congress, Maui, HI, USA. https://www.medicine20congress.org/index.php/med/med2014/paper/view/2209

Africa Data Hub (2024). *Silencing women* [database]. https://www.africadatahub.org/femicide-kenya

Baker, B. (2018). *Returning to tech, and assessing commitment*. Medium. https://medium.com/@brianaclairbaker/returning-to-tech-c7f35462c551

boyd, d. (2008). Why youth (heart) social network sites: The role of networked publics in teenage social life. In D. Buckingham (Ed.), *Youth, identity, and digital media* (pp. 1–26). MIT Press.

Capella-Castro, A. A. (2021). *Ley Olimpia: Examining policymaking around digital violence* [Unpublished undergraduate thesis, University of San Francisco]. https://repository.usfca.edu/cgi/viewcontent.cgi?article=1047&context=honors

Ceci, L. (2024, May 24). *YouTube: Global advertising revenues as of Q1 2024*. Statistica. https://www.statista.com/statistics/289657/youtube-global-quarterly-advertising-revenues/#:~:text=YouTube's%20worldwide%20advertising%20revenues%20amounted,the%20first%20quarter%20of%202023.

Citizen TV. (2023, May 15). *Monday report: Sexual & Gender-based violence* [Video]. YouTube. https://www.youtube.com/watch?v=F5SNQOv7CjQ

Creswell, J. W. (2007). *Qualitative inquiry and research design: Choosing among five approaches* (2nd ed.). Sage Publications.

Döring, N., & Mohseni, M. (2020). Gendered hate speech in YouTube and YouNow comments: Results of two content analyses. *Studies in Communication and Media, 9,* 62–88. https://doi.org/10.5771/2192-4007-2020-1-62

Gender Violence Recovery Centre (GVRC). (2022). *Facts about GBV*. https://gvrc.or.ke/facts-about-gbv/

Jenkins, H., Purushotma, R., Weigel, M., Clinton, K., & Robison, A. J. (2009). *Confronting the challenges of participatory culture*. MIT Press. https://doi.org/10.7551/mitpress/8435.003.0011

Kagonye, F. (2021). *Kenya's first non-governmental gender-based violence call centre launched in Kayole*. The Standard. https://www.standardmedia.co.ke/evewoman/lady-speak/article/2001405430/kenyas-first-non-governmental-gender-based-violence-call-centre-launched-in-kayole

Kassova, L., & Addy, R. (2022). *How Africa's first gender desk succeeded (and lessons for future initiatives)*. AKAS. https://fullerproject.org/how-africas-first-gender-desk-succeeded/

Kenya News Agency. (2023). Four in 10 women in Kenya have faced physical or sexual violence from an intimate partner, KDHS reveals. https://www.kenyanews.go.ke/four-in-10-women-in-kenya-have-faced-physical-or-sexual-violence-from-an-intimate-partner-kdhs-reveals/

Lowery, T. (2023, February 20). *What is social justice? A short guide for activists-in-the-making*. Global Citizen. https://www.globalcitizen.org/en/content/what-is-social-justice-guide-for-activists-equity

Lynn Ngugi. (n.d.). *About*. https://www.youtube.com/@LynnNgugi

Lynn Ngugi. (2023). *I stayed in an abusive marriage for years, could not find the strength to walk out but I finally did*. YouTube. https://www.youtube.com/watch?v=xb1eHFXYIBs

McLuhan, M. (1964). *Understanding media: The extensions of man*. McGraw-Hill.

Milberry, K. (2012). *Media ecology*. Oxford Bibliographies. https://doi.org/10.1093/obo/9780199756841-0054

Miller, K., & Demirbilek, M. (2023). The role of social media in the fight against gender violence. In D. Mishra (Ed.), *Cyberfeminism and gender violence in social media* (pp. 90–99). IGI Global. https://doi.org/10.4018/978-1-6684-8893-5.ch006

Nation Media Group. (n.d.). *About NMG*. https://www.nationmedia.com/who-we-are/

Ndaka, F. M. (2023). *Wakurugenzi* networks: Reframing Kenyan vernaculars of gender/gendering in Abel Mutua's YouTube channel. *Eastern African Literary and Cultural Studies, 9*(1), 19–40. https://doi.org/10.1080/23277408.2022.2106609

Papacharissi, Z. (2014). Affective publics and structures of storytelling: Sentiment, events and mediality. *Information, Communication & Society, 19*(3), 307–324. https://doi.org/10.1080/1369118X.2015.1109697

Postman, N. (1970). The reformed English curriculum. In high school. In A. C. Eurich (Ed.), *1980: The shape of the future in American secondary education* (pp. 160–168). Pitman.

Psychotherapy and Counselling Federation of Australia (PACFA). (n.d.). *What is therapy?* https://pacfa.org.au/portal/Portal/Community/What-is-Therapy.aspx

Shishko, B. (2022). Storytelling in the digital era: Perspectives on age and gender. *TRAMES, 26*(4), 397–411. https://doi.org/10.3176/tr.2022.4.03

United Nations High Commissioner for Refugees (UNHRC). (n.d.). *Gender-based violence*. https://www.unhcr.org/what-we-do/protect-human-rights/protection/gender-based-violence

Usikimye Kenya. (n.d.). *Usikimye survivors' stories*. https://www.youtube.com/playlist?list=PLKSO2AQfdRPmME_zMNAgsW2herUwAjqfI

Vahedi, L., Stark, L., Ding, R., Masboungi, C., Erskine, D., Poulton, C., & Seff, I. (2024). A qualitative investigation of gender-based violence prevention and response using digital technologies in low resource settings and refugee populations. *European Journal of Psychotraumatology, 15*(1), 1–16. https://doi.org/10.1080/20008066.2024.2347106

World Bank. (n.d.). *Social inclusion*. https://www.worldbank.org/en/topic/social-inclusion

World Bank Report. (2019). *Gender-based violence (violence against women and girls)*. https://www.worldbank.org/en/topic/socialsustainability/brief/violence-against-women-and-girls

World Vision. (2022). *Facts, FAQs, history, what you need to know about gender-based violence*. https://www.wvi.org/stories/facts-faqs-history-what-you-need-know-about-gender-based-violence

YouthActionNet. (2015, October 28). *Saying 'no' to gender-based violence in Kenya*. https://www.youtube.com/watch?v=KaHy3Rml7WM

YouTube. (n.d.). *Community guidelines*. https://www.youtube.com/howyoutubeworks/policies/community-guidelines/

Chapter 13

# Community Radio in Building Resilience Against Gender-based Violence in Tanzania: A Case of Radio Sengerema

*Dianus Josephat Ishengoma*

*University of Dar es Salaam, Tanzania*

## Abstract

Gender-based violence (GBV) represents a profound violation of human dignity that substantially impacts millions of individuals, and Sub-Saharan Africa faces particularly severe challenges. This study assesses Sengerema community radio's contribution to addressing GBV, with a particular focus on community participation in radio dialogues. Its mixed-methods research design comprises collecting data through in-depth interviews with radio managers and editors, focus group discussions with programme producers, presenters, and news reporters, as well as a quantitative content analysis of 100 weekly radio programmes. The findings reveal that the radio station has undertaken some initiatives to involve community members in dialogues on GBV, and men exhibit a higher level of participation in these dialogues than women. While the radio station devoted effort to influencing attitudes towards GBV, its capacity to effectively tackle the issue is constrained. Challenges include financial limitations, inadequate support from politicians and local leaders, and deeply entrenched cultural practices. The study recommends increasing dedicated programmes on GBV, involving local leaders in broadcasting plans, providing education to address the cultural factors that obstruct women's participation in

Gender and Media Representation: Perspectives from Sub-Saharan Africa, 191–206
doi:10.1108/978-1-83608-406-820251014

decision-making, and increasing creativity and innovation to ensure financial sustainability to improve effectiveness.

*Keywords*: Gender-based violence; community media; social justice; women; communication; Tanzania

## Introduction

The UN Inter-Agency Standing Committee Task Force on Gender and Humanitarian Assistance (2005) defines GBV as any act committed against a person's will based on socially ascribed gender differences between males and females. They note that GBV is often used interchangeably with the term 'violence against women' due to the subordinate positions women hold in society that make them more vulnerable to socioeconomic injustices. The CARE International Report (2014) covering 2011–2013, however, highlights that men and boys can also be subjected to GBV, particularly when they go against prescribed social norms. GBV is a widespread violation of human rights with a particular prevalence in developing countries (Muluneh et al., 2020, p. 2). In Africa, GBV remains a pervasive problem contributing to human rights violations, increasing women's vulnerability to reproductive health issues, and limiting their participation in productive roles (PEPFAR, 2016, p. 65). GBV affects not only women, but also children, men, and entire families in that it perpetuates a culture of fear, mistrust, and intimidation (Muluneh et al., 2020, p. 2). Consequently, several countries, especially in Sub-Saharan Africa, have incorporated GBV strategies into budgeting and planning policies to address sociocultural values that contribute to GBV (PEPFAR, 2016, p. 66).

Tanzania, like other African countries, still experiences widespread cases of GBV in its communities. The Tanzania Demographic and Health Survey for 2015–2016 (Ministry of Health [Tanzania Mainland], Ministry of Health [Zanzibar], National Bureau of Statistics, Office of the Chief Government Statistician, & ICF, 2023) highlights that more than 20% of women aged 15–49 in Tanzania have experienced sexual violence, and approximately 44% of married women have faced both physical and sexual violence. Statistics from the Inspector General of Police, Tanzania (2021, p. 21) indicate that 42,414 cases of GBV were reported across the country in 2020. The report highlights that the most prevalent forms of GBV are rape, human trafficking, homicide, child desertion, and kidnapping. The Sengerema district in the Mwanza region of Tanzania is a studied area rife with GBV incidents (Statistics from the Inspector General of Police, Tanzania, 2017, pp. 75–78) which is infamous for such physical and psychological violence.

The national government of Tanzania has been promoting gender equality and combating GBV through the enactment of laws and formulation of policies. For example, freedom from GBV is a goal of Tanzania's Development Vision 2025, which aims to create a strong economy and enhance the quality of life (PEPFAR, 2016, p. 65). Notable legislative changes include the 1998 amendment to the Sexual Offences (Special Provisions) Act, the 2011 Female Genital Mutilation Act, and the strengthening of the Marriage Act, which mandates marriage equality (Tanzania Women Lawyers Association [TAWLA] (2014, p. 42). Such institutional reforms to proactively prevent GBV as the establishment of gender focal points in each ministry and the creation of gender desks within the Police Force have also been enacted (Simmons et al., 2016, p. 37).

While the government has intensified its efforts to promote gender equality and combat GBV, community media have additional roles to play that complement these efforts within communities. Early communication models derived from modernisation and dependency theories of development in 1980s have faced substantial criticism for neglecting a fundamental element of participatory (Mefalopulos, 2008, p. 4). As a result, the participatory communication approach, advocating for the engagement of communities in addressing development challenges, emerged (Freire, 1997, p. 30). This approach underscores the importance of involving communities in the fight against GBV and highlights the vital role of community radio in this endeavour.

Many scholars have proposed different definitions of what constitutes 'community radio'. Onyenankeya and Salawu (2023) define community radio as a localised radio station serving a small geographic area and often supported by local listeners or social groups. Studies conducted by the Media Institute of Southern Africa (2000) reveal diverse responses when people are asked about the meaning of community radio. Some respondents treated community radio as a medium for communicating local activities and covering community events mostly in languages to facilitate understanding, whereas other respondents insisted that community radio should air programmes that address the development challenges in its community. This chapter adopts a working definition of community radio that integrates the various features addressed by many scholars: community radio is a broadcasting radio station located in a specific geographical area; funded by the government, donors, or the community of interest; that aims to address challenges affecting people in that area and which has a significant influence on the community members through programming and coverage.

In Tanzania, community radio has emerged as a participatory medium that plays a crucial role in addressing a wide range of development challenges, including poverty, agriculture, elections, women's affairs, conflict, human rights, gender inequality, education, and cultural beliefs (Faisal & Alhassan, 2018; Khan et al., 2017; Wabwire, 2013). Community radio helps address cultural barriers and disseminate information on GBV by providing platforms, incentives, and dialogue tailored to the needs of the communities (Wabwire, 2013, p. 43). While scholars in Tanzania recognise the importance of community radio in addressing sociocultural inequalities and injustices (Bamwenda, et al., 2015; Manenosabin & Charles, 2019; Mwidima, 2019), there remains a gap in evidence regarding its role in combatting GBV, particularly in rural areas. This chapter investigates the Sengerema community radio station's interventions in building resilience against GBV and the extent to which community members participate in radio dialogues on GBV.

### Brief Overview of Community Radio

The history of community radio can be traced to the 1940s in Latin America, when the mainstream media as a mode of communication failed to address poverty and injustices in marginalised communities (Okinyi, 2019, p. 158). In Europe, community radio began to serve as an alternative to public broadcasting in the 1960s (Fraser & Estrada, 2001, p. 30). In Africa, its significance grew with democratic processes in the 1990s and was supported by organisations like UNESCO that recognise community radio's potential as a tool for the promotion and amplification of free expression by the voices of marginalised communities (Mrutu, 2008, p. 3). In Tanzania, private mainstream radio stations emerged in the 1990s but had limited reach to marginalised communities (Katunzi, 2014, p. 446). Community radio stations began operating in 1993, focussing on local issues like farming, literacy, and health (Myers, 2011, p. 11). The rise of these stations reflects the implementation of Structural Adjustment Policies in the late 1980s and early 1990s that advocated for the liberalisation of radio airwaves and promoted democratic reforms (Mpehongwa, 2024, p. 35).

Radio Sengerema was established in 2001 as an initiative managed by the Sengerema Multipurpose Community Telecentre, with the primary goal of facilitating the diffusion of technology to spur development in rural areas of Sengerema and the nearby communities. In September 2003, the radio became an independent subsidiary of the telecentre and shifted its aims not only to the diffusion of technology in rural areas but also the provision of other information beneficial to society. Sengerema community radio is now a long-serving station and has helped address development challenges through education and information sharing in the Sengerema community and its Lake region neighbours (Bamwenda et al., 2015, p. 24). One assistant radio manager asserted that the station has been instrumental in disseminating information on disease prevention for such killers as cholera and HIV/AIDS and on scientific farming methods. Additionally, it fosters gender equality by providing platforms that challenge gender stereotypes, promote equal opportunities, and advocate for human rights (Bamwenda et al., 2015, p. 25). It is thus an appropriate platform for a case study of how community radio can and does address GBV in Sub-Saharan Africa.

## Theoretical Framework

This study's theoretical framework is rooted in participatory communication theory (PCT), first introduced by Freire in 1968 as a response to earlier development and communication paradigms like modernisation and dependency (Freire, 1997). PCT asserts the fundamental importance of people's power in achieving sustainable development and makes participation a crucial element in sustainable development strategies. This theory places a strong emphasis on dialogical and horizontal communication, the empowerment of communities, ownership, and the consideration of cultural context as major factors in generating the necessary development outcomes (Sylvester, 2016). PCT considers development as a result of collaboration and the involvement of all stakeholders such that communication plays a pivotal role (Ali & Sonderling, 2017, p. 82). The theory posits that development failures, poverty, and conflicts stem from top-down planning and a lack of involvement of local communities in programme identification and design for specific local contexts (Ali & Sonderling, 2017, p. 81; Mosse, 2001,

p. 28), whereas two-way communication fosters trust, explores opportunities, facilitates knowledge and experience sharing, and creates a broad-based consensus, all of which contribute to the success and sustainability of development efforts (Mefalopulos, 2008, p. 4). PCT further advocates for a culture of specificity and encourages a people-centred, holistic development model and has been used by several scholars (e.g., Dunu, 2015; Khan et al., 2017; Manenosabin & Charles, 2019) to establish the role of communication platforms in engaging communities to address development challenges. The foundational principles of PCT, namely engagement, empowerment, open dialogue, and endogenous action (Ali & Sonderling, 2017, p. 94), served as guiding concepts for developing the key questions and assumptions regarding community radio intervention in addressing GBV issues. This chapter demonstrates community radio as a unique medium that aligns with the core principles of PCT by promoting community participation as feedback, sharing, and interrogation in dialogues related to GBV.

## Methodology

The study was conducted at Radio Sengerema in Sengerema district, located in the Mwanza region of Tanzania. This radio station was selected as a case study because it is situated in a rural area in the Lake Zone of Tanzania where according to Statistics from the Inspector General of Police, Tanzania (2021, p. 11) incidents of GBV are common. A mixed research approach, incorporating qualitative and quantitative methodologies, was adopted to provide a comprehensive understanding of the phenomenon and enable complementary analysis of qualitative information with quantitative data (Creswell & Creswell, 2018, p. 337). The research utilised a quantitative content analysis from a sample of 100 weekly radio programmes, in-depth interviews with two radio managers and five editors, and focus group discussions (FGDs) with 12 programme producers, news reporters, and radio presenters. Whereas in-depth interviews were held with editors and managers selected purposefully from the radio station to gain insight into their experiences and perspectives on involving community members in radio programmes to address GBV, FGDs were employed to collect data from two separate groups of six participants each, composed of radio programme producers and presenters. Purposive sampling was utilised to select 100 recent radio programmes from five weekly special broadcasts aired by Radio Sengerema over the six months between February and July 2019 for content analysis. The selection of recent programmes reflects the lack of accessible records for earlier broadcasts, and the chosen programmes specifically focussed on development issues in which GBV was a central concern that Radio Sengerema aimed to address. The five weekly programmes subjected to quantitative content analysis were: *Haki ya Mwananchi* [The Rights of a Citizen]; *Sauti ya Walemavu* [The Voice of the Physically Handicapped); *Pambazuko* [Sunrise]; *Ukurasawa Vijana* [Youth Corner]; and *Maadili Mema* [Good Ethics]. The coding of the transcripts of these programmes' broadcasts included themes on the availability of GBV content and the types of sources involved (female or male, experts or laypeople, etc.), of violence discussed, and of community participation. These themes and concepts were analysed using a content analysis matrix and descriptive and inferential statistics. Qualitative data collected through in-depth interviews and FGDs was recorded and stored using notetaking and tape-recording and was manually analysed using the protocols for thematic analysis outlined by Robert Weber (2008). To ensure the respondents' safety and meet ethical standards, the researcher obtained a research clearance from the University of Dar es Salaam, Tanzania that was then presented to relevant authorities in the study areas, including the Mwanza Regional Administrative Secretary, Sengerema District Administrative Secretary, and the Sengerema radio manager. All participants were informed about the study's purpose and their roles before their consent.

## Findings and Discussion

These findings are the results of data collected from three different kinds of sources: in-depth interviews with radio editors and managers, FGDs with programme producers and reporters, and 100 radio programme segments. The discussion is organised around a qualitative description of themes coded throughout the study, and each of the themes is complemented by quantitative data derived from the content analysis of the broadcasts.

### Radio Programmes on Building Resilience Against GBV

Radio Sengerema has taken diverse steps to build resilience against GBV practices within the community. During their interviews, the radio managers and editors emphasised that the radio station's policy and practices dictated that approximately 90% of the radio content cater to the needs and aspirations of the community, while the remaining 10% cover general content, including national issues. Editors and managers attested that the radio station puts such emphasis on community concerns, that GBV, which is common in the area, has been prioritised in their programming. They explained how a wide range of programme formats, from radio news bulletins to documentaries and special segments, have played a pivotal role in shifting people's perspectives on GBV practices in the community:

> We have managed to change the minds of community members regarding their perception of GBV in this community, and now we are glad that these incidents are being minimized, if not abandoned. (Male interview respondent, Sengerema, 2019)

To fulfil the station's mandate to focus on severe issues in the community for change, the station made a concerted effort to translate statistical data into accessible information and provide platforms for discussions on the various special issues and needs of individuals who have experienced GBV. Additionally, the radio manager and editors emphasised the importance of educating and supporting individuals with special needs, who are particularly vulnerable to all forms of violence. They further explained that the radio station has established a supportive system that facilitates gatherings for vulnerable individuals, such as those with disabilities, to share their experiences and collectively discuss strategies to safeguard their lives.

This statement from an interview respondent well captures quite a few of the responses provided by the editors:

> We have a program titled *Sauti ya Walemavu* (The Voice of People with Disability), which provides a platform for individuals with disabilities and other victims of violence to engage in discussions aimed at putting an end to violence against them. (Male interview respondent, Sengerema, 2019)

The radio station has also used its programming that educates the community to combat GBV by informing women and children about the social and cultural factors linked to GBV. During FGDs, radio producers and reporters highlighted that the radio initiatives have fostered a deep understanding of the root causes of violence against women and children, particularly those stemming from cultural backgrounds. This education also includes practical information about how to escape violence and utilise legal avenues to report it. The radio producers stated that they have also focussed on educating their listeners about the country's laws on GBV by engaging legal experts on the programmes. They added that many community members commit GBV because they do not know that Tanzanian and international law prohibits these acts.

The editors and producers expressed similar perspectives on the kind of education that Radio Sengerema provided:

> We have managed to provide extensive education, especially to women and children who are the primary targets of violence. This education focuses on resisting cultural practices associated with GBV and on how to report such incidents when they occur in their community. (Male interview respondent, Sengerema, 2019)

> People commit these crimes without being informed of the laws that prohibit these acts; therefore, it has been our role as the Radio Sengerema to educate people through our programs, news coverage, and bringing perpetrators to the program. (Female interview respondent, Sengerema, 2019)

The editors and producers also stated that they play a major role in helping women liberate themselves from patriarchal ideologies and socially sanctioned GBV. They noted that in Sengerema, a patriarchal society, programme producers work hard to encourage women to liberate themselves both culturally and economically by highlighting opportunities available to women in the community. In other words, they argue that building women's confidence is crucial to the fight against GBV:

> Women have no say in the family; they only depend on the men
> who, consequently, use this loophole as a way to commit violence
> against women. But since our programs engage more women,
> we have witnessed different changes in women's live. (IDIs, male
> respondent, Sengerema, 2019)

These findings demonstrate that Radio Sengerema has undertaken several initiatives to combat GBV in their Lake Region community. The station heavily prioritises local community concerns, translates statistical data about GVB into easily accessible information, provides education about the law to the community, and actively challenges harmful cultural practices that contribute to violence. Respondents were confident that these efforts have led to a transformation of public perceptions and empowerment of marginalised groups, especially women and individuals with special needs, and Radio Sengerema's success confirms such studies as Obagboye (2021) and Muluneh et al. (2020) that identify four kinds of initiatives are needed to address the challenges of GBV in communities: addressing community attitudes and cultural barriers, empowering communities, providing timely information on GBV, and strengthening laws and policies. What is more, Radio Sengerema confirms the assumptions of PCT by demonstrating the importance of community media in empowering the community to participate in addressing development challenges.

### Community Members Participate in Radio Dialogues on GBV

This theme gave insight into how community members were engaged in addressing GVB in their programming. The responses from interviews and FGDs indicate that members of the Sengerema community, but particularly its men, had more opportunities to participate in radio programmes addressing GBV compared to individuals from outside the region. The radio producers highlighted that since the primary clients of the radio programmes in Sengerema are the community members themselves, the content produced is inherently linked to the community's interests. One radio producer highlighted how participation is incorporated into interview segments:

> We first consult with local government leaders in Sengerema
> before approaching individual community members to express
> their views, later on, we merge the ideas and input from our com-
> munity leaders with those provided by our community members
> to ensure that our programs are inclusive and comprehensive.
> (Male/female interview respondent, Sengerema, 2019)

Two distinct types of direct community participation in production were reported by the manager and editors. The first was the participation of community members in the preparation of the programmes as sources of stories or information, who have given permission for the sharing of their experience in the programmes produced. The second was sharing their views about the content of a programme during or after its broadcast through the provision of a platform. In other words, community members also participate by giving feedback on programming by calling, sending an SMS, or posting on Facebook, WhatsApp, or other social media:

> We invite both women who have experienced violence and men who are often seen as the main perpetrators, to discuss these issues together. We also involve experts, such as those from the Gender Desk, to provide their perspectives. (Female FGD respondent, Sengerema, 2019)

Furthermore, it was established that the emphasis on programme participation is often on victims of violence, presumed perpetrators, and those influenced by or connected to instances of violence. To facilitate such involvement, the radio station collaborates with influential organisations and major mainstream media outlets to disseminate the radio's agenda effectively:

> We involve stakeholders like the BBC and UNESCO, especially for addressing youth violence during puberty. We also include parents, leaders, and experts such as doctors and gender professionals from the community. (Male FGD respondent, Sengerema, 2019)

When discussing the phenomenon of lower rates of participation among women in comparison to men in these programmes, both interview and FGD respondents highlighted the heavier burden of domestic responsibilities on women in Sengerema. They are often obliged to remain at home, where they tend to family and reproductive roles that leave limited time to engage with radio programmes. Furthermore, respondents pointed out that the patriarchal system entrenched in Sengerema significantly limits women's roles in decision-making, further restricting their availability to participate in initiatives like radio programmes. As one producer put it:

> Women in this region have limited time available for engagements such as attending radio programs. The prevailing patriarchal culture in this society constrains women's freedoms significantly. Consequently, women have fewer opportunities to participate in radio programs addressing gender-based violence. (Female interview respondent, Sengerema, 2019)

These findings show that Radio Sengerema has initiated significant efforts to engage community members in discussions about GBV, and the limited participation of women in these programmes highlights the tenacity of deep-rooted patriarchal structures in Africa that deny women recognition and perpetuate gender inequalities (Dunu, 2015, p. 178; O'Brien, 2019, p. 793). Addressing these disparities is crucial. Initiatives must challenge these norms by actively involving women in radio programming and other development efforts and promoting gender diversity in decision-making processes to dismantle entrenched patriarchy and effectively address issues like GBV.

## Ways of Community Participation in the Programme

A content analysis of 100 segments from five weekly programmes supplemented the thematic analysis of data gathered from FGDs and interviews. Four methods of community participation were identified: mobile calls or SMS during live or recorded broadcasts (42.75%), live participation in the studio (31.3%), involvement as sources of GBV-related information (22.9%), and participation through the station's social media accounts (3.05%, Table 13.1). The analysis of 100 segments supports the answers from interviews and FGDs on the opportunities for the community members to participate in community radio programmes.

## Type of Community Participants in GBV Radio Programmes

Six categories of community members participating in GBV radio programmes as either news sources or guests were identified: indigenous women only, indigenous men only, both indigenous men and women, community experts, political and religious leaders and members of civil society. The indigenous participants were categorised into three groups to highlight the differences between programmes that involved only women, only men, and those that involved both men and women simultaneously.

Around 24% of the participants were from civil society, 23% were community experts, and 15% were community leaders. Programmes with indigenous participants included 19% involving both indigenous men and women, 12% with men only, and 7% with women only (Fig. 13.1).

These findings indicate a significant involvement from civil society and experts and less participation from indigenous men and women. The notable gender gap, with men more active, reflects persistent patriarchal ideologies and gender stereotypes that undermine women's influence in social and economic development (Kumari & Joshi, 2015, p. 45).

Table 13.1.   Ways of Participating in the Radio Programmes (Content Analysis).

| Category | Frequency | Percentage (%) |
| --- | --- | --- |
| Through calls/SMS during the programme on GVB | 56 | 42.7 |
| Through the station's social media accounts | 4 | 3.1 |
| Participating in the studio during a live or recorded programme on GBV | 41 | 31.3 |
| Being used as a source of information or news on GBV | 30 | 22.9 |
| Total | 131 | 100.0 |

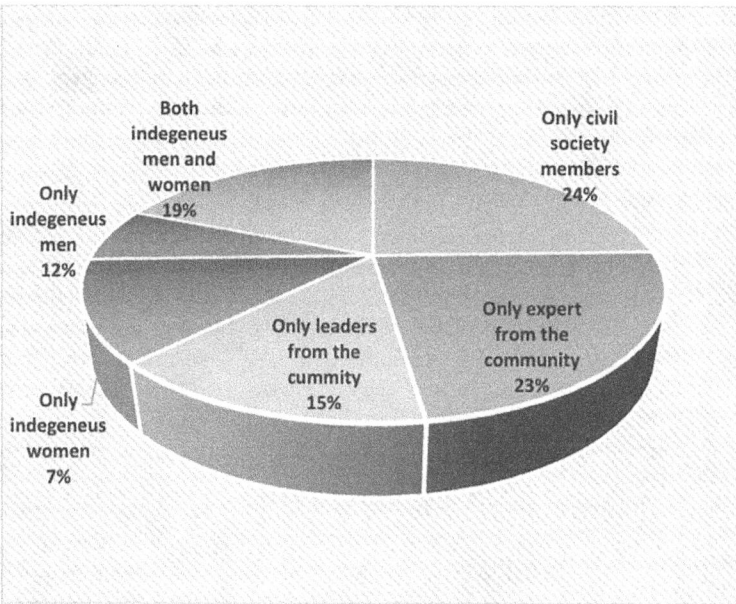

Fig. 13.1.   Members Participating in Sengerema Community Radio. *Source*: Field Data (2019).

## Challenges to Sengerema Community Radio's GBV Programming

Radio producers, editors, and reporters provided rich, detailed data about the many and diverse challenges they have faced in addressing GBV in their programmes. Participants' answers revealed three categories as the most important challenges.

### Poor Cooperation from Local Leaders and Politicians

Participants reported that local community and political leaders appear to obstruct efforts to disclose the perpetrators of GBV on Radio Sengerema. They reported that these leaders sometimes cooperated with the perpetrators. Respondents alleged that leaders took bribes from the girl's parent or the culprits of childhood rape in cases that Radio Sengerema was investigating and that this corruption also resulted in failure to prosecute such cases of GBV due to a 'lack' of evidence:

> I once decided to cover a story on a girl-child who was raped and impregnated in the Mbayanda area. In the process of covering this story, the parents were not ready to collaborate with me. When I tried to investigate further, I discovered that the village leaders and parents had resorted to corruption to muddle the case. (Male FGD respondent, Sengerema, 2019)

This concern raised by radio producers echoes Medie's (2013) argument that responses to GBV, whether through media or legal measures, are always also shaped by power structures and political will. Many African states have laws criminalising GBV, including rape, but enforcement is often weak, few cases reach the courts, and victims are pressured to seek reconciliation instead of prosecution. Journalists and reporters, as part of the system, are limited by these circumstances.

*Cultural Challenges*

Participants also cited cultural challenges rooted in the traditional patriarchal values of the Sengerema region as an obstacle to the radio's efforts to address GBV. In Sengerema, men are perceived as authority figures, and women have less power in resource ownership and decision-making. During discussions, it was highlighted that radio journalists often needed to seek permission from men to interview women and children about GBV incidents, and these men were sometimes reluctant to grant such permission due to fear of implication in scandals. These patriarchal values prevented producers from addressing crucial issues related to GBV:

> As you know, the Sengerema community lives under the traditional patriarchal system whereby the final say comes from men. This male chauvinism has affected our programs or stories because for important issues we cannot interview women without the consent of men, especially in rural areas. This problem has been a hindrance because most of the time men will not allow their wives to express themselves freely in our programs. (Female FGD respondent, Sengerema, 2019)

This cultural stereotyping of women increases their vulnerability to GBV because radio producers face difficulties in obtaining information on GBV, particularly when women and children are affected within their families:

> Many women in this area endure gender-based violence like battery and rape but hesitate to report it due to cultural barriers, particularly the culture of silence. They fear societal labels and potential isolation from both women and men if they speak out against their husbands or perpetrators. (Male FGD respondent, Sengerema, 2019)

Cultural barriers contributing to the silence among GBV victims necessitate collective action from the community, government, and other entities at all levels. These barriers are further highlighted by Shivram and Mu-azu (2017), which explored the impact of FM radio broadcasts in local dialects on rural communities in the Tamale metropolis of northern Ghana using survey methods to collect data from select communities. Their findings revealed that cultural beliefs, religious convictions, and the political landscape of a given society significantly influence the development and progress of media. Addressing these cultural factors through community education is crucial to enhancing women's participation in decision-making and overcoming sociocultural barriers that disadvantage them in development.

*Financial Challenges*

During FGDs, insufficient funding emerged as a critical issue affecting both the production and outreach of Radio Sengerema's GBV-related programming. Participants highlighted, for example, the practical problems posed by limited transportation budgets to reach rural victims and perpetrators. They also noted how the absence of essential facilities like vehicles and modern production equipment constrained journalists' ability to cover GBV stories effectively across diverse audiences:

> The challenges occur when we want to visit news sources. We sometimes lack money for transport, as we have no car for news or programs and, sometimes, when we ask for the bus fare, we are neglected unless a special leader is visiting that particular place. (FGD, female respondent, Sengerema, 2019)

Financial challenges are a widely recognised major obstacle to the sustainability of community radio stations. Wesso (2007) highlighted the reluctance of local businesses to advertise on community radio stations. Furthermore, Mrutu (2008) and Katunzi (2014) found that fees imposed by signal providers create a significant, sometimes insurmountable burden, especially for smaller, community-oriented stations without substantial financial backing from the government or private sector. Indeed, Mrutu (2008) proposes that when a community radio station fails due to financial challenges, governments should intervene to save that radio station for the interest of the people.

## Conclusion

Radio Sengerema demonstrates that community radio has the potential to address community-specific issues. This study explored this rural Tanzanian community radio station's endeavours to tackle GBV as part of its development agenda. While the station predominantly focuses on development topics, expanding its coverage of GBV as a developmental issue is essential. The research also highlights the pivotal role of radio programmes in educating and informing the community and fostering positive shifts in attitudes towards GBV. These programmes have ignited debates on GBV, empowered women to share their experiences, advocated for marginalised voices, and fostered community involvement in exposing GBV misconduct. These milestones, while significant, demonstrate the ongoing need for such further efforts as increasing dedicated programmes on GVB. Indeed, the findings reveal a limited level of community engagement in the radio programmes and a marked gender disparity: women are less involved than men. This observation highlights the shortage of opportunities for community involvement in GBV programmes and the urgent need for increased creativity and innovation, especially in empowering women.

Respondents identified three major categories of hindrances to the radio station's efforts in addressing GBV in the Sengerema area during interviews and FGDs: political corruption, persistent patriarchal values, and funding. These obstacles are consistent with previous studies examining what significantly impacts a community radio's effectiveness in addressing the development agenda (Katunzi, 2014; Mrutu, 2008; Wesso, 2007). To overcome these challenges, it is crucial to employ PCT strategies, like involving local leaders and politicians in radio plans, providing community education to address cultural barriers that hinder women's participation in decision-making, and promoting the sustainability of community radio stations. Despite Radio Sengerema's efforts to address GBV issues, there is still considerable room for improvement that can maximise its impact on the prevalence of GBV and foster positive community transformation.

# References

Ali, A. C., & Sonderling, A. (2017). Factors affecting participatory communication for development: The case of local development organization in Ethiopia. *Jurnal Komunikasi, 33*(1), 80–97. https://doi.org/10.17576/JKMJC-2017-3301-06

Bamwenda, G., Mashindano, O., Nzuki, M., & Hassan, A. (Eds.). (2015). *Poverty and environment initiative (PEI): A study to assess institutional capacity and mapping of best practices and development opportunities in Sengerema District*. Economic and Social Research Foundation.

Care International Report. (2014). *Challenging gender-based violence worldwide: CARE's program evidence* (p. 25). Retrieved June 9, 2014, from http://care.ca/sites/default/files/publications/Challenging%20GBV%20Worldwide-CARE_s%20program%20evidence.pdf

Creswell, J. W., & Creswell, J. D. (2018). *Research design: Qualitative, quantitative and mixed method approaches* (5th ed.). Sage Publications.

Dunu, I. V. (2015). Women participation in community radio in Nigeria: Towards marginalization or exclusion? Analysis of selected campus community radio stations. *European Scientific Journal, 11*(20), 177–193. https://eujournal.org/index.php/esj/article/view/5960

Faisal, A. M., & Alhassan, A. (2018). Community access and participation in community radio broadcast: Case of Radio Gaakii, Ghana. *Journal of Development and Communication Studies, 5*(2), 85–102. https://doi.org/10.4314/jdcs.v5i2

Fraser, C., & Estrada, S. R. (2001). *Community radio handbook*. UNESCO.

Freire, P. (1997). *Pedagogy of the oppressed* (Rev. ed.). Continuum.

IASC Task Force on Gender and Humanitarian Assistance. (2005). *Guidelines: Gender-based violence interventions in humanitarian assistance: Focusing on prevention of and response to sexual violence in emergencies*. Inter-Agency Standing Committee. https://interagencystandingcommittee.org/iasc-sub-working-group-gender-and-humanitarian-action/iasc-guidelines-gender-based-violence-interventions-humanitarian-settings-2005/

Inspector General of Police, Tanzania. (2021). *Crime statistics and road safety events January – December 2020* [*Takwimu za hali ya uhalifu na matukio ya usalama barabarani Januari–Desemba 2020*]. Tanzania Police Force Ministry of Internal Affairs; National Statistics Office Ministry of Finance and Planning. https://www.nbs.go.tz/nbs/takwimu/Crime/Crime_Report_January_to_%20December_2020.pdf

Inspector General of Police. (2017). *Crime and traffic incidents statistics report January–December 2016.* https://www.nbs.go.tz/nbs/takwimu/trade/CrimeStats_Jan-Des2016English.pdf

Katunzi, A. (2014). Assessment of community radio in Tanzania: Case study of Orkonerei Radio Service FM. *African Communication Research, 7*(3), 445–577.

Khan, A. A., Khan, M. R., Hassan, M. Ahmed, F., & Shah R. H. (2017). Role of community radio for community development in Bangladesh. *The International Technology Management Review, 6*(3), 94–102. https://doi.org/10.2991/itmr.2017.6.3.3

Kumari, A., & Joshi, H. (2015). Gender stereotyped portrayal of women in the media: Perception and impact on adolescent. *IOSR Journal of Humanities and Social Science, 20*(4, v. 2), 44–52. https://iosrjournals.org/iosr-jhss/pages/20(4)Version-2.html

Medie, A. P. (2013). Fighting gender-based violence: The women's movement and the enforcement of rape law in Liberia. *African Affairs, 112*(448), 377–397. https://doi.org/10.1093/afraf/adt040

Manenosabin, F., & Charles, P.M. (2019). The contributions of community radios in fostering social services in Tanzania: An evaluation of "Maendeleo vijijini" program by Radio SAUT FM in Misungwi district. *Social Sciences, 8*(5), 255–260. https://doi.org/10.11648/j.ss.20190805.16

Media Institute of Southern Africa. (2000). *Community-level baseline research into community media attitudes and needs in Zambia and Namibia.* MISA.

Mefalopulos, P. (2008). *Development communication sourcebook: Broadening the boundaries of communications.* World Bank. https://hdl.handle.net/10986/6439

Ministry of Health (Tanzania Mainland), Ministry of Health (Zanzibar), National Bureau of Statistics, Office of the Chief Government Statistician, and ICF. (2023). *Tanzania Demographic and Health Survey and Malaria Indicator Survey 2022 Key Indicators Report.* Ministry of Health (Tanzania Mainland), Ministry of Health (Zanzibar), National Bureau of Statistics, Office of the Chief Government Statistician, and ICF. https://dhsprogram.com/pubs/pdf/PR144/PPR144.pdf

Mosse, D. (2001). People's knowledge, participation and patronage: Operations and representations in rural development. In B. Cook & U. Kothari (Eds.), *Participation: The new tyranny?* (pp. 16–35). Zed Press.

Mpehongwa, G. (2024). Assessment of community radio social impact in Tanzania. *International Journal of Communication and Public Relation, 9*(3), 34–47. https://doi.org/10.47604/ijcpr.2496

Mrutu, E. (2008). *Community radio in Africa – Case Study: Tanzania* [Licentiate thesis, Finland University of Tampere]. Trepo. https://trepo.tuni.fi/handle/10024/76497

Muluneh, M. D., Stulz, V., Francis, L, & Agho, K. (2020). Gender-based violence against women in sub-Saharan Africa: A systematic review and meta-analysis of cross-sectional studies. *International Journal of Environmental Research and Public Health, 17*(3), 903. https://doi.org/10.3390/ijerph17030903

Mwidima, P. C. (2019). The integration of community radios in achieving the 'Big Results Now' goals in Tanzania. *International Journal of Science and Research, 8*(7), 1842–1848. https://www.ijsr.net/getabstract.php?paperid=ART20199953

Myers, M. (2011). *Voices from villages: Community radio in the developing world.* CIMA. https://cima.ned.org/publication/voices-from-villages-community-radio-in-the-developing-world/

Obagboye, G. T. (2021). Addressing gender-based violence in Africa (Nigeria and Botswana). *Saudi Journal of Humanities and Social Sciences, 6*(10), 405–413.

O'Brien, A. (2019). Women in community radio: A framework of gendered participation. *Feminist Media Studies, 19*(6), 87–802. https://doi.org/10.1080/14680777.2018.1508051

Okinyi, N. P. (2019). Communities' participation in Kenya through community radio broadcasting stations in Kenya on development: A critical review. *Global Media Journal, 17*(32), 158–164.

Onyenankeya, K., & Salawu, A. (2023). Community radio acceptance in rural Africa: The nexus of language and cultural affinity. *Information Development, 39*(3), 567–580. https://doi.org/10.1177/02666669211073458

PEPFAR. (2016). *Annual report to Congress.* https://www.state.gov/wp-content/uploads/2019/08/PEPFAR-2016-Annual-Report-to-Congress.pdf

Shivram, G. P., & Mu-azu, I. A. (2017). The impact of FM Radio broadcast in local dialect on rural community development in Ghana. *Journal of Applied and Advanced Research, 2*(3), 114–121. https://doi.org/10.21839/jaar.2017.v2i3.76

Simmons, K., Mihyo, Z., & Messner, L. (2016). *Lessons from the gender-based violence initiative in Tanzania.* USAID, PEPFAR, & AIDSFree. https://pdf.usaid.gov/pdf_docs/pa00m477.pdf

Sylvester, E., Z. (2016). Major development communication paradigms and practices: Implications for graphic communication. *African Research Review, 10*(3), 317–337. https://doi.org/10.4314/afrrev.v10i3.21

Tanzania Women Lawyers Association (TAWLA). (2014). *Gender equality and women empowerment (GEWE II): Review of laws and policies related to gender-based violence of Tanzania mainland.* https://www.svri.org/sites/default/files/attachments/2016-07-05/Tanzanian%20review%20GBV%20report%202014%20by%20TAWLA%20TAMWA%20CRC%20TGNP%20ZAFELA.pdf

Wabwire, J. (2013). The role of community radio in development of the rural poor. *New Media and Mass Communication, 10*, 40–47. https://iiste.org/Journals/index.php/NMMC/article/view/4391

Weber, R. P. (2008). *Basic content analysis: Quantitative applications in the social science.* Sage Publications.

Wesso, H. M. (2007). Community radio sustenance in the era of convergence. In *The national community radio conference: Sustaining community radio in the era of convergence*, Durban, 12–13 March.

Chapter 14

# Community Radio as an Enabler of Women's Empowerment in Kenya: A Systematic Review of Scholarly Evidence

*Joseph Njuguna*

*Murang'a University of Technology, Kenya*

## Abstract

Community radio's ability to meet the information needs of rural and marginalised populations has piqued scholarly interest globally, and many studies have explored how women leverage these tools for survival. This chapter systematically reviews peer-reviewed journal articles on how community radio has empowered Kenyan women during the last decade. From an eligible corpus of 17 articles, results show a declining trajectory of studies, especially from 2016 on. Most studies targeted women from slums and rural, semi-arid areas. The women were characterised as illiterate, information-poor, culturally marginalised, and with underutilised potential and explored how they perceived community radio as empowering their health, political, and environmental decision-making and actions. The women identified radio's empowering experiences related to raising awareness and knowledge on health, climate, politics, and business issues and to feedback channels that helped articulate a voice to participate in family decisions, fight backward cultural practices, aspire to elective politics, and fight for

Gender and Media Representation: Perspectives from Sub-Saharan Africa, 207–222

doi:10.1108/978-1-83608-406-820251015

gender equality. Some women credited radio content (e.g. testimonies from successful businesswomen) with the growth of their businesses.

*Keywords*: Systematic review; community radio; media; women; empowerment; Kenya; 2024

# Introduction

Debates over gender and development are about how best to empower women to acquire the agency to exploit opportunities to meet instrumental and intrinsic needs as envisaged in Goal 5 of the UN Sustainable Development Goals (UN Women, 2022). Despite the crucial role women play in society, such obstacles as information poverty continue to obstruct their development (Mulauzi & Sitali, 2010). Media, especially community radio, is considered central to addressing the information poverty of women because it affords them important spaces of self-expression and agency to address long-established mechanisms and processes of marginalisation, gender inequality, and inequity (Khader, 2018).

The dis(empowering) nature of such media as radio is evident in the choice of content, the framing of content, and the voices that publish that content. Whereas portraying women in non-stereotypical and unbiased roles is associated with their empowerment and positive perceptions of their issues and how they are perceived (Kabeer, 2005; Sullivan, 2011), stereotypical and biased portrayal serves to entrench discrimination. The accessibility and power of the radio as a critical knowledge site for information have triggered significant consideration of the medium as the public sphere that brings communities together and unlocks the unheard voices of women. Community radio stations, by virtue of their not-for-profit status and community participation (ownership), provide alternatives to commercial radio stations and broadcast the voices of those who feel discriminated against and underrepresented by mainstream media (Mhagama, 2016). Such platforms are 'intimate media', a term that I use here to flag how women can freely access information on such intimate topics as rape and domestic violence and discuss them in appropriate social spaces (like markets and listening groups) with their womenfolk (Heywood & Tomlinson, 2019).

Media's role in fostering gender equality has been championed at international forums like the 1995 UN World Conference of Women in Beijing which initiated the Beijing Declaration and Platform for Action to advance gender equality in selected areas of concern. In recognition of media's significant impact in shaping the society's understanding of gender equality, UNESCO (2024) has been supporting campaigns for gender-sensitive reporting and balanced coverage of gender issues. Debates on how radio empowers women mainly focus on how women use such platforms to access information, amplify their voices on issues that concern them, and enable their rightful participation in political decision-making (Rimmer, 2021; Tijani-Adenle, 2022). Media empowerment of women has also gained global scholarly interest in an attempt to understand how experiences with radio content production and consumption affect the decisions that women make (Rimmer, 2021).

In Kenya, women account for about 51% of the population, according to statistics from the most recent population census (Kenya National Bureau of Statistics, 2019). Kenya enjoys a vibrant media landscape, spurred by a liberalised media sector and widening democratic space, such that an average of 84% of urban and rural populations are exposed to radio broadcasts (Githaiga & Wildermuth, 2022). At the time of writing, there are 58 community radio stations, most of which are located in low-income peri-urban areas and use different local dialects to reach targeted audiences. Despite the growth of community radio, studies show that women still suffer from ignorance and discrimination. Such communication scholars from the Global South as Kassilly and Onkware (2010) have called for studies that problematise the community radio phenomenon from an African context to explore its enduring value for emancipating the underprivileged from information poverty. More than two decades later, however, there is still no synthesised evidence on how the emergence of community radio stations has impacted the lives of women in African contexts. This study addresses this lacuna by systematically reviewing scholarly articles on the role of radio in empowering Kenyan women, and its results will provide a robust body of knowledge on how this research domain has progressed and the areas of radio empowerment that have emerged to prepare the ground for future research.

## Literature Review

Although the concept of women's empowerment has lacked a common definition, increasing scholarly convergence points to a common thread that underlies its meaning – supportive mechanisms that foster self-belief, self-esteem, and agency in women to make informed choices and enable them to participate equitably (with men) in matters that affect them (Cornwall, 2016; Kabeer, 2005; Rimmer, 2021). The philosophy behind community radio is about according voices to the underprivileged and underrepresented in society. Such radio broadcasts are considered mouthpieces for, by, and about the community, and they arose from the need for an alternative voice to critique a monopolistic mainstream media that neglected social injustices against the marginalised. Studies on community radio foreground participatory communication as key to sustainable development. By allowing communities to co-create content, development is brought to traditionally ignored audiences. In other words, community radio enables members to participate as producers and consumers of content that they 'own'.

Anecdotal evidence abounds on how community radio stations have helped address obstacles to women's development across the globe. For example, the Aymara women in Bolivia established Radio Wiñay Jatha to advocate for the plight of their indigenous communities by providing a forum for the voices of the Aymara women to safeguard their culture and promote their human rights (Buckley, 2011). India has also spearheaded community radio stations to boost women. For example, the portable station Namma Dhwani has empowered women by showcasing their talent through their participation in producing content and raising awareness about sanitation, nutrition, and education (Nirmala, 2015). Other community radio stations and broadcasts have been recognised as important voices and information sources in women's agricultural practices, disaster preparedness, and the promotion of women's rights (Ngugi, 2015). Prasad and Deepak (2019) explored indicators of community radio empowerment among women in India and uncovered positive correlations between women's community radio exposure and their political aspirations and business performance. In her thesis, Rimmer (2021) explores how lack of voice affects the empowerment of selected female radio volunteers in Northern England and positions community radio as a crucial site of feminist pedagogy and consciousness-raising that helps to validate women's knowledge and fight the hegemonic tendencies of the white-male-dominated media.

Programmes from community radio stations have been cited as enablers of behavioural change to abandon practices like female genital mutilation and gender-based violence in countries like Somalia and Sudan (Arestoff & Djemai, 2016). Rwanda is a role model in women's empowerment, and its community radio has been instrumental in disseminating educative programmes on gender equality issues (Niyonzima & Bhuju, 2021). Burundi's *Radio Ijwiry'Umukenyezi* (Voice of Women) has been crucial to reviving the hopes of poor women after the country's 2015–2020 civil unrest (Githaiga & Wildermuth, 2022). Women are targeted with content on agricultural productivity, peace messages, and women-led debates on human rights, and Agaba and Isabirye (2024) investigate how community radio helps fight those traditions that hamper women's progress. The radio broadcasts catalysed positive change in people's mindsets and social transformation of their respondents. The role of radio in economic empowerment of women was explored in a study by Usoroh (2021), who interviewed Nigerian women in Bogije, an outpost of Lagos, about how media formats like drama, talks shows, and interviews with prominent businesspeople impacted the women's business decisions. Soyinka et al. (2022) examined the contribution of community radio to knowledge of gender issues using focus groups of women from Badargry, Lagos, and they confirmed that radio programmes facilitated lively debates around gender issues like the education of girls, reproductive health, and prospects of women's election to political positions. In a similar study, Oduaran and Okorie (2019) found that 50% of female radio listeners in South Africa appreciated how community radio stations highlight the problem of women's rights in South Africa. Fombad and Jiyane's (2019) study of two community radio stations in KwaZulu-Natal also found that radio broadcasts were critical to information access for the women's decision-making.

With no systematic reviews to explicate community radio's impact on women in specific contexts and regions, this study focuses on Kenya. It analyses the peer-reviewed scholarly work to identify the characteristics of the studies (growth for the last decade, areas of research), the characteristics of the targeted women, and the themes of radio empowerment derived from their results. For this study, radio empowerment involves enabling women to acquire agency from an informed perspective through five response categories about the radio content, namely 'information gained', 'awareness created', 'attitudes shaped', 'resources mobilised', and 'participation enabled'.

## Methodology

The four-step approach proposed by Preferred Reporting Items for Systematic Reviews and Meta-Analyses was adopted to identify studies for review (see Moher et al., 2015). This involves identifying initial citations from relevant sources (e.g. databases), screening citations using inclusion and exclusion criteria, selecting the most eligible citations, and determining the final list of studies to review. Articles were searched using the Google Scholar, Scopus, Academia.edu, AJOL, and Web of Science databases. For inclusion, articles had to focus on radio (or media) and women, be based on Kenyan women (in any region), be written in English, and have been published between 2014 and 2024 in peer-reviewed journals with fulltext access. Grey literature (reports, news stories, dissertations, position papers, etc.) was excluded to avoid potential bias.

Boolean operators (AND/OR) were used to conduct string searches of different combinations of terms like ('community radio') OR ('radio') OR ('media') AND ('Kenyan women') AND ('women in Kenya') to screen titles, abstracts, keywords, and the full text of relevant papers. A few articles were manually identified through bibliographic chaining. Eligible articles ($n = 17$) were then downloaded for analysis. The thematic characteristics of the reviewed studies (e.g. key areas of radio and women coverage and radio empowerment themes) were identified through an inductive process of content analysis by reading them several times to enable coding of emergent themes. Two trained research assistants conducted the analyses with an intercoder reliability of 94%.

## Results and Discussion

### *Temporal Growth of Articles*

The average annual scholarly production was 1.7 articles. A time-series analysis since 2014 (Fig. 14.1) showed a peculiar research pattern: studies peaked only in the first two years (2014–2016), and there were no studies in 2017. From 2018, when three articles were published, there was a downward trend of research activity, culminating in only two articles between 2023 and 2024. Thus, the number of studies on radio and women empowerment in Kenya demonstrates a downward trajectory with research, gaining traction in the first four years (about 59% of the studies) but diminishing for the remainder of the decade. Decreased academic interest in radio could be attributed to the surge in new media technologies that has seen campaigns gradually move from traditional platforms to social media – where most audiences have also shifted, as suggested by such scholars as Cornwall (2016).

Table 14.1.   Summary of Studies Reviewed.

| Author(s) | Focus of Study | Location | Method (and Sample) | Key Results |
|---|---|---|---|---|
| Mulwa and Mathooko, (2014) | Media and contraceptive use | Kibera slums, Nairobi city | Survey ($n = 37$ women), media content analysis | >80% aware of contraceptives from radio content |
| Bosibori et al. (2018) | Vernacular radio and family planning | Rural Kisii, Nyanza region | Survey ($n = 322$ women); Interview medical staff | Radio is key in FP awareness; culture and illiteracy slow uptake |
| Githaiga and Wildermuth (2022) | Radio and women empowerment | Mathare slums, Nairobi city | Survey ($n = 36$ women); 13 interviews | Ghetto radio gave women voice, talent, and entrepreneurship acumen |
| Mogambi and Ochola (2015) | Pastoralists empowerment through radio | Arid North Eastern, Samburu | Survey ($n = 80$ women); interviewed leaders and comm. radio staff | Radio gave women voice to fight vices like FGM, GBV, and ensure equality |
| Nyambane et al. (2015) | Radio and fighting cervical cancer | Kenyatta Nat Hospital, NBI | Survey ($n = 126$ women); interview medical staff | Radio content effective in promoting prevention/care |
| Kirui et al. (2014) | Climate change info. sources for ASAL farmers | Marigat, Baringo (Rift valley region) | Survey ($n = 95$ women) | 89% prefer (use) radio as sources of climate info that is reliable and with local angle |
| Ngigi and Muange (2022) | Gender in climate info. source preference | Embu, Nakuru, Nyeri, and Siaya | Survey ($n = 156$ couples) | Radio and social groups provided better climate info |
| Odini (2013) | Media as health info. Sources | Vihiga, western region | Survey ($n = 150$ women) | 59% regularly listen to radio for health information |
| Yaya et al. (2018) | Media and malaria prevention | Selected African countries | Malaria Indicator Survey (MIS) ($n = 5,291$ women from Kenya) | Radio was key in promoting about 58% women's use of anti-malaria drugs and ITNs |

| Author (year) | Topic | Location | Method | Findings |
|---|---|---|---|---|
| Mwinyihaji (2012) | Muslim women rights on radio | n/a | Desk research | Women journalists can vie for elections and fight abuses |
| Okinda et al. (2020). | Women's political knowledge thru radio | Rural Kakamega, West region | Survey (n = 400 women) | Radio encouraged them to vote, criticise poor leadership, want to vie for posts, etc. |
| Ndzovu (2019) | Radio preaching by Musl. women | Mombasa, Coast region | Interviews to female radio producers | Muslim women given voice and are role models to others |
| Sterling and Huyer (2010) | Comm. radio as voice for women | Makueni, Eastern region | Survey (n = 170 women), FGDs with 33 women groups | Women able to articulate issues and hear themselves on air |
| Obilo and Vundi (2018) | Preferred information channels for empowerment among women traders | Siaya, Nyanza region | Survey (n = 64 women fish traders) | 77% prefer radio Ramogi (trusted, is vernacular and gives regular updates) |
| Obuya and Emojong (2024) | Community radio in family planning among women | Migori, Nyanza region | Survey (n=400 women); interviews and content analysis of radio programs | 78% listen to Gima Dhano programme of radio Rameny – leads to positive attitudes and high uptake of contraceptives |
| Mbatha et al. (2023) | Community radio and women's health awareness | Kibera slums, Nairobi | Survey (n=100 women under Linda Mama health program) | Radio has created awareness and influenced women to sign up with the programme |
| Wahome et al. (2020) | Health information sources and abortion attitudes | Nakuru, Rift Valley region | Survey (n = 367 women seeking abortion); 10 interviews with health care providers | Radio is significant in influencing abortion attitudes; social groups are also key (78%) |

### Areas of Focus

Studies mainly focussed on five areas of empowerment by community radio: health, environment, freedom of expression, political participation, and economic advancement. Seven studies (41%) investigated radio's role in addressing women's health concerns about such topics as family planning (Bosibori et al., 2018; Mulwa & Mathooko, 2014; Obuya & Emojong, 2024), abortion (Wahome et al., 2020), cervical cancer (Nyambane et al., 2015), general health information sources (Odini, 2013), malaria (Yaya et al., 2018), and free intrapartum care through the government of Kenya's Linda Mama programme (Mbatha et al., 2023). The next most researched issue was how radio contributes to women's political participation (18%), with studies focussing on radio and women's participation in electoral politics (Okinda et al., 2020), Muslim women's use of radio for political legitimacy (Mwinyihaji, 2012), and radio's influence on women's decision to vote (Okinda et al., 2020).

Studies also focussed on the contribution of radio to Kenyan women's freedom of expression and access to information for decision-making. For example, Muslim women's experiences of Islamic preaching on radio broadcasts (Ndzovu, 2019) and Kamba women's participation in Radio Mang'elete community debates (Sterling & Huyer, 2010). Two studies explored the role of information sources like radio in the dissemination of information about climate change (Kirui et al., 2014) and the gender differences in the preferred media for accessing climate information (Ngigi & Muange, 2022). The sample included only one article that directly focussed on empowering women economically, which assessed how Siaya women's fish businesses were boosted by radio content (Obilo & Vundi, 2018).

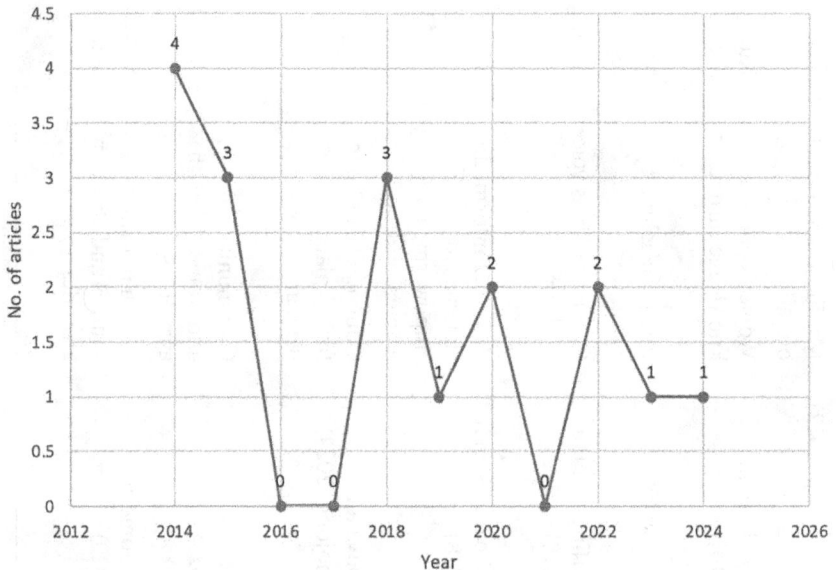

Fig. 14.1. Growth of Articles (2014–2024).

Two articles assessed the general contribution of radio to women's day-to-day lives in the slums (Githaiga & Wildermuth, 2022) and in semi-arid environments (Mogambi & Ochola, 2015).

The results show that the work of the academic research community on radio and women's empowerment in Kenya has been focussed on health, politics, and freedom of expression issues. The bulk of the studies explore women's agency in exploiting the affordances of radio to disentangle themselves from health problems, marginalisation, and unequal access to opportunities. These studies align with emerging scholarly and policy debates geared at the full emancipation of women (see Conroy-Krutz, 2018; Fombad & Jiyane, 2019; Mhagama, 2016). Studies have also shown that health, environment, and politics take centre stage in global media coverage and research (Gatua et al., 2010; Nirmala, 2015). Like in other developing countries, these issues are the fulcrum of survival for women in Kenya such that they attract debate and academic interest, especially from those with a feminist approach.

### Characteristics and Rationale of Women Targeted

Studies have well demonstrated the powerful impact of community radio's life-changing content and opportunities of participation for marginalised and dis-empowered people (Akhter, 2010; Fombad & Jiyane, 2019; Nirmala, 2015). The reviewed studies justify targeting women for various reasons. Some, which focus on public health, describe rural women as 'ignorant', 'illiterate', and 'with low decision-making power' on matters of family planning despite their higher fertility rate (Bosibori et al., 2018; Mulwa & Mathooko, 2014; Wahome et al., 2020). Some studies cite the annual Kenya Demographic and Health Surveys that attribute women's suffering to poverty, retrogressive cultures, and ignorance (Bosibori et al., 2018). Flagging the double tragedy of childbearing and poverty in hostile environments like semi-arid areas, one study foregrounded women as beasts of burden at the household level (Mogambi & Ochola, 2015). Others suggest that the women are 'information-poor' with little or no voice on their socioeconomic welfare to emphasise the urgency to leveraging such media as radio to empower them (Ngigi & Muange, 2022; Sterling & Huyer, 2010). Studies also categorise the women subjects as amenable to manipulation, misinformation, and underutilisation especially when their rights and equal opportunities are not well-articulated (Ndzovu, 2019; Nyambane et al., 2015; Odini, 2013).

The studies focussed on women in Kenya's regions that were described as malaria-prone, drought-stricken, Muslim-dominated, urban slums, rural, and in proximity to Lake Victoria. The studies focussed on slums around Nairobi: Mathare (Githaiga & Wildermuth, 2022), Kibera (Mulwa & Mathooko, 2014), and Kibra (Mbatha et al., 2023). However, one study (Nyambane, et al, 2015) targeted all women seeking health care at Kenyatta National Hospital within Nairobi city. The studies also examined rural settings in the western region in Kakamega (Odini, 2013; Okinda et al, 2020) and Kisii (Bosibori et al., 2018) and the semi-arid regions of the northeast (Mogambi & Ochola, 2015), east (Sterling & Huyer, 2010), and the Rift Valley (Kirui et al., 2014; Wahome et al., 2020) as well as Kenya's coastal region (Ndzovu, 2019) and Nyanza region (Obilo & Vundi, 2018; Obuya & Emojong, 2024). Two studies were based on desk review and did not focus on any particular region (Mwinyihaji, 2012; Yaya et al., 2018). One study (Ngigi & Muange, 2022) was a nationwide survey. It was evident that women from underprivileged regions formed the bulk of participants in the 17 reviewed studies.

Results demonstrate convergence with other studies that position women from impoverished backgrounds as the greatest beneficiaries and targets of community radio stations (e.g. Cornwall, 2016). Despite their role in family and community development, women largely remain invisible and voiceless due to lack of access to information, illiteracy, and subjection to retrogressive cultural practices that diminish their potential. Scholars argue that women's roles must be considered when evaluating the communication for development programmes since women are often more negatively affected by structural inequalities than men (Gatua et al., 2010; Heywood, 2020). Kenya has the largest slum in Africa, Nairobi's neighbourhood of Kibera, which potentially is attracting disproportionate research interest on how vulnerable women eke out a living and the role played by slum community radio stations in their socioeconomic empowerment.

## *Themes of Radio Empowerment in the Reviewed Studies*

Grounded coding was used to identify common words and phrases that define the empowering nature of radio from the results of the studies. Such terminology as 'confidence', 'awareness', 'knowledge', 'skills', 'promotion', and 'empower' among others were associated with women's experiences and perceptions of radio as tools of empowerment, irrespective of the nature of studies. These terminologies related to women gaining new knowledge (e.g. about health issues like cancer, contraceptives, and climate change); changing attitudes about health issues (like malaria prevention); gaining new literacies about family planning; giving feedback on talk shows on topics related to health, cultural inhibitions, access to information, rights, etc.; and boosting business from information heard on the radio. The aggregated studies uncovered three themes on how community radio has empowered Kenyan women.

### Creating and Sustaining Awareness/Knowledge

This theme was a common thread woven through most reviewed studies. For example, women indicated that continued exposure to radio content raised their awareness, knowledge, and capacities to understand health issues like family planning options (Bosibori et al., 2018; Mulwa & Mathooko, 2014), their rights (Mogambi & Ochola, 2015; Mwinyihaji, 2012), and climate change (Ngigi & Muange, 2022) as well as access to business credit (Obilo & Vundi, 2018). Most studies reported more than 70% of their women respondents as attributing the acquisition of these skills to their regular consumption of radio programmes (e.g. talk shows), their trust in the radio for accurate details, and community radio stations' use of the local language to circulate messages. One study credited radio with having contributed new literacies on health awareness and disease prevention based on how the testimonies from the invited guests had encouraged about 86% of the women listeners to adopt healthier alternatives for family planning (Mulwa & Mathooko, 2014). In another, more recent study, slum women foregrounded radio as responsible for their awareness of their benefits under the government's Linda Mama programme that provides free pre-natal, natal, and post-natal services (Mbatha et al., 2023).

The power of radio to address information poverty among women was evident in studies that examined radio as a medium that provides easy access to reliable, detailed, and relevant information about climate (Kirui et al., 2014; Ngigi & Muange, 2022), malaria prevention (Yaya et al., 2018), and general health (Odini, 2013). In most of these studies, women credited radio messages for the informed decisions they took, the health risks they avoided, and the change in their attitudes towards health issues and weather. This positioned information circulated by the community as their power in decision-making. The ability of community radio to raise awareness and knowledge about issues affecting women in Kenya is consistent with studies that have examined how community programmes impart new agricultural practices in India (Nirmala, 2015) and sensitisation towards the legal rights of Niger women (Heywood, 2020) in addition to teaching voting rights to Turkish women (Akhter, 2010).

### Voices for Civic Participation

Studies, especially those focussed on women in politics, religion, and slums and semiarid areas underscored radio's role in helping women voice their concerns and opinions. For example, women credited listening to community radio for their confidence to engage in radio conversations on Ghetto Radio in the Mathare slums, on Ramogi FM in Siaya county, and on the Gima Dhano programme on Rameny radio in Migori. Through its regular updates, use of local language, and open channels of feedback, community radio afforded spaces for women to air their pressing issues. Some women in the northeastern region of Kenya confirmed the role of Serian Radio programmes in boosting their willingness to openly discuss joining elective politics and fighting practices like female genital mutilation, gender-based violence, and the denial of educations to girls among the pastoralist communities (Mogambi & Ochola, 2015).

The opportunity to participate in 'speaking about their issues' made some respondents believe they have become change agents. For example, studies on the Muslim women who serve as hosts and producers on Radio Salam and Radio Rahma positioned these women as role models in the fight against vices like drugs, female genital mutilation, and discrimination who used the radio platform to champion participation in electoral politics and exert their religious acumen by giving and broadcasting regular Islamic sermons (Mwinyihaji, 2012; Ndzovu, 2019). Most women (81%) in the study conducted by Okinda et al. (2020) also foregrounded the role of radio messages in their attitudes and intention to vote in the 2022 general elections. Through the Mang'elete community radio, Kamba *mwethias* (women groups) were able to use an interactive radio technology (AIR) to anonymously record and send their concerns to the radio station for discussions. The technology helped them to articulate their concerns, and hearing themselves on the radio increased their sense of agency in their overall empowerment (Sterling & Huyer, 2010). All the studies heralded the opportunity to contribute to content on radio through feedback as game-changing in women's struggles for equal and equitable participation in decisions affecting them.

The drive for inclusive participation of women in public and social affairs has gained currency. As the reviewed studies show, there has been a concerted campaign to use community radio stations to give agency to women and a forum in which to use their voices to confront long-standing barriers to their development. These findings support other studies (e.g. Arestoff & Djemai, 2016; Conroy-Krutz, 2018; Khader, 2018) on how women have become change agents, role models, elected leaders, and influenced policy action, thanks to their participation in community radio shows.

### Economic Empowerment

Although most studies did not expressly mention women's economic empowerment as an outcome of radio exposure, a few participants in these studies did credit their (or their children's) survival on being employed by as radio show producers and hosts (like Serian Radio in Samburu), on the promotion of their talent (e.g. Ghetto Radio in Mathare slums), or business (e.g. the Mtaani Show on Ghetto radio), and training opportunities to become DJs and video vixens (e.g. Serian Radio). Some women credited radio testimonies from successful businesspeople with their business's growth through credit, the purchase of equipment, and advertising (Githaiga & Wildermuth, 2022; Obilo & Vundi, 2018). These findings about the role of community radio in boosting the economic livelihoods of women supports the conclusions of Heywood (2020), Nirmala (2015), and Fombad and Jiyane (2019), who found that, as in the reviewed articles, women in Niger, India, and South Africa, respectively, benefitted from entrepreneurship programmes aired on the radio.

## Conclusion

This systematic review is a pioneer effort at synthesising studies on community radio's empowering influences on Kenyan women as documented in scholarly work published between 2014 and 2024. It has pointed to the academic interest that community radio as a tool of women empowerment has generated and helps chart new research directions. The trajectory of the growth of the studies is modest, with increased interest in radio as an intervention in health, political, and environmental issues among women. Although only 17 studies were identified for review, the results demonstrate broad scholarly agreement about the place and promise of community radio in improving the welfare of Kenyan women.

As a population of study, most women were rationalised as vulnerable, marginalised, without a voice, and highly amenable to paternalistic exploitation thanks to retrogressive cultures and information poverty. Community radio is a formidable grassroots tool that can help raise awareness of the diverse issues affecting women, fight information poverty, and support the agency of women in charting their own empowerment. Data from the reviewed studies indicate that most women listen to the radio and prefer it as the most reliable source of information for addressing their varied concerns. These results expand the body of scholarly knowledge by contextualising them in Kenya, a country with a vibrant and rapidly expanding community radio network.

Researching the implications of community radio on women's empowerment is imperative, especially in the Kenyan context (and most of the developing world) because radio, with its integration with social media tools, gains currency as a tool to address gender discrimination. Continuous interrogation of questions around radio and the empowerment of Kenyan women in the age of digital communication and communities would give a more holistic understanding of how such 21st-century tools can be integrated to help boost community radio stations' potential to interact with more women. More empirical data are required to establish if participation has led to tangible stakeholder policy action and behaviour changes, and this should be investigated alongside the provisions of local, regional, and international gender empowerment instruments. For a more comprehensive picture of the situation in Kenya, future studies would incorporate more search tools and databases and analyse the methodologies employed, and cover a broader study period with larger sample sizes. Grey literature from reputable publishers on radio and women in Kenya would also add value to the scholarly results. Finally, women's empowerment as a fluid concept would benefit from studies that employ exploratory factor analysis to develop validated scales to measure it.

## References

Agaba, E., & Isabirye, J. (2024). Community radio and the promotion of gender equality. A case study of Nyabihoko Sub-county, Ntungamo District. *IAA Journal of Communication, 10*(1), 1–13. https://doi.org/10.59298/IAAJC/2024/101.113.10000

Akhter, Z. (2010). Voice of the voiceless: Women enlightenment Bou and community radio. *Turkish Online Journal of Distance Education, 11*(1), 35–41. https://dergipark.org.tr/en/download/article-file/156028

Arestoff, F., & Djemai, E. (2016). Women's empowerment across the life cycle and generations: Evidence from sub-Saharan Africa. *World Development, 87*, 70–87. https://doi.org/10.1016/j.worlddev.2016.06.002

Bosibori, N., Kurgat, K., & Akwala, A. (2018). Vernacular radio programmes and family planning promotion among reproductive women in rural areas: A case of Nyamaiya Ward, Kenya. *IOSR Journal of Humanities and Social Science, 23*(9 v. 3), 87–98. https://www.iosrjournals.org/iosr-jhss/papers/Vol.%2023%20Issue9/Version-3/L2309038798.pdf

Buckley, S. (Ed.). (2011). Bolivia: Radio Wiñay Jatha – Voice of Aymara women. In *Community media: A good practice handbook*. United Nations Educational, Scientific and Cultural Organization. Communication and Information Sector. www.unesco.org/webworld.

Conroy-Krutz, J. (2018). Media exposure and political participation in a transitional African context. *World Development, 110*, 224–242. https://doi.org/10.1016/j.worlddev.2018.05.002

Cornwall, A. (2016). Women's empowerment: What works? *Journal of International Development, 28*(3), 342–359. https://doi.org/10.1002/jid.3210

Fombad, M., & Jiyane, G. (2019). The role of community radios in information dissemination to rural women in South Africa. *Journal of Librarianship and Info Science, 51*(1), 47–58. https://doi.org/10.1177/0961000616668960

Gatua, M., Patton, T., & Brown, M. (2010). Giving voice to invisible women: 'FIRE' as a model of a successful women's community radio in Africa. *Howard Journal of Communications, 21*(2), 164–181. https://doi.org/10.1080/10646171003727441

Githaiga, G., & Wildermuth, N. (2022). Radio, mobile communications, and women's empowerment: Experiences in Mathare, Nairobi. *The African Journal of Information and Communication, 30*, 1–22. https://doi.org/10.23962/ajic.i30.13753

Heywood, E. (2020). Radio journalism and women's empowerment in Niger. *Journalism Studies, 21*(10), 1344–1362. https://doi.org/10.1080/1461670X.2020.1745668

Heywood, E., & Tomlinson, M. (2019). The contribution of citizen views to understanding women's empowerment as a process of change: The case of Niger. *Feminist Media Studies, 20*(5), 713–729. https://doi.org/10.1080/14680777.2019.1642230

Kabeer, N. (2005). Gender equality and women's empowerment: A critical analysis of the third millennium development goal. *Gender and Development, 13*(1), 13–24. https://doi.org/10.1080/13552070512331332273

Kassilly, B., & Onkware, K. (2010). Struggles and success in engendering the African public sphere: Kenyan women in politics. *Kenya Studies Review, 3*(3), 71–83.

Kenya National Bureau of Statistics. (2019). *2019 Kenya population and housing census, Volume 3, Distribution of population by age and sex.* https://www.knbs.or.ke/wp-content/uploads/2023/09/2019-Kenya-population-and-Housing-Census-Volume-3-Distribution-of-Population-by-Age-and-Sex.pdf

Khader, S. (2018). Passive empowerment: How women's agency became women doing it all. *Philosophical Topics, 46*(2), 141–1363. https://muse.jhu.edu/article/764816

Kirui, V., Waiganjo, M., & Cheplogoi, S. (2014). Evaluating access and use of dissemination pathways for delivering climate information and services to women farmers in semi-arid Kenya. *International Journal of Advanced Research, 2*(9), 44–53. https://www.journalijar.com/uploads/479_IJAR-3657.pdf

Mbatha, P., Odek, A., & Njenga, R. (2023). The role of community radio in creating awareness on health issues: A case study of Pamoja FM's Linda Mama delivery program. *African Multidisciplinary Journal of Research (AMJR), Special Issue I*, 325–349. https://journals.spu.ac.ke/index.php/amjr/article/view/207

Mhagama, P. (2016). The importance of participation in development through community radio: A case study of Nkhotakota community radio station in Malawi. *Critical Arts: A South–North Journal of Cultural & Media Studies, 30*(1), 45–61. https://doi.org/10.1080/02560046.2016.1164384

Mogambi, H., & Ochola, A. (2015). Community radio and empowerment of women among pastoralist communities in northern Kenya. *Online Journal of Communication and Media Technologies, 5*(4), 29–63. https://doi.org/10.29333/ojcmt/2525

Moher, D., Shamseer, L., Clarke, M., Ghersi, D., Liberati, A., Petticrew, M., Shekelle, P., Stewart, L., & PRISMA-P Group. (2015). Preferred reporting items for systematic review and meta-analysis protocols (PRISMA-P) 2015 statement. *Systematic Reviews, 4*(1), 1–9. https://doi.org/10.1186/2046-4053-4-1

Mulauzi. F., & Sitali, W. (2010). Using information and communication technologies (ICT) to provide information to fight poverty, diseases and ignorance among rural women in Zambia. *Zambia Library Association Journal, 25*(1), 5–18. https://hdl.handle.net/10520/AJA0049853X_511

Mulwa, P. M., & Mathooko, P. (2014). Effects of mass media messages on women's decision-making on contraceptive use in Kenya. *International Journal of Social Sciences and Entrepreneurship, 1*(13), 261–281.

Mwinyihaji, E. (2012). Kenyan Muslim women in media and politics: Fighting for legitimacy. *Global Journal of Human–Social Science: C Sociology, 12*(C9), 39–42. https://socialscienceresearch.org/index.php/GJHSS/article/view/459

Ndzovu, H. (2019). Broadcasting female Muslim preaching in Kenya: Negotiating religious authority and the ambiguous role of the voice. *African Journal of Gender and Religion, 25*(2), 14–40. https://doi.org/10.14426/ajgr.v25i2.879

Ngigi, M., & Muange, E. (2022). Access to climate information services and climate-smart agriculture in Kenya: A gender-based analysis. *Climate Change, 174*, 21. https://doi.org/10.1007/s10584-022-03445-5

Ngugi, P. (2015). Using community radios as a tool for development. *Journal of Mass Communication & Journalism, 5*(6), 1–8. https://www.hilarispublisher.com/open-access/using-community-radios-as-a-tool-for-development-2165-7912-1000263.pdf

Nirmala, Y. (2015). The role of community radio in empowering women in India. *Media Asia, 42*(1–2), 41–46. https://doi.org/10.1080/01296612.2015.1072335

Niyonzima, D., & Bhuju, K. (2021). The role of community radio in promoting gender equality in Rwanda. In S. Jamil, B. Çoban, B. Ataman, & G. Appiah-Adjei (Eds.), *Handbook of research on discrimination, gender disparity, and safety risks in Journalism Advances in Linguistics and Communication Studies* (pp. 343–365). IGI Global. https://doi.org/10.4018/978-1-7998-6686-2.ch018

Nyambane, R., Mberia, H., & Ndati, N. (2015). The role of radio and television in reducing the burden and severity of cervical cancer among women in Kenya with special focus on Kenyatta National Hospital in Nairobi Kenya. *International Journal of Education and Research, 3*(6), 1–12. http://www.ijern.com/journal/2015/June-2015/01.pdf

Obilo, M., & Vundi, N. (2018). Preferred channels of information for empowerment among fish traders in Siaya County, Kenya. *Strategic Journal of Business & Change Management, 5*(4), 2199–2205. https://www.strategicjournals.com/index.php/journal/article/view/1019

Obuya, J., & Emojong, O. (2024). Efficacy of Ngima Dhano community radio programme in the uptake of contraceptives among women in Cham GiWadu Division, Kenya. *International Journal of Media, Journalism and Mass Communications, 10*(1), 37–48. https://doi.org/10.20431/2454-9479.1001003

Odini, S. (2013). Accessibility and utilization of health information by rural women in Vihiga County, Kenya. *International Journal of Science and Research, 5*(7), 2319–7064. Article NOV164666.

Oduaran, C., & Okorie, N. (2019). Community radio, women and family development issues in South Africa: An experiential study. *Journal of International Women's Studies, 20*(7), 102–112. https://vc.bridgew.edu/jiws/vol20/iss7/7

Okinda, I., Nyambuga, C., & Ojwang, B. (2020). Influence of radio on women voters' political knowledge on the 2013 Kenyan general elections. *Acta Universitatis Danubius, 14*(1), 86–107. https://dj.univ-danubius.ro/index.php/AUDC/article/view/399

Prasad, R., & Deepak, N. (2019). Community radio and women empowerment: A pragmatic investigation. *New Media and Mass Communication, 83*, 10–21. https://doi.org/10.7176/NMMC/83-02

Rimmer, A. (2021). Breaking the silence: Community radio, women, and empowerment. *Community Development Journal, 56*(2), 338–355. https://doi.org/10.1093/cdj/bsz030

Soyinka, A., Olajide, J., Biobaku, L., & Affar, M. (2022). Radio's contributions to knowledge of gender equality among women in rural Badagry, Nigeria. *Covenant Journal of Communication, 9*(2), 76–93. https://journals.covenantuniversity.edu.ng/index.php/cjoc/article/view/3212

Sterling, R., & Huyer, S. (2010). 89.1 FM: The place for development: Power shifts and participatory spaces in ICTD. *The Journal of Community Informatics*, *6*(1). https://doi.org/10.15353/joci.vi.2435

Sullivan, B. (2011). *The new age of radio: How ICTs are changing rural radio in Africa.* Farm Radio. https://farmradio.org/publications/new-age-radio-icts-changing-rural-radio-africa/

Tijani-Adenle, G. (2022). Women FM (W.FM): The women-focused radio station amplifying the voices of Nigerian women. In M. Lindgren & J. Loviglio (Eds.), *The Routledge companion to radio and podcast studies* (pp. 327–338). Routledge. https://doi.org/10.4324/9781003002185

UNESCO. (2024). *Media and gender equality.* https://www.unesco.org/gender-equality/media-and-gender-equality/

UN Women. (2022). *Facts and figures: Women's leadership and political participation.* https://www.unwomen.org/en/what-we-do/leadership-and-political-participation/facts-and-figures

Usoroh, U. (2021). The role of radio in fostering economic empowerment of rural women in Bogije Ibeju-Lekki, Lagos. *Journal of Resources Development and Management*, *75*, 74–87. https://doi.org/10.7176/JRDM/75-06

Wahome, A., Mberia, H., & Sikolia, G. (2020). Influence of health message sources on attitude towards abortion among women in Nakuru County, Kenya. *International Journal of Scientific and Research Publications*, *10*(5), 205–210. http://doi.org/10.29322/IJSRP.10.05.2020.p10124

Yaya, S., Uthman, O., Amouzou, A., & Bishwajit, G. (2018). Mass media exposure and its impact on malaria prevention behaviour among adult women in sub-Saharan Africa: Results from malaria indicator surveys. *Global Health Research and Policy*, *3*, 1–9. https://doi.org/10.1186/s41256-018-0075-x

# Chapter 15

# Gendered Power Relations and Culture of Silence: An Exploration of Female Interns' Sexual Harassment Experiences in Nigerian Newsrooms

*Bimbo Lolade Fafowora*

*Rhodes University, South Africa*

## Abstract

Women journalists constantly grapple with such challenges as sexism and sexual harassment from male colleagues, news sources, and, more recently, online audiences. Although studies have examined sexual harassment of women in media, little attention has been paid to female interns or trainee journalists. This study explores female interns' experiences concerning sexism and sexual harassment within newsrooms in Nigeria using the propositions of radical feminist theory and the culture of silence to understand how gendered power dynamics mediate the experiences of female interns within Nigerian newsrooms and ascertain the prevalence of sexual harassment. An online questionnaire was distributed to female interns in media organisations across southwestern Nigeria. While few of the interns acknowledged experiencing a form of sexual harassment, the findings reveal the influence of a prevalent culture of silence around sexual harassment cases in Nigeria. The study also identified a lack of (awareness

Gender and Media Representation: Perspectives from Sub-Saharan Africa, 223–238

doi:10.1108/978-1-83608-406-820251016

about) internal mechanisms for regulating or addressing workplace sexual harassment in Nigerian media organisations.

*Keywords*: Sexual harassment; gendered power dynamics; women in media; culture of silence; radical feminist theory; female interns; Nigerian media

## Introduction

Feminist advocates and scholars have had to contend with the challenge of sexual harassment for over four decades now (Samuels, 2003). Sadly, women's experiences of sexual harassment have not changed much despite changes in legislation against sexual harassment, especially in the workplace. Workplace sexual harassment (WSH) remains an endemic scourge that continues to undermine women's authority and reinforce sexist stereotypes in the workplace through sexual objectification (McLaughlin et al., 2017). WSH affects women in various sectors of society globally. For instance, a 2016 study of 28 European Union countries reports that 55% of women have experienced some form of sexual harassment in their lifetime (European Union Agency for Fundamental Rights, 2014; Directorate-General for Communication, 2016). Similarly, Fitzgerald and Cortina (2018) estimated that half of the women working in the United Kingdom will experience at least one form of sexual harassment in the workplace during their lifetime. In the United States, 59% of women reported having experienced physical or verbal sexual harassment (Graf, 2018). Although sexual harassment is hard to define because its constituents are subjective and context-dependent, this chapter adopts the International Labour Organisation's (ILO, 2020) definition for standardisation purposes. The ILO policy brief (p. 1) describes WSH as

> any physical, verbal or non-verbal conduct of a sexual nature and other conduct based on sex, affecting the dignity of women and men, which is unwelcome, unreasonable, and offensive to the recipient; and a person's rejection of, or submission to, such conduct is used explicitly or implicitly as a basis for a decision which affects that person's job; or conduct that creates an intimidating, hostile or humiliating working environment for the recipient.

While men can also be victims of sexual harassment, studies show that men experiences of WSH are less documented (Carstensen, 2016; Farkas et al., 2020). Despite ongoing advocacy for the eradication of gender inequality and sexism in the workplace, sexism still exists in various professions, including journalism. Indeed, because of the gendered nature of the journalistic profession, women in media still grapple with various challenges related to sexism, including low wages, violence, subversion, and sexual harassment (Harris et al., 2016). Research from 20 countries across three continents, namely Africa, Asia, and Europe, shows that

41% of women media professionals have experienced some form of sexual harassment in the workplace, and half of women media professionals from six African countries reported having experienced sexual harassment (Blumell & Mulupi, 2022b). In Nigeria, 38.1% of women media professionals have experienced sexual harassment (Blumell & Mulupi, 2021).

Sexual harassment most often occurs in a context of unequal power relations (International Labour Organisation, 2020). Moagi (2023, pp. 64–65) notes that WSH is 'a prominent feature of unfair labour practises and a means for discrimination and gender inequality in many institutions globally. Sexual harassment in the media industry has severe implications for women's careers, leading to career stagnation, reduced job satisfaction, and mental health issues, ultimately hindering their professional growth and advancement such that women leave the profession or feel isolated, marginalised, and excluded from opportunities (Akinbobola, 2020; Blumell et al., 2023). While there has been extensive research on sexual harassment (Karami et al., 2021), few studies have examined WSH in relation to the experiences of interns in media organisations. This chapter broadens the discussion on WSH to include a group that embodies an intersection of vulnerabilities because of their gender and status in the organisational and socioeconomic hierarchy. With a focus on female interns in media organisations in southwestern Nigeria,[1] the study seeks to answer the following questions: What are the sexual harassment experiences of female interns in Nigerian newsrooms? How do victims of sexual harassment handle harassment and seek redress? What organisational policies and internal regulatory mechanisms are available for victims of sexual harassment to report perpetrators and seek redress? The rationale for investigating the current state of sexual harassment in Nigerian newsrooms stemmed from my experience of sexual harassment as an intern about two decades ago, but recent studies indicate that sexual harassment remains a prevalent and persistent challenge for women journalists in Nigeria, hindering their career aspirations (Akinbobola, 2020; Blumell et al., 2023). Using the propositions of radical feminist theory and the concept of the culture of silence, I argue that sexual harassment is mostly driven by the need for control or domination rather than sexual gratification (Thompson, 2001). I also argue that prevailing sociocultural gender norms and the culture of victim-blaming or stigmatisation may prevent victims of sexual harassment from speaking up or seeking redress (Fernando & Prasad, 2018; Hershcovis et al., 2021).

## Literature Review

Sexual harassment has been a subject of increasing academic attention since the early 1970s (see MacKinnon, 1979). The problematisation of sexual harassment gave women not only an avenue to identify a set of unacceptable behaviours

---

[1]The specific administrative divisions cannot be ascertained as the data collection was done virtually and the questionnaire was not designed to collect location data to further protect respondents' identities.

against them in the workplace, but also an opportunity to lodge complaints and mobilise to seek redress and tackle the scourge (Bacchi & Jose, 1994). Despite concerted efforts to stem the tide of sexual harassment, it continues to constitute a menace to women all over the world, leading to increased advocacy and academic interest to understand and tackle it. In a systematic review of studies of sexual harassment across various contexts from 1977 to 2020, Karami et al. (2021) found that sexual harassment has been studied using such different variables as age, race or ethnicity, sexual orientation, geographical location, and whether it took place in social or professional spaces. They contend that WSH was the most researched theme in sexual harassment studies, and their review identified studies of sexual harassment in such various other social spaces as schools, homes, online spaces, hospitals, and the military and a focus on feminism, media, politics, and sexual harassment that constitutes a new trend in the 21st century. The findings of Karami et al. (2021) are not only indicative of the prevalence of sexual harassment in the workplace, but also confirm that sexual harassment is tied to sexism and the unequal gendered power dynamic of the workplace (see McLaughlin et al., 2012; Moagi, 2023). In other words, gender and sexism still play a pivotal role in mediating the experiences of women in media across the world.

Women journalists grapple with discrimination and sexual harassment not only from male colleagues but also in the field from news sources, often in positions of authority, who request sexual favours in exchange for interviews (Lachover, 2005). For instance, Kabah (2019) notes the male dominance in newsrooms in his investigation of the gendered experiences of female journalists in Tamale, the capital of the Northern Region of Ghana. The experiences of Ghanaian women journalists exemplify quid-pro-quo relationships; in other words, sexual favours are requested in exchange for material benefits (Anderson, 2006). Harris et al.'s (2016) study of the impact of gender on the risks female journalists face in conflict reportage notes that women are more susceptible to risks like targeted killings and sexual harassment than their male counterparts due to their gender. In a study of the lived experiences of women journalists in Sub-Saharan Africa, Akinbobola (2020) identified sexual harassment as a challenge that denigrates women in media and hinders women's entrance into and progression in the journalistic profession. Indeed, Akinbobola (2020) reports that sexual harassment is the second-most-shared challenge confronting women journalists in countries across Sub-Saharan Africa, and some of the participants in the study narrated experiences of sexual harassment as a condition for work in their respective media organisations. A cross-continental study of the impact of sexual harassment on job satisfaction in the news industry across 16 countries in Sub-Saharan Africa, southeast Asia, and North Africa and the middle east flagged the prevalence of both verbal and physical forms of sexual harassment in newsrooms and regional differences in the frequency of sexual harassment (Blumell et al., 2023): Sub-Saharan Africa reported the highest frequency of sexual harassment and the lowest level of job satisfaction. More importantly, Blumell et al. (2023) note that while sexual harassment has significant negative consequences on women journalists, few women report their harassers.

Blumell et al.'s (2023) findings echo arguments about the culture of silence and secrecy that permeates discussions about experiences of and the prevalence of sexual harassment in the workplace across the globe (Spiliopoulou & Witcomb, 2023). North (2016), for example, reports findings from a survey of the sexual harassment experiences of female journalists in Australia shows that not only that sexual harassment is an ongoing and systemic problem in the Australian media industry, but also that there is a lack of awareness of what behaviours constitute sexual harassment and how to lodge complaints. This research highlights the importance of arguments for the institution of legal rights and established processes to empower women and victims of sexual harassment to lodge complaints and seek redress (North, 2016).

## Theoretical Framework

### Radical Feminist Theory

Feminist scholarship views sexual harassment as a fallout of women's disadvantaged position in society, which has not only marginalised them, but also made them subjected to domination and control (Uggen & Blackstone, 2004). In other words, feminist scholars view the phenomenon as a means through which men exercise power over women. Wilson and Thompson (2001, p. 61) describe WSH as 'an inappropriate use of power that isolates, undermines, and degrades women'. Bacchi (1999) similarly conceptualised WSH as an intrusive male behaviour intended to denigrate and humiliate women. Thus, sexual harassment is considered an act rooted in power and control over an individual because of their gender.

Radical feminist scholars argue that sexual harassment is embedded in societal structures of oppression. They argue that gender and sex are social constructs by which men assert authority and dominate women. They also propose that patriarchy, also referred to as male supremacy or male dominance, is a central organising system of society such that women constitute an oppressed 'sex class' (Grosser & Tyler, 2021; Thompson, 2001). Thus, they perceive sexual harassment as an offshoot of patriarchy used to intimidate and silence women in various contexts, including the workplace, and view male domination and control as a social system that perpetuates gendered power imbalances (Thompson, 2001). Radical feminist scholars also argue that sexual harassment impedes women's experiences of equal opportunity in employment and other sectors of society. Although radical feminists do not consider male dominance and women's subjugation universal and unalterable, they take pride in identifying and naming domains or systems of male domination with a view to challenging the status quo and dismantling the existing order of domination.

Radical feminists further contend that sexuality is central to women's suppression (Thompson, 2001). They argue that WSH is a form of gender discrimination experienced mostly by women (Holland & Cortina, 2016). Contrary to the general belief that sexual harassment is a result of attraction, studies have identified it as a behaviour motivated by a desire for control and domination rather than a desire for sex (Bargh et al., 1995; Wilson & Thompson, 2001). Hence both younger women, who are more likely to be in subordinate positions, and their older counterparts in positions of authority are prone to experiencing sexual harassment (McLaughlin et al., 2012; North, 2016). This argument is useful to this study because it encapsulates female journalist interns' experiences of sexual harassment within feminist scholarship.

## Culture of Silence and Sexual Harassment

Paulo Freire (1970) first used the concept of a 'culture of silence' in his *Pedagogy of the Oppressed* to explain the dynamics of power and domination within oppressive cultures. In explaining the culture of silence, Freire posits that unequal social relations create a culture of silence whereby the subordinate or oppressed are unable to express their experiences and struggles openly. Freire argues further that a prevalent culture of silence may cause oppressed individuals to internalise their oppression, suppress their self-image, and develop feelings of powerlessness such that for the oppressed to break free from the culture of silence, they must develop critical consciousness by recognising the oppressive structures and actively seek liberation and social transformation. Although the culture of silence was originally conceptualised to describe impoverished and illiterate underclasses across the world, feminist scholars have employed it to generate insights into why sexual harassment still lingers in various contexts despite years of awareness, advocacy, and litigation (Fernando & Prasad, 2018; Ford et al., 2021).

Cultures of silence around WSH not only result from individual actions alone, but also exist within organisational structures and social networks. Fernando and Prasad (2018) identified line managers, HR personnel, and ordinary colleagues as examples of people complicit in perpetuating silence or secrecy on sexual harassment cases in the workplace. Morrison and Rothman (2009), in their examination of the interplay between power and silence in organisational contexts, note that employee silence results from a combination of psychological and behavioural effects relative to an individual's position on the spectrum of power. In other words, employees' judgement calls about when to keep silent and when to speak up are shaped and intensified by power differentials between managers and subordinates, and employees in positions of relatively low power are more likely to choose silence over speaking up, especially if the latter portends danger or amounts to futility. Similarly, in theorising silence in relation to WSH, Ford et al. (2021, p. 516) explicate that organisations that trivialise discourses around sexual harassment or consider it a 'private matter' or an 'issue to be resolved through [complicated] bureaucratic processes' encourage the perpetuation of sexual harassment and victims' silence.

A study on the prevalence and reporting of sexual harassment in public spaces in the UK showed that 80% of victims of sexual harassment in the country do not lodge a formal complaint (UN Women UK, 2021). Some studies on sexual harassment explicate that sexual harassment thrives because victims seldom report violations and abuse due to the fear of stigmatisation or discouragement resulting from delayed or denied justice (McLaughlin et al., 2017; Spiliopoulou & Witcomb, 2023). Indeed, some studies have also shown that women who do report their abusers sometimes do not get redress as they were either avoided or asked to provide considerable evidence to substantiate the accusation (Fernando & Prasad, 2018, pp. 1574–1584). While a lot of people are complicit in perpetuating the culture of silence around WSH, Fernando and Prasad (2018) note that creating channels for victims to report harassment that ensure victims' complaints are taken seriously and their concerns validated is crucial to ending the damages of sexual harassment. It is also important that perpetrators are held accountable to prevent reoccurrence.

## Methodology

This study focuses on the sexual harassment experiences of female interns from media organisations in southwestern Nigeria between 2018 and 2023. Data were collected using a self-administered online questionnaire, a method particularly suitable for data from widely distributed samples and research on sensitive matters because it offers respondents a measure of anonymity (Babbie, 2021). The sample consisted of 96 respondents, of whom 22 were excluded because they fell outside the gender (female), age (18–28), and temporal criteria of the study, leaving a total of 74 respondents, whose responses were analysed descriptively to get an overview of the interns' experiences of sexual harassment. The average age of respondents was 22.

The results presented contain preliminary data collected through consolidated criteria for reporting qualitative research: a 32-item checklist, a three-part online questionnaire comprising demographic questions, an adaptation of the Likert scale, and open-ended questions to elicit rich responses on the respondents' experiences of sexual harassment. One of the open-ended questions was targeted at recruiting participants for in-depth interviews. None of the 74 respondents were keen on being interviewed. The questionnaire was developed using relevant literature to adequately define and identify the key indicators of sexual harassment (Benya et al., 2018; World Health Organization, 2007). Respondents were recruited through Facebook, LinkedIn, and WhatsApp using the snowball or referral technique, which is particularly useful for researching vulnerable or hard-to-reach groups (Babbie, 2021). The questionnaire was also distributed through the researcher's personal and professional networks of friends, journalists, journalism educators, and students. Data analysis and presentation are descriptive because of the small sample size. The researcher does not attempt to generalise the findings of this exploratory study.

## Ethics and Consent

Sexual harassment is sensitive research because of its research focus and the target population. Researchers must be sensitive to how their investigations may pose psychological risks to respondents by triggering such distressing emotions as guilt, shame, and embarrassment (Liamputtong, 2007). Rhodes University's Human Research Ethics Committee approved this study and its protocols for informed consent, data usage, and potential emotional impact. The consent form advised respondents who experienced adverse emotional reactions to discontinue and seek professional help. The researcher was also careful about question phrasing in the questionnaire, anonymisation, and prioritisation of respondents' well-being over research outcomes in accordance with feminist research ethics.

## Presentation and Discussion of Findings

This section provides an overview of the descriptive data collected from a 32-item e-questionnaire on female interns' sexual harassment experiences in media organisations in Nigeria. The purpose of this research is not to examine the prevalence of sexual harassment in the Nigerian media industry but rather to draw attention to female interns' experiences of sexual harassment and how such incidents are handled when they occur. The data are presented in tables and figures to highlight instances of behaviours that constitute sexual harassment as identified by previous research.

### Sexual Harassment Experiences of Female Interns in Nigerian Newsrooms

The foremost objective of the study was to describe the sexual harassment experiences of female interns in newsrooms. Nineteen statements containing different indicators of sexual harassment were designed on a Likert-type scale to elicit responses to answer the first research question (Table 15.1). Cumulatively, the survey responses showed that 64% of the respondents did not experience sexual harassment, whereas 36% had experienced it in various forms (Fig. 15.1). A little more than a third indicated that they had experienced a form of harassment at least once or twice during the period of their internship. A few of the respondents experienced some of the indicators three or more times, and even fewer noted that they had experienced sexual harassment more than five times. This finding is consistent with Akinbobola (2020) and Blumell and Mulupi (2021), who reported sexual harassment as one of the lingering challenges for women in Nigerian newsrooms. It is also indicative of gender and patriarchal norms as an organising system for power and dominance in Nigerian media.

## Perpetrators and Respondents' Handling Experiences of Sexual Harassment

### How Sexual Harassment Experiences Are Handled by Interns

The second objective of the study was to identify how interns handled their experiences of sexual harassment. Three questions were used to collect data to meet this objective, and they focussed on identifying the perpetrators, the action taken by the harassed intern, and the outcome, especially for those who experienced harassment and lodged a complaint. The perpetrators identified included administrators, male superiors/supervisors, male news sources, and male co-interns (see Table 15.2). Specifically, 17.5% of the respondents reported being sexually harassed by individuals above them in the organisational hierarchy, and this finding corroborates Brown and Flatow's (1997) finding that WSH results from power differentials between men and women within an organisation such that talented younger women are susceptible to sexual harassment as a means of control by men. Seven of the 74 respondents reported being propositioned by male news

Table 15.1. Interns' Experiences of Sexual Harassment.

| Sexual Harassment Indicators | Number of Times Experienced | | | | | |
|---|---|---|---|---|---|---|
| | Zero | One–Two | Three–Five | > Five | NR | Total |
| Sexually suggestive stories or offensive jokes | 39 (53%) | 21 (28%) | 6 (8%) | 3 (4%) | 5 (7%) | 74 (100%) |
| Discussions of a personal or sexual nature | 37 (50%) | 24 (32%) | 7 (9%) | 2 (3%) | 4 (5%) | 74 (100%) |
| Crude and offensive sexual remarks | 43 (58%) | 22 (30%) | 2 (3%) | 2 (3%) | 5 (7%) | 74 (100%) |
| Mistreatment because of their gender | 44 (59%) | 15 (20%) | 8 (11%) | 3 (4%) | 4 (5%) | 74 (100%) |
| Unwanted sexual attention | 44 (59%) | 15 (20%) | 3 (4%) | 5 (7%) | 7 (9%) | 74 (100%) |
| Sexually suggestive materials | 56 (76%) | 7 (9%) | 4 (5%) | 1 (1%) | 6 (8%) | 74 (100%) |
| Sexist remarks | 47 (64%) | 15 (20%) | 3 (4%) | 3 (4%) | 6 (8%) | 74 (100%) |
| Romantic sexual relationship | 42 (57%) | 15 (20%) | 7 (7%) | 4 (5%) | 6 (8%) | 74 (100%) |
| Unwanted invitation for dates | 44 (59%) | 13 (18%) | 9 (12%) | 2 (3%) | 6 (8%) | 74 (100%) |
| Subtle offer of reward or special treatment to engage in sexual behaviour | 47 (64%) | 15 (20%) | 4 (5%) | 1 (1%) | 7 (9%) | 74 (100%) |
| Subtle threats for not being sexually cooperative | 50 (68%) | 11 (15%) | 7 (9%) | 0 (0%) | 6 (8%) | 74 (100%) |
| Discomfort from being touched on their bare hand, arm, shoulders, or waist | 42 (57%) | 16 (22%) | 6 (8%) | 4 (5%) | 6 (8%) | 74 (100%) |
| Stroking or fondling on the legs or neck, breast, or buttocks | 49 (66%) | 11 (15%) | 5 (7%) | 4 (5%) | 5 (7%) | 74 (100%) |

*(Continued)*

Table 15.1.    *(Continued)*

| Sexual Harassment Indicators | Number of Times Experienced | | | | | | |
| --- | --- | --- | --- | --- | --- | --- | --- |
| | Zero | One–Two | Three–Five | > Five | NR | Total | |
| Unwanted sexual advances resulting in them pleading or physically resisting | 53 (72%) | 8 (11%) | 5 (7%) | 2 (3%) | 6 (8%) | 74 (100%) | |
| Implied better treatment or promised a permanent position if sexually cooperative | 54 (73%) | 11 (15%) | 3 (4%) | 0 (0%) | 6 (8%) | 74 (100%) | |
| Pressured to respond positively to sexual or social invitations to be well-treated | 55 (74%) | 9 (12%) | 3 (4%) | 1 (1%) | 6 (8%) | 74 (100%) | |
| Fear of being treated poorly if they did not cooperate sexually | 54 (73%) | 12 (16%) | 1 (1%) | 1 (1%) | 6 (8%) | 74 (100%) | |
| Treated badly for refusing to have sex | 51 (69%) | 10 (14%) | 5 (7%) | 2 (3%) | 6 (8%) | 74 (100%) | |
| Coercive/forced sexual intercourse | 56 (76%) | 9 (12%) | 2 (3%) | 1 (1%) | 6 (8%) | 74 (100%) | |

Cummulative summary of respondents' experiences of sexual harassment

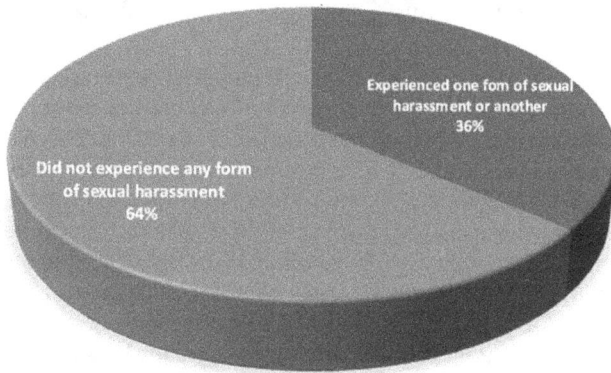

Fig. 15.1. Distribution of Respondents Who Experienced Sexual Harassment Compared to Those Who Did Not.

Table 15.2. Distribution of Identified Perpetrators of Sexual Harassment in This Study.

| Perpetrators | Frequency | Percentage |
|---|---|---|
| Male superiors or supervisors | 13 | 48 |
| Male news sources | 7 | 26 |
| Male co-interns | 6 | 22 |
| Male administrator | 1 | 4 |
| Total | 27 | 100 |

sources, a finding that adds nuance to studies by Lachover (2005) and Kabah (2019) that also documented experiences of sexual harassment between female journalists and male news sources. In short, the pervasiveness of sexual harassment in the news industry has serious negative implications for the uptake of women journalists because it can constitute an entry barrier for young and aspiring female journalists or impede their career progression.

### *Actions Taken by the Respondents Who Experienced Sexual Harassment*

To further understand how the respondents handled their experiences of sexual harassment, those who reported the sexual harassment were asked to indicate the steps they took to seek help or redress. This question was followed by two open-ended questions asking the respondents their reasons for reporting or not. Only six of the 27 respondents who reported having experienced a form of sexual harassment took steps to report it, while 20 did not. Although the sample for this study is not large enough to make generalisations, the proportion of interns who failed to report their harassers supports the narrative about a prevailing culture of silence around WSH globally (see Alaggia & Wang, 2020; Blumell & Mulupi, 2021, 2022; North, 2016; Sadia Jamil, 2020).

Respondents who did not report their harassers were asked to state the reason(s) for their (in)action; three stated that they did not report because they were ashamed or afraid of putting the perpetrator in trouble. This finding is crucial to highlighting the culture of blaming and shaming victims of sexual harassment instead of holding their perpetrators accountable and corroborates Alaggia and Wang (2020), who also found that victims of sexual harassment do not report their experiences because they fear retribution, being disbelieved, shame, and self-blame. Blumell and Mulupi's (2022) study of sexist behaviours in newsrooms in South Africa and Nigeria also established the prevalence of sociocultural and religious ideologies that encourage victim-blaming and slut-shaming victims of sexual harassment because of prevailing beliefs that place the responsibility for avoiding sexual harassment on women. A surprising finding was the respondents' fears of retribution against the perpetrator – two of the respondents preferred to endure sexual harassment rather than report the perpetrator because they did not want him to run into trouble or lose his job. While one can surmise that such a reaction might result from sociocultural and religious conditioning, further exploration of the factors involved in this reaction is needed.

### *Awareness of Organisational Policies for Mitigating Sexual Harassment in Newsrooms*

Responses to the question used to assess respondents' awareness of policies or internal structures available for victims of sexual harassment in their organisations indicates a gross lack of awareness of any such entity: only 20 respondents answered in the affirmative (see Fig. 15.2). While many media organisations in Nigeria have a designated human resources department, the extent to which these personnel highlight sexual harassment in their organisational policy or resolve cases of sexual harassment is not clear. Respondents' lack of awareness of policies for dealing with sexual harassment cases might be indicative of a lack of such

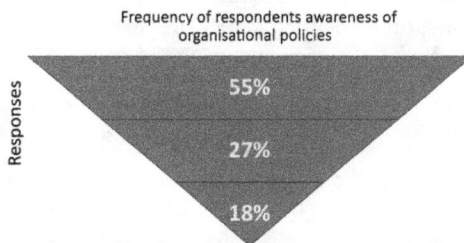

Frequency of respondents awareness of
organisational policies

Responses

55%

27%

18%

Fig. 15.2.    Distribution of Respondents' Awareness of Organisational Policies or Internal Regulatory Mechanisms for Addressing Sexual Harassment.

policy or a lack of awareness about existing policies. These data corroborate the finding that there is also a significant lack of awareness about newsroom policies to combat sexual harassment among women in the Australian media industry (North, 2016). What is more, respondents' lack of awareness of available policies for dealing with sexual harassment in their respective organisations clarifies why those who did report their harassers mostly chose to report to external entities like parents, friends, or the police.

## Conclusion

This chapter explored the experiences of sexual harassment among female interns, vulnerable due to their gender and hierarchical positions, in Nigerian newsrooms. The study established the silence about sexual harassment against women in Nigerian newsrooms as evidence of patriarchy and gendered power imbalances in Nigerian newsrooms. Interns' experiences of sexual harassment ranged from subtle forms, like sexually suggestive jokes and sexist remarks, to outright solicitation and coercion to have sex. Many of the respondents chose not to report their harassers, and the extant literature on WSH indicates that this might be because of prevailing sociocultural gender norms, the fear of victim-blaming stigmatisation, shame, or a lack of organisational policies (or awareness of them) for addressing sexual harassment.

Some methodological challenges arose due to the sensitive nature of the research. First, the use of solely online surveys and a small sample limits the study's generalisability. Second, the high attrition rate and respondents' reluctance to participate in follow-up interviews hindered the collection of more nuanced data. Nevertheless, the research provides a valuable reference point for discussions on sexual harassment in Nigerian media organisations. I recommend reviewing and developing methods for researching sexual harassment in conservative contexts like Nigeria to gain a deeper understanding of the phenomenon that is so crucial for effective policy formulation. While the scope of the current study was female interns in Nigerian newsrooms, studies show that males can also be victims of WSH (Berdahl et al., 1996; Farkas et al., 2020; Gerrity, 2000; Lee, 2000). Future studies on sexual harassment should expand their scope to include young men as part of the vulnerable group. This would help to create a further understanding of male experiences of sexual harassment, especially within conversational contexts and as interactions with toxic masculinity.

## References

Akinbobola, Y. (2020). *Barriers to women journalists in Sub-Saharan Africa*. African Women in Media (AWiM).

Alaggia, R., & Wang, S. (2020). 'I never told anyone until the #metoo movement': What can we learn from sexual abuse and sexual assault disclosures made through social media? *Child Abuse & Neglect, 103*, Article 104312. https://doi.org/10.1016/j.chiabu.2019.104312

Anderson, E. (2006). Recent thinking about sexual harassment: A review essay. *Philosophy & Public Affairs*, *34*(3), 284–312. https://doi.org/10.1111/j.1088-4963.2006.0069.x

Babbie, E. (2021). *The practice of social research*. Cengage Learning.

Bacchi, C. L. (1999). *Women, policy and politics: The construction of policy problems*. Sage Publications.

Bacchi, C., & Jose, J. (1994). Historicising sexual harassment. *Women's History Review*, *3*(2), 263–270. https://doi.org/10.1080/09612029400200050

Bargh, J. A., Raymond, P., Pryor, J. B., & Strack, F. (1995). Attractiveness of the underling: An automatic power → sex association and its consequences for sexual harassment and aggression. *Journal of Personality and Social Psychology*, *68*(5), 768–781. https://doi.org/10.1037/0022-3514.68.5.768

Berdahl, J. L., Magley, V. J., & Waldo, C. R. (1996). The sexual harassment of men? Exploring the concept with theory and data. *Psychology of Women Quarterly*, *20*(4), 527–547. https://doi.org/10.1111/j.1471-6402.1996.tb00320.x

Benya, F. F., Widnall, S. E., & Johnson, P. A. (Eds.). (2018). *Sexual harassment of women: Climate, culture, and consequences in academic sciences, engineering, and medicine*. National Academies Press. https://www.ncbi.nlm.nih.gov/books/NBK519467/

Blumell, L. E., Mulupi, D., & Arafat, R. (2023). The impact of sexual harassment on job satisfaction in newsrooms. *Journalism Practice*, 1–20. https://doi.org/10.1080/17512 786.2023.2227613

Blumell, L. E., & Mulupi, D. (2021). 'Newsrooms need the metoo movement.' Sexism and the press in Kenya, South Africa and Nigeria. *Feminist Media Studies*, *21*(4), 639–656. https://doi.org/10.1080/14680777.2020.1788111

Blumell, L. E., & Mulupi, D. (2022a). 'A playing field where patriarchy plays': Addressing sexism in South African and Nigerian newsrooms. *Journalism Practice*, *16*(4), 582–602. https://doi.org/10.1080/17512786.2020.1807391

Blumell, L. E., & Mulupi, D. (2022b). *Sexual harassment in the media: Africa report*. WAN_IFRA. https://wan-ifra.org/2022/01/sexual-harassment-in-newsrooms/#:~:text=2022-01-26.%20New%20data%20from%20a%20global%20study%20analysing%20sexual%20harassment

Brown, C. M., & Flatow, G. M. (1997). Targets, effects, and perpetrators of sexual harassment in newsrooms. *Journalism & Mass Communication Quarterly*, *74*(1), 160–183. https://doi.org/10.1177/107769909707400113

Carstensen, G. (2016). Sexual harassment reconsidered: The forgotten grey one. *NORA – Nordic Journal of Feminist and Gender Research*, *24*(4), 267–280. https://doi.org/10.1080/08038740.2017.1292314

Directorate-General for Communication. (2016). *Special Eurobarometer 449: Gender-based violence* (Volume A) [electronic dataset]. Publications Office of the European Union. https://data.europa.eu/data/datasets/s2115_85_3_449_eng

European Union Agency for Fundamental Rights. (2014). *Violence against women: An EU-wide survey. Main results report*. Publications Office of the European Union. https://fra.europa.eu/en/publication/2014/violence-against-women-eu-wide-survey-main-results-report

Farkas, A. H., Scholcoff, C., Machen, J. L., Kay, C., Nickoloff, S., Fletcher, K. E., & Jackson, J. L. (2020). The experience of male physicians with sexual and gender-based harassment: A qualitative Study. *Journal of General Internal Medicine*, *35*, 2383–2388. https://doi.org/10.1007/s11606-020-05695-4

Fernando, D., & Prasad, A. (2018). Sex-based harassment and organizational silencing: How women are led to reluctant acquiescence in academia. *Human Relations*, *72*(10), 1565–1594. https://doi.org/10.1177/0018726718809164

Fitzgerald, L. F., & Cortina, L. M. (2018). Sexual harassment in work organizations: A view from the 21st century. In C. B. Travis, J. W. White, A. Rutherford, W. S. Williams, S. L. Cook, & K. F. Wyche (Eds.), *APA handbook of the psychology of women: Perspectives on women's private and public lives* (pp. 215–234). American Psychological Association. https://doi.org/10.1037/0000060-012

Ford, J. L., Ivancic, S., & Scarduzio, J. (2021). Silence, voice, and resilience: An examination of workplace sexual harassment. *Communication Studies, 72*(4), 513–530. https://doi.org/10.1080/10510974.2021.1953092

Freire, P. (1970). *Pedagogy of the oppressed* (M. B. Ramos, Trans.). Herder and Herder.

Gerrity, D. A. (2000). Male university employees' experiences of sexual harassment-related behaviors. *Psychology of Men & Masculinities, 1*(2), 140–151. https://doi.org/10.1037/1524-9220.1.2.140

Graf, N. (2018, April 4). *Sexual harassment at work in the era of #MeToo*. Pew Research Center. https://pewresearch.org/social-trends/2018/04/04/sexual-harassment-at-work-in-the-era-of-metoo

Grosser, K., & Tyler, M. (2021). Sexual harassment, sexual violence and CSR: Radical feminist theory and a human rights perspective. *Journal of Business Ethics, 177*, 217–232. https://doi.org/10.1007/s10551-020-04724-w

Harris, J., Mosdell, N., & Griffiths, J. (2016). Gender, risk and journalism. *Journalism Practice, 10*(7), 902–916. https://doi.org/10.1080/17512786.2016.1166449

Hershcovis, S. M., Vranjes, I., Berdahl, J. L., & Cortina, L. M. (2021). See no evil, hear no evil, speak no evil: Theorizing network silence around sexual harassment. *Journal of Applied Psychology, 106*(12), 1834–1847. https://doi.org/10.1037/apl0000861

Holland, K. J., & Cortina, L. M. (2016). Sexual harassment: Undermining the wellbeing of working women. In M. Connerley & J. Wu (Eds.), *Handbook on well-being of working women. International handbooks of quality-of-life* (pp. 83–101). Springer. https://doi.org/10.1007/978-94-017-9897-6_6

International Labour Organisation (ILO). (2020). *Sexual harassment in the world of work.* https://ilo.org/resource/brief/brief-ndeg2-sexual-harassment-world-work

Kabah, K. P. A. (2019). Gender and journalism: A perspective of female journalists in the Tamale metropolis in Ghana. *International Journal of Research and Scientific Innovation, 6*(8), 98–102. https://rsisinternational.org/journals/ijrsi/digital-library/volume-6-issue-8/98-102.pdf

Karami, A., Spinel, M. Y., White, C. N., Ford, K., & Swan, S. (2021). A systematic literature review of sexual harassment studies with text mining. *Sustainability, 13*(12), 6589. https://doi.org/10.3390/su13126589

Lachover, E. (2005). The gendered and sexualised relationship between Israeli women journalists and their male news sources. *Journalism, 6*(3), 291–311. https://doi.org/10.1177/1464884905054062

Lee, D. (2000). Hegemonic masculinity and male feminisation: The sexual harassment of men at work. *Journal of Gender Studies, 9*(2), 141–155. https://doi.org/10.1080/713677986

Liamputtong, P. (2007). *Researching the vulnerable: A guide to sensitive research methods. Researching the vulnerable.* Sage Publications.

MacKinnon, C. A. (1979). *Sexual harassment of working women: A case of sex discrimination.* Yale University Press.

McLaughlin, H., Uggen, C., & Blackstone, A. (2012). Sexual harassment, workplace authority, and the paradox of power. *American Sociological Review, 77*(4), 625–647. https://doi.org/10.1177/0003122412451728

McLaughlin, H., Uggen, C., & Blackstone, A. (2017). The economic and career effects of sexual harassment on working women. *Gender & Society, 31*(3), 333–358. https://doi.org/10.1177/0891243217704631

Moagi, A. L. (2023). Sexual harassment and other workplace challenges for African women. *African Journal of Gender, Society & Development, 12*(1), 63–86. https://doi.org/10.31920/2634-3622/2023/v12n1a4

Morrison, E. W., & Rothman N. B. (2009). Silence and dynamics of power. In J. Greenberg & M. S. Edwards (Eds.), *Voice and silence in organizations* (pp. 111–134). Emerald.

North, L. (2016). Damaging and daunting: Female journalists' experiences of sexual harassment in the newsroom. *Feminist Media Studies, 16*(3), 495–510. https://doi.org/10.1080/14680777.2015.1105275

Sadia Jamil, S. (2020). Suffering in silence: The resilience of Pakistan's female journalists to combat sexual harassment, threats and discrimination. *Journalism Practice, 14*(2), 150–170. https://doi.org/10.1080/17512786.2020.1725599

Samuels, H. (2003). Sexual harassment in the workplace: A feminist analysis of recent developments in the UK. *Women's Studies International Forum, 26*(5), 467–482. https://doi.org/10.1016/j.wsif.2003.08.004

Spiliopoulou, A., & Witcomb, G. L. (2023). An exploratory investigation into women's experience of sexual harassment in the workplace. *Violence Against Women, 29*(9), 1853–1873. https://doi.org/10.1177/10778012221114921

Thompson, D. (2001). *Radical feminism today*. Sage Publications.

Uggen, C., & Blackstone, A. (2004). Sexual harassment as a gendered expression of power. *American Sociological Review, 69*(1), 64–92. https://www.jstor.org/stable/3593075

UN Women UK. (2021). *All-party parliamentary group for UN women*. APPG for UN women. https://www.unwomenuk.org/site/wp-content/uploads/2021/03/APPG-UN-Women_Sexual-Harassment-Report_2021.pdf

Wilson, F., & Thompson, P. (2001). Sexual harassment as an exercise of power. *Gender, Work & Organization, 8*(1), 61–83. https://doi.org/10.1111/1468-0432.00122

World Health Organization. (2007). *WHO ethical and safety recommendations for researching, documenting and monitoring sexual violence in emergencies*. WHO. https://www.who.int/publicatio.ns/i/item/9789241595681

# Index